FORMULA ONE 2025

Copyright © 2025 Headline Publishing Group Limited

First published in 2025 by Welbeck

This edition published by Welbeck

An Imprint of HEADLINE PUBLISHING GROUP

1

Apart from any use permitted under UK copyright law, this publication may only be reproduced, stored, or transmitted, in any form, or by any means, with prior permission in writing of the publishers or, in the case of reprographic production, in accordance with the terms of licences issued by the Copyright Licensing Agency.

Cataloguing in Publication Data is available from the British Library

ISBN 978-103541-875-6

Printed and bound in the UK by Bell & Bain Ltd

MIX
Paper | Supporting
responsible forestry
FSC® C104740
FSC
www.fsc.org

Headline's policy is to use papers that are natural, renewable and recyclable products and made from wood grown in well-managed forests and other controlled sources. The logging and manufacturing processes are expected to conform to the environmental regulations of the country of origin.

HEADLINE PUBLISHING GROUP
A Hachette UK Company
Carmelite House
50 Victoria Embankment
London EC4Y 0DZ

The authorised representative in the EEA is Hachette Ireland,
8 Castlecourt Centre, Dublin 15, D15 XTP3, Ireland (email: info@hbgi.ie)

Editor: Conor Kilgallon
Design: Russell Knowles and Luke Griffin
Picture research: Paul Langan
Production: Marion Storz

www.headline.co.uk
www.hachette.co.uk

All stats and facts correct as at 31st December 2024.

FORMULA ONE 2025

TEAMS | DRIVERS | TRACKS | RECORDS

BRUCE JONES

WELBECK

// CONTENTS

ANALYSIS OF THE 2025 SEASON   8

McLAREN   10   **ASTON MARTIN**   28   **WILLIAMS**   46
Lando Norris   12   Fernando Alonso   30   Alex Albon   48
Oscar Piastri   13   Lance Stroll   31   Carlos Sainz   49

FERRARI   16   **ALPINE**   34   **SAUBER**   50
Charles Leclerc   18   Pierre Gasly   36   Nico Hulkenberg   52
Lewis Hamilton   19   Jack Doohan   37   Gabriel Bortoleto   53

RED BULL RACING   20   **HAAS**   38
Max Verstappen   22   Esteban Ocon   40
Liam Lawson   23   Oliver Bearman   41

MERCEDES   24   **RB**   42
George Russell   26   Yuki Tsunoda   44
Andrea Kimi Antonelli   27   Isack Hadjar   45

TALKING POINTS 2025

Top Designer Adrian Newey Seeks a New Challenge   54   The Ferrari Driver Academy Bears Some Fresh Fruit   58
Norris Victory Boosts Britain To 21 F1 Winners   56

KNOW THE TRACKS 2025   60

Melbourne   62   Barcelona   70   Baku   80
Shanghai   63   Montreal   71   Marina Bay   81
Suzuka   64   Red Bull Ring   72   Circuit of the Americas 82
Sakhir   65   Silverstone   73   Mexico City   83
Jeddah   66   Spa-Francorchamps   76   Interlagos   84
Miami   67   Hungaroring   77   Las Vegas   85
Imola   68   Zandvoort   78   Lusail   86
Monaco   69   Monza   79   Yas Marina   87

REVIEW OF THE 2024 SEASON   88

Bahrain GP   90   Canadian GP   100   Azerbaijan GP   108
Saudi Arabian GP   91   Spanish GP   101   Singapore GP   109
Australian GP   92   Austrian GP   102   United States GP   110
Japanese GP   93   British GP   103   Mexico City GP   111
Chinese GP   94   Hungarian GP   104   Sao Paulo GP   114
Miami GP   95   Belgian GP   105   Las Vegas GP   115
Emilia Romagna GP   96   Dutch GP   106   Qatar GP   116
Monaco GP   97   Italian GP   107   Abu Dhabi GP   117

FINAL RESULTS 2024   118

FORMULA ONE RECORDS   120

2025 SEASON FILL-IN CHART   126

Opposite: Lando Norris and Max Verstappen celebrate after filling the top places in the Emilia Romagna GP.

Mercedes AMG mechanics attend to their pre-race tasks on George Russell's F1 W15 before last year's British GP.

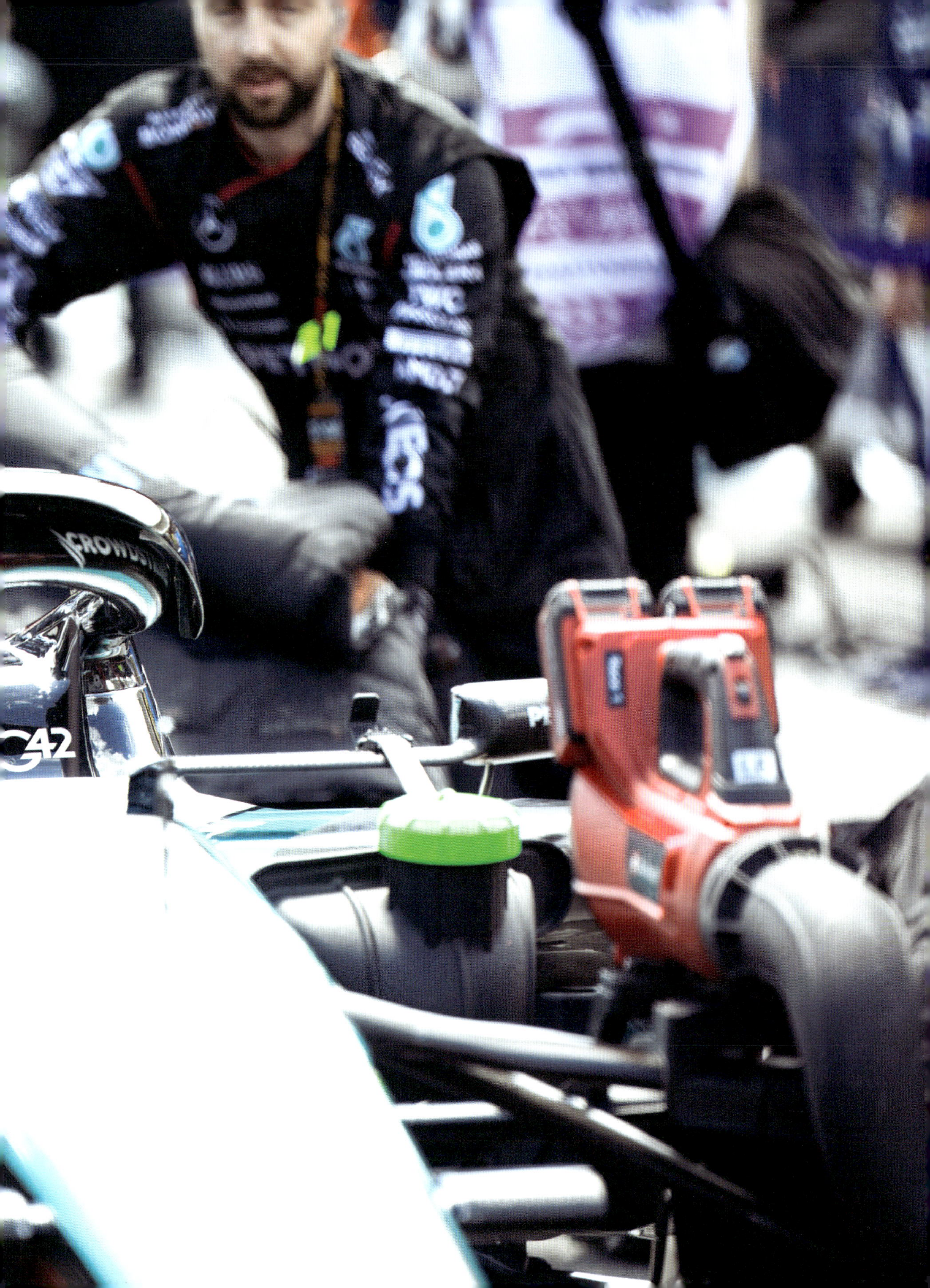

// ANALYSIS OF THE 2025 SEASON

Far from being another stroll to glory for Max Verstappen and Red Bull Racing, last year was a hard-earned victory as McLaren, Ferrari and Mercedes all pushed hard. This year is the last under the current technical regulations, so teams will have half an eye on 2026, but the good news is that at least four teams fancy their chances on taking this year's honours.

Max Verstappen raced to a fourth title in four years with Red Bull Racing last year, but future F1 fans will do well to look beyond that record in the history books as it was a belter of a season; four teams produced winners as their cars suited different conditions to produce one of the most unpredictable championships in years. If this season can see McLaren, Ferrari and Mercedes start on an equal footing, then we will be in for a treat.

When Lewis Hamilton announced that he was leaving Mercedes to join Charles Leclerc at Ferrari, it set the driver market spinning, with Carlos Sainz Jr ending up signing for Williams, a team still attempting to rediscover its form.

However, the most inexplicable part of the driver market was Red Bull Racing getting its second driver Sergio Perez to extend his contract when he simply wasn't delivering. Indeed, after making it four podium visits in the first five rounds, he never placed that well again and cost the team the constructors' title. Not long before Christmas 2024, though, a decision to move Perez on was reached and Liam Lawson was selected over the more experienced Yuki Tsunoda to step up from RB.

It will feel strange to see Hamilton sporting the red of Ferrari after driving for just McLaren then Mercedes in his 18 years in F1. There was some concern that he was losing his edge with a lacklustre run in Brazil, but he was man of the race next time out in Las Vegas. How he settles in alongside Ferrari will be a story of its own.

McLaren had a spell when it bounced back from a poor start to have the best car on the grid, but it will be doing everything in its power to make sure that it delivers consistently for both Lando Norris and Oscar Piastri, who now know what it takes to win a Grand Prix.

George Russell established himself as Mercedes' team leader in 2024 and a sudden trend of introducing young talent to F1 means that he will be the old hand to teenage rookie Andrea Kimi Antonelli.

Aston Martin became ever more at sea last year and the fact that it is being joined by F1's most successful designer, Adrian Newey, is the best news it has had in years. However, don't expect much until 2026 when he will surely have one of the best cars waiting for the introduction of F1's new rules.

Alpine appeared to rediscover its mojo late last year and Pierre Gasly has rookie Jack Doohan alongside him for 2025. Haas has an all-new line-up with Esteban Ocon and Ollie Bearman but,

perhaps more importantly, it also now has technical support from Toyota. RB remains as Red Bull's waiting room and promising FIA F2 Championship runner-up Isack Hadjar will be able to show how he ranks against Tsunoda, who must feel unfortunate to have been overlooked for promotion.

Once great team Williams will be praying that the late-season accidents that cost it so much money don't happen again but having Sainz join Alex Albon will certainly give them a boost. Not much can be expected from Sauber's final year before it is rebranded as Audi, but Nico Hulkenberg will score when points are possible while rookie Gabriel Bortoleto finds his feet.

The sprint race format will remain the same as it was in 2024, with Fridays at the six Grands Prix that have a sprint race earmarked for free practice sessions and qualifying for the sprint. The Saturday at these meetings will now start with the sprint race and then qualifying for the Grand Prix itself. The rounds at which these sprint races are scheduled are China, Miami, Belgium, the USA, Brazil and Qatar.

And the ten existing teams will be watching with interest as an 11th team – Cadillac – prepares to join in 2026.

McLAREN

It had seemed that Red Bull Racing was heading for a third consecutive constructors' title last year, but then McLaren hit its stride, and the wins began to flow. This year, either Lando Norris or Oscar Piastri could become world champion.

McLaren's form came on in leaps and bounds through last year and Lando Norris was able to take four victories – but not the title.

Recent converts to F1 can be forgiven for thinking that the teams have always employed a cast of many hundreds, but it was very different when Bruce McLaren decided in 1966 to build F1 cars rather than simply racing them. There were fewer than ten people working for the team when he set up a workshop close to London's Heathrow airport, and they were all motivated to succeed by this charismatic Kiwi.

It took until 1968 for McLaren to win in F1, but the team was able to expand as it was earning a great deal of money from dominating the North American Can Am sports car series, winning the majority of the races and selling customer cars to the bulk of the field.

Tragedy struck in 1970 when Bruce was killed testing his latest Can Am car at Goodwood, but the team was led on by Teddy Mayer and four years later had its first world champion: Emerson Fittipaldi. The M23 chassis was still competitive two years later and James Hunt used one to pip Ferrari's Niki Lauda.

However, the team wasn't quick to master ground effects at the end of the decade and it took a major restructuring of the team, with Ron Dennis taking control, for it to rise again. World titles for Lauda (1984) and Alain Prost (1985 and 1986)

KEY PERSONNEL & 2024 ROUND-UP

ANDREA STELLA

There has been a new dynamism at McLaren since Andrea became team principal before the 2023 season. This Italian mechanical engineer began his F1 career with Ferrari, rising from the test team to work first with Michael Schumacher and later with Kimi Raikkonen in their title-winning years. In 2015, he joined McLaren and was head of race operations for three years before being promoted to be first performance director and then executive director of racing in 2019.

FROM REVERSE TO FAST FORWARD

As in 2023, McLaren started slowly and then found its stride. Lando Norris was on the podium by the third round and a winner by the sixth. Oscar Piastri was developing as fast as the MCL38 was and, after Norris was told to hand him his first win in Hungary, became a winner in more traditional style in Baku. Rivals complained of flexing wings giving McLaren advantage, but the FIA said all was fine and it moved ahead of Red Bull Racing.

2024 DRIVERS & RESULTS

Driver	Nationality	Races	Wins	Pts	Pos
Lando Norris	British	24	4	374	2nd
Oscar Piastri	Australian	24	2	292	4th

put the team at the front. Then Prost was joined by Ayrton Senna for 1988, along with Honda engines, and sparks flew as F1's two fastest drivers jostled for dominance. The French and Brazilian drivers took one title apiece before Prost said the atmosphere was too poisonous between them and moved on to Ferrari for 1990. Senna triumphed that year, as he did to make it three titles in 1991.

Then came the Williams years and it wasn't until McLaren landed Mercedes engines that a McLaren driver was crowned again. This was Mika Hakkinen and he did it again in 1999. Although it seemed most unlikely that the Finn wouldn't carry on in this vein, Michael Schumacher and Ferrari then took control for the next five years.

McLaren simply couldn't regain its lofty standards, and it took until 2007 when it had its next shot at glory, with both Fernando Alonso and rookie Lewis Hamilton going for gold. Yet, after a blunder or two, Ferrari's Kimi Raikkonen pipped them at the final round. Hamilton put that right in 2008, winning five rounds

on his way to winning the title by the narrowest of margins – a single point – ahead of Ferrari's Felipe Massa.

However, this was something that couldn't be built on, despite Hamilton and Jenson Button's best efforts in 2010 as Red Bull Racing rose to prominence, and McLaren gradually fell from its perch. Worse was to follow after a deal was done to race with Honda engines again from 2015 and they tumbled to rank ninth out of the ten teams that year. Indeed, even Alonso couldn't get the cars to shine.

It took a change to Renault engines for a modicum of form to be discovered as Mercedes continued to dominate in 2018. McLaren advanced to fourth in 2019, then third overall in 2020, with Carlos Sainz grabbing second place at Monza in this COVID-restricted season. Finally, in 2021, now with Mercedes power once more, Daniel Ricciardo put McLaren back in the winner's circle when he headed home team-mate Lando Norris in a McLaren one-two at the Italian GP.

Despite no further wins in 2022 and

2023 as Max Verstappen steamrollered the opposition in his Red Bull, team principal Zak Brown seemed to be guiding the team in the right direction, suggesting that great days were just around the corner.

"We lost too many points at the start of last year when we weren't competitive enough. Once our car improved, we proved we have the qualities as a team, and the qualities in Lando and Oscar, to contend for both titles."

Andrea Stella

Lewis Hamilton enjoys his breakthrough win for McLaren in Canada in 1997 and then kept on winning.

LANDO NORRIS

Last season was one in which McLaren caught, then outpaced, Red Bull. Lando became a winner and suddenly realized that he had an outside title shot. The final outcome could be different this year if he starts with the best car.

Lando knows that he must improve his race starts in 2025.

The ambition was clear when Lando began to rise through kart racing. He wanted to get to the top.

Lando's success in kart racing was prodigious, with his 2013 season yielding the World KF Junior and European KFJ titles, only to be improved on the following year when he became World KF champion at the age of 14. On intervening weekends, Lando even gained his first car racing experience, racing in the Ginetta Junior series, as much to learn the British circuits as anything else.

In 2015, Lando raced here, there and everywhere, winning the MSA Formula title in Britain, but also racing in the British, German and Italian F4 series.

This maximalist approach continued in 2016 when Lando kicked off his year by winning the Toyota Racing Series title in New Zealand, then came back to the northern hemisphere and won the European and NEC Formula Renault titles, as well as taking four wins in the BRDC F3 series.

What impressed most on his way up was his 2017 campaign, when he claimed nine wins to dominate the FIA F3 Euro series. He also had a test with McLaren for being chosen as the 2016 McLaren Autosport BRDC Young Driver. Lando then stepped up to FIA F2 in 2018 and, although he won just once, ended the year as runner-up to George Russell to prove that he was ready for F1.

McLaren signed Lando as team-mate to Carlos Sainz and he learnt so well from the Spaniard that he finished third in the 2020 season-opener in Austria.

McLaren dropped a rank to fourth overall in 2021, but Lando continued his progress to be sixth in the drivers' championship, just missing out on winning the Italian GP which was won by team-mate Daniel Ricciardo, although Lando outscored him across the year.

Lando remained top McLaren driver in 2022, ranking seventh, then again in 2023 when he ended up sixth after a poor start was followed by six second places.

TRACK NOTES

Nationality:	**BRITISH**
Born:	**13 NOVEMBER 1999, GLASTONBURY, ENGLAND**
Teams:	**McLAREN 2019–25**

CAREER RECORD

First Grand Prix:	**2019 Australian GP**
Grand Prix starts:	**128**
Grand Prix wins:	**4**
	2024 Miami GP, Dutch GP, Singapore GP, Abu Dhabi GP
Poles:	**9**
Fastest laps:	**12**
Points:	**1007**
Honours:	**2024 F1 RUNNER-UP, 2018 FIA F2 RUNNER-UP, 2017 EUROPEAN F3 CHAMPION, 2016 EUROPEAN FORMULA RENAULT CHAMPION & NORTHERN EUROPE FORMULA RENAULT CHAMPION & TOYOTA RACING SERIES CHAMPION & McLAREN AUTOSPORT BRDC YOUNG DRIVER AWARD, 2015 MSA FORMULA CHAMPION, 2014 WORLD KF KART CHAMPION, 2013 WORLD KF JUNIOR KART CHAMPION & EUROPEAN KFJ KART CHAMPION & KF JUNIOR SUPER CUP WINNER**

ENJOYING THE THRILL OF THE CHASE

After the first five of last year's Grands Prix, Lando ranked fifth, his best finish being second in Shanghai, while Max Verstappen was doing as he had done in 2022 and 2023 and was pulling clear of the field, his advantage already 25 points. Next time out, though, Lando won the Miami GP. McLaren had begun to sort its MCL38 to the drivers' liking and the developments would keep coming through the course of the season. In fact, with Ferrari and Mercedes also doing better, Red Bull's two years of domination were coming to an end. Lando won again at Zandvoort, kicking sand in the face of Max's home supporters. However, there was an unusual factor that counted against Lando winning more Grands Prix, and this was an extraordinary inability to convert pole positions into leading both into and out of the first corner. It took him until his fifth attempt, at the Singapore GP, to get it right. He knew then that he would have to win each of the final six races and pray for a mistake from Max, but Lando didn't have quite enough firepower to get the job done.

OSCAR PIASTRI

This is a driver with 'future world champion' written all over him. A Grand Prix winner in his second year in the sport's top level, he is also with a team that is expected to provide him with a winning machine.

Oscar came on strongly in 2024 and will make a push to become team leader in 2025.

For drivers from the Antipodes, there is always the knowledge that if they want to reach the top in racing they will have to trade the familiarity of their homeland for Europe, because that is where racing's proving ground continues to be based. It's where the stars of tomorrow gather to prove that they are better than their rivals, worthy of operating at the next level as they try to scramble their way up the single-seater racing ladder.

Oscar had headed out from Australia when still racing karts to finish sixth in the World OK Junior series and this result encouraged him, as a 15-year-old, to try his hand at single-seaters, starting in the United Arab Emirates F4 championship.

From here, Oscar headed to Britain, and he learnt fast to end the 2017 season as runner-up in British F4. Then, he stepped up to the more hotly contested European Formula Renault Championship, learning the circuits as he ranked eighth overall. Oscar remained in Formula Renault for the following year and seven wins were enough to win the European series.

The FIA F3 series is a level at which many a hotshot comes unstuck, wilting under the ever-increasing level of competition. Not Oscar, as he made it two titles in two years after a final round shoot-out with Theo Pourchaire and Logan Sargeant.

The task of completing his hat trick was going to be tougher still, as that meant winning the FIA F2 series – the final category before F1 – with Prema Racing. However, taking six wins meant that he completed the feat in style, finishing 60 points clear of the next driver. The Alpine team noted his remarkable progress and got Oscar on to its books, giving him his first taste of F1. Then Oscar spent the following year attending Grands Prix as its reserve driver before Alpine thought it had signed him for 2023, only to find that McLaren had got him first. When one looks at the subsequent divergent fortunes of the two teams, that proved a lucky escape, and he grabbed a second place in Qatar in his maiden season.

TRACK NOTES

Nationality:	**AUSTRALIAN**
Born:	**6 APRIL 2001, MELBOURNE, AUSTRALIA**
Teams:	**McLAREN 2023–25**

CAREER RECORD

First Grand Prix:	**2023 BAHRAIN GP**
Grand Prix starts:	**46**
Grand Prix wins:	**2**
	2024 Hungarian GP, Azerbaijan GP
Poles:	**0**
Fastest laps:	**3**
Points:	**389**
Honours:	**2021 FIA F2 CHAMPION, 2020 FIA F3 CHAMPION, 2019 EUROPEAN FORMULA RENAULT CHAMPION, 2017 BRITISH FORMULA 4 RUNNER-UP**

LOOKING LIKE A FUTURE CHAMPION

If Oscar's maiden season of F1 was impressive in the way that he went about his business and got better and better through the year, then his second campaign was clear evidence that he had much more to give. Two wins for the rapidly improving McLaren team was a worthy return, especially as he was asked after a while to play the supporting role to team leader Lando Norris, who was better placed in the points table to challenge Red Bull Racing's Max Verstappen. It's bizarre, but his maiden win in Hungary felt disappointing, but this was down to the way that Norris was asked to hand the lead back to Oscar as he had been in control before the final pit stops. Fortunately, his second win, on the streets of Baku, was a simple, unchallenged victory. Oscar did more than enough to suggest that he has all the tools required to fight Lando for supremacy within the team in 2025 in what should be an enthralling battle.

Lando Norris had his best season to date in 2024 but ended it as runner-up.

FERRARI

Last year was an increasingly positive one for Ferrari as the team collected wins with both drivers, but this year is going to feel different as Lewis Hamilton lines up alongside Charles Leclerc in what ought to be an intriguing battle for supremacy.

Ferrari stepped up to become a serious challenger to Red Bull Racing last year and will be looking to take more victories this year.

Ferrari has been in the World Championship since it began in 1950 and running cars at the top level since the 1930s. However, it hasn't always been at the point of the pinnacle and there have been many years when it has fallen away from the pace. Yet, as we head into its 76th year at the sport's top level, with 248 Grand Prix wins to its name, there is a sense that it is working its way back to becoming a title-challenging team again.

Enzo Ferrari was a mechanic, a racing driver and then a team owner. After running the Alfa Romeo works team from 1932, he went out on his own after World War Two. The wins started flowing from 1951, after which he had matters all his own way when Alfa Romeo withdrew at the end of that year. Having mastered new rules for 1952, he provided a car that Alberto Ascari used to achieve considerable success as he romped to the title and then did it all again in 1953.

Mercedes then took control of F1, and it wasn't until Ferrari adopted the Lancia chassis that the team claimed its third drivers' title when Juan Manuel Fangio prevailed in 1956. Two years later, Mike Hawthorn prevailed over Vanwall's Stirling Moss.

There was change on the way in F1,

KEY PERSONNEL & 2024 ROUND-UP

LOIC SERRA

This 53-year-old Frenchman trained in mechanical engineering and his early career was spent working on tyres and suspension for Michelin. He had his first contact with F1 when Michelin supplied tyres. In 2006, when Michelin quit F1, he joined the BMW Sauber team. Then, when BMW withdrew from F1 at the end of 2009, Loic moved to Mercedes and rose to the position of performance director. Joining Ferrari means that he will be able to continue his long-running spell of working with Lewis Hamilton.

VASSEUR GUIDES THE TEAM FORWARD

Both Charles Leclerc and Carlos Sainz Jr won Grands Prix for Ferrari in 2024, and there was a great step forward in selecting superior race strategies, a weak point in previous campaigns. Team principal Frederic Vasseur's calming hand on the tiller has been noticeable, especially in not inflating errors that would previously have blown the team off course. Sainz missed a round with suspected appendicitis, but academy driver Ollie Bearman impressed when he stood in.

2024 DRIVERS & RESULTS

Driver	Nationality	Races	Wins	Pts	Pos
Ollie Bearman	British	1	0	7	18th
Charles Leclerc	Monegasque	24	3	356	3rd
Carlos Sainz	Spanish	23	2	290	5th

with Cooper and Lotus showing that cars might be better by being smaller and moving the engine from the front to the tail. Ferrari resisted this but was ready in 1961 when new rules made F1 a formula for cars with smaller 1.5-litre engines and Phil Hill took the title. Then, only the genius of former multiple motorbike world champion John Surtees kept Ferrari in the hunt as he battled to get the volatile management structure to focus on F1 as much as it did on sports car racing, narrowly taking the 1964 title.

With Lotus and BRM and then Brabham and McLaren innovating as they went, Ferrari fell into a bit of a demise, hampered by political interference from within and a desire to keep using Ferrari's favoured flat-12 format rather than following its rivals in using a V8. Apart from flashes of genius from Jacky Ickx when he nearly won the title, it took until Niki Lauda, designer Mauro Forghieri and young team chief Luca di Montezemolo got things sorted in the mid-1970s for Ferrari to return to the top. Two titles in three years for the Austrian

gave the team momentum, but success stalled again after Lotus introduced ground effects in 1977.

Two years later, Jody Scheckter and Gilles Villeneuve ended up first and second, but Williams was on the rise, and despite Alain Prost's nearly successful chase of McLaren's Ayrton Senna in 1990 and Gerhard Berger ending Ferrari's three-year winning drought in 1994, wins remained hard to come by. In fact, Scheckter's success proved to be Ferrari's last drivers' title for 21 years as British teams dominated. The driver who helped the team succeed again was Michael Schumacher and he then added four more titles under the guidance of Jean Todt and Ross Brawn.

The 2007 title was the last to be won by a Ferrari driver, when Kimi Raikkonen pipped McLaren's Fernando Alonso and Lewis Hamilton, before Felipe Massa fell agonisingly short the following year. However, since then it has been wins that have been collected rather than titles by Charles Leclerc and Carlos Sainz.

FOR THE RECORD

Team base:	**Maranello, Italy**
Active in Formula One:	**From 1950**
Grands Prix contested:	**1,098**
Wins:	**248**
Pole positions:	**253**
Fastest laps:	**263**
Constructors' titles:	**16**
Drivers' titles:	**15**

THE TEAM

Chairman:	**John Elkann**
Team principal:	**Frederic Vasseur**
Deputy team principal:	**Jerome d'Ambrosio**
Technical director, chassis & aerodynamics:	**Loic Serra**
Technical director, power unit:	**Enrico Gualtieri**
Head of aerodynamics:	**Loic Bigois**
Sporting director:	**Diego Ioverno**
Head of supply chain:	**Enrico Racca**
Driving academy director:	**Jock Clear**
Head of track engineering:	**Matteo Togninalli**
Chassis:	**Ferrari SF25**
Engine:	**Ferrari V6**
Tyres:	**Pirelli**

The personnel changes for this year initially had Loic Serra joining from Mercedes to report to Enrico Cardile, but he was promoted to becoming the team's chassis technical director when Cardile moved on to Aston Martin. Former F1 racer Jerome d'Ambrosio also joins from Mercedes and will be deputy team principal, reporting to Frederic Vasseur.

"It was frustrating to finish last year 14 points behind McLaren, as it is a very small margin, less than two percent of the total, but our target is never to be second. We don't need to look for motivation as we already have it."

Fred Vasseur

Michael Schumacher made Ferrari great again, such as with this 2004 title win in Japan.

CHARLES LECLERC

It will be intriguing to see how Charles responds to having seven-time world champion Lewis Hamilton as his team-mate, and whether they can work together harmoniously to help Ferrari climb to the top of the pile.

Charles has a new challenge in his seventh season with Ferrari following Lewis' arrival.

Guided into karts by his father Herve who competed in the Monaco Formula 3 race five times before hanging up his helmet and starting a family, Charles and his younger brother Arthur took little persuasion to try kart racing and Charles was clearly talented. Title success followed, starting in cadet karts, and he was a front runner right up to finishing as runner-up in the World KZ kart series in 2013 when he was 16.

Then it was time for single-seaters and Charles raced to second overall in the Formula Renault ALPS series, but this was considered enough for him to advance to the FIA F3 Championship in 2015. With so little car racing experience, this ought to have been a two-year project, but the wins flowed from early in his campaign and he went on to rank fourth.

So, it was next stop GP3 for Charles in 2016 and he raced to three wins and the title for ART Grand Prix ahead of Alex Albon, with Ferrari signing him up to its driver academy. The FIA F2 series was Charles' next target, and he was a dominant champion in that for Prema Racing.

So it was that Ferrari propelled him into F1 in 2018, placing him at a team that used its customer engines: Sauber. His impact was impressive, and he would qualify regularly way further up the grid than team-mate Marcus Ericsson.

Ferrari had seen enough and his second year in F1 was as a works driver, and he has remained with the team ever since. He slotted in seamlessly

and would have won on his second outing but for an engine problem that dropped him from the lead at Sakhir, then cleared. By year's end, with wins at Spa-Francorchamps and Monza in the bag, he ranked fourth, one place ahead of team-mate Sebastian Vettel.

It looked as though 2022 might be his year, with early-season wins in the Bahrain and Australian GP, but Max Verstappen came on strongly to dominate for Red Bull, leaving Charles as runner-up.

TRACK NOTES

Nationality:	MONEGASQUE
Born:	16 OCTOBER 1997,
	MONTE CARLO, MONACO
Teams:	SAUBER 2018,
	FERRARI 2019–25

CAREER RECORD

First Grand Prix: **2018 AUSTRALIAN GP**

Grand Prix starts:	147
Grand Prix wins:	8

2019 Belgian GP, Italian GP, 2022 Bahrain GP, Australian GP, Austrian GP, 2024 Monaco GP, Italian GP, United States GP

Poles:	26
Fastest laps:	10
Points:	1430
Honours:	2022

F1 RUNNER-UP, 2017 FIA F2 CHAMPION, 2016 GP3 CHAMPION, 2015 MACAU F3 RUNNER-UP, 2014 FORMULA RENAULT ALPS RUNNER-UP, 2013 WORLD KZ KART RUNNER-UP, 2012 UNDER 18 WORLD KART RUNNER-UP & EURO KF KART RUNNER-UP, 2011 ACADEMY TROPHY KART CHAMPION, 2010 JUNIOR MONACO KART CUP CHAMPION, 2009 FRENCH CADET KART CHAMPION

CAPPED BY WINNING IN MONACO

Having ranked fifth in 2023 as Red Bull Racing dominated, Charles might have expected a similar result last year, but it was soon clear that Ferrari had a more competitive car. It wasn't a match for the Red Bulls, but it was the best of the rest, shown by team-mate Carlos Sainz winning the third round. Then, after finishing consistently on the podium, Charles made the step up that he was seeking and scored his first win since the 2022 Austrian GP. Better still, he did it on home ground in Monaco and this was extra special for Charles as, not only did he become the first Monegasque driver to do so, but he did it in commanding style by starting from pole and leading every one of the 78 laps. More than that, it propelled him closer to points leader Max Verstappen and further clear of Lando Norris in the points table at this one-third distance point of the season. Further wins at Monza and COTA excited the tifosi but, by then, McLaren had moved ahead of Ferrari, and he was to lose further ground.

LEWIS HAMILTON

After 12 years and six drivers' titles with Mercedes, Lewis is making the leap to team up with Charles Leclerc at Ferrari. Perhaps the change will do him good and bring more wins, but he may also have to adapt to a new team landscape.

After 12 years with Mercedes, Lewis jumped at the chance to become a winner with Ferrari.

Lewis could have been one of a host of young kart racers who had the talent but not the money to proceed. This all changed, though, when Lewis cheekily asked McLaren principal Ron Dennis at an awards dinner if he would help out. Dennis did, guiding Lewis all the way to F1.

Lewis had his first full year of car racing in 2002 in British Formula Renault. After ranking third, he returned in 2003 and his ten wins made him champion. F3 followed in 2004 and this was another two-year project, with Lewis winning the F3 Euro title with a remarkable 15 wins in 2005. GP2 came next and Lewis edged out Nelson Piquet Jr to win that title too.

Fittingly, McLaren gave Lewis his F1 break in 2007 and he feared no one, not even his own team-mate Fernando Alonso. They fought tooth and nail, Lewis taking four wins, but both were edged out by Ferrari's Kimi Raikkonen when he took the title at the final round.

Lewis got his revenge in 2008 and landed the first of his seven F1 titles. McLaren lost its competitiveness over the next few years and, although Lewis kept on winning races, titles were out of his reach. So, he joined Mercedes in 2013 and the 11 wins that he claimed in 2014 brought him his second crown.

What followed was a run of five titles in the next six years, interrupted only by team-mate Nico Rosberg pipping him in 2016.

It had looked as though he would be champion in 2021, but Max Verstappen just got ahead. Mercedes' form has dropped, precipitating his move to Ferrari.

A RETURN TO WINNING WAYS

Seventh place in the opening race was not the dream way to start the 2024 season, with Red Bull Racing way out front. Fortunately for Lewis, matters improved and the first of his two wins came at the British GP when he mastered changing track conditions to end a 57-race winning drought. The second win came two rounds after that, at Spa-Francorchamps. Lewis thought that he had finished second, but then team-mate George Russell's car was discovered in post-race inspection to be underweight, so he was awarded the full 25 points for victory. Yet, Mercedes failed to find consistently competitive performance from its W15s and both drivers would be frustrated at subsequent races when they couldn't run either at or near the front of the field. Qualifying only 11th for the Dutch GP was indicative of this and it was compounded by being pushed back three positions for impeding Sergio Perez. Lewis enjoyed one last podium visit for Mercedes, for second place in Las Vegas.

TRACK NOTES

Nationality:	**BRITISH**
Born:	**7 JANUARY 1985, STEVENAGE, ENGLAND**
Teams:	**McLAREN 2007–12, MERCEDES 2013–24, FERRARI 2025**

CAREER RECORD

First Grand Prix: **2007 AUSTRALIAN GP**

Grand Prix starts: **356**

Grand Prix wins: **105**
2007 Canadian GP, United States GP, Hungarian GP, Japanese GP, 2008 Australian GP, Monaco GP, British GP, German GP, Chinese GP, 2009 Hungarian GP, Singapore GP, 2010 Turkish GP, Canadian GP, Belgian GP, 2011 Chinese GP, German GP, Abu Dhabi GP, 2012 Canadian GP, Hungarian GP, Italian GP, United States GP, 2013 Hungarian GP, 2014 Malaysian GP, Bahrain GP, Chinese GP, Spanish GP, British GP, Italian GP, Singapore GP, Japanese GP, Russian GP, United States GP, Abu Dhabi GP, 2015 Australian GP, Chinese GP, Bahrain GP, Canadian GP, British GP, Belgian GP, Italian GP, Japanese GP, Russian GP, United States GP, 2016 Monaco GP, Canadian GP, Austrian GP, British GP, Hungarian GP, German GP, United States GP, Mexican GP, Brazilian GP, Abu Dhabi GP, 2017 Chinese GP, Spanish GP, Canadian GP, British GP, Belgian GP, Italian GP, Singapore GP, Japanese GP, United States GP, 2018 Azerbaijan GP, Spanish GP, French GP, German GP, Hungarian GP, Italian GP, Singapore GP, Russian GP, Japanese GP, Brazilian GP, Abu Dhabi GP, 2019 Bahrain GP, Chinese GP, Spanish GP, Monaco GP, Canadian GP, French GP, British GP, Hungarian GP, Russian GP, Mexican GP, Abu Dhabi GP, 2020 Styrian GP, Hungarian GP, British GP, Spanish GP, Belgian GP, Tuscan GP, Eifel GP, Portuguese GP, Emilia Romagna GP, Turkish GP, Bahrain GP, 2021 Bahrain GP, Portuguese GP, Spanish GP, British GP, Russian GP, Sao Paulo GP, Qatar GP, Saudi Arabian GP, 2024 British GP, Belgian GP

Poles:	**104**
Fastest laps:	**67**
Points:	**4862.5**

Honours: 2008, 2014, 2015, 2017, 2018, 2019 & 2020 F1 WORLD CHAMPION, 2007, 2016 & 2021 F1 RUNNER-UP, 2006 GP2 CHAMPION, 2005 EUROPEAN F3 CHAMPION, 2003 BRITISH FORMULA RENAULT CHAMPION, 2000 WORLD KART CUP & EUROPEAN FORMULA A KART CHAMPION, 1999 ITALIAN INTERCON A CHAMPION, 1995 BRITISH CADET KART CHAMPION

RED BULL RACING

It had looked as though 2024 was going to be just another title-winning year for Red Bull, but the mood turned tense, senior staff left and Sergio Perez struggled, so it will take work for the team to get its mojo back.

Max Verstappen races to his seventh win from the opening ten races in 2024's Spanish GP, but then life became a whole lot tougher.

Triple world champion Jackie Stewart set the ball rolling when he and his elder son Paul created the Stewart GP team from the latter's Formula 3000 outfit Paul Stewart Racing, and stepped up to F1 in 1997. The cars were beautifully presented and the team gained a reward from a season spent finding its feet in F1's midfield when Rubens Barrichello scooped a surprise second place finish at, of all places, Monaco.

There was no clear progress as McLaren and Ferrari fought over honours through the next two seasons, but the team had a remarkable day in the 1999 European GP at the Nurburgring when not only did Johnny Herbert master wet/dry conditions to give the team its first win, but Barrichello followed him home in third. This bumper day helped the team rank fourth.

It was clear that more budget was required, and Stewart Sr brokered a deal for the team to be rebadged as Jaguar

Racing from 2000. Sadly, as was seen over the next five years, being taken under the wing of a motor manufacturer doesn't often lead to harmonious management

as people with little experience of the sport interfere.

There were highlights, flashes of speed, such as third places for Eddie Irvine in

KEY PERSONNEL & 2024 ROUND-UP

CHRISTIAN HORNER

This former British racing driver worked his way through the junior single-seater formulae, reaching Formula 3000 in 1997, but was never quite the winning ticket. However, he achieved his F1 dream in 2005 when his experience of running the family's Arden team in F1's feeder formula, F3000, was thought ideal to run Red Bull Racing when it morphed out of Jaguar Racing. He was the youngest team principal in the paddock, but his experience grew alongside the team, and he has guided it to six constructors' titles.

A BRILLIANT START BUT GRADUAL DECLINE

For a team to win seven of the first ten Grands Prix of a season and yet fail to win the constructors' title is almost unthinkable, yet this was what befell Red Bull Racing last year. No blame can be apportioned to Max Verstappen, as he took each of those wins. Sergio Perez, though, struggled increasingly with the RB20, then lost confidence. Add to that the rise in form of Ferrari, McLaren and Mercedes, and so a most unusual season unfolded but Max was still able to grab a fourth title.

2024 DRIVERS & RESULTS

Driver	Nationality	Races	Wins	Pts	Pos
Max Verstappen	Dutch	24	9	437	1st
Sergio Perez	Mexican	24	0	152	8th

FOR THE RECORD

Team base:	**Milton Keynes, England**
Active in Formula One:	**As Stewart GP 1997–99, Jaguar Racing 2000–04, Red Bull Racing 2005 on**
Grands Prix contested:	**527**
Wins:	**123**
Pole positions:	**104**
Fastest laps:	**99**
Constructors' titles:	**6**
Drivers' titles:	**8**

THE TEAM

Team principal:	**Christian Horner**
Motorsport consultant:	**Helmut Marko**
Technical director:	**Pierre Wache**
Chief engineer, car engineering:	**Paul Monaghan**
Head of aerodynamics:	**Enrico Balbo**
Head of performance engineering:	**Ben Waterhouse**
Head of racing:	**Gianpiero Lambiase**
Head of strategy:	**Hannah Schmitz**
Chassis:	**Red Bull RB21**
Engine:	**Honda RBPT V6**
Tyres:	**Pirelli**

Monaco in 2001 and Monza in 2002, plus strong qualifying performances from Mark Webber – but no wins.

So, in 2005, the team was effectively reinvented. It kept its base in Milton Keynes but had a whole new feel and a rebirth as Red Bull Racing, with Christian Horner brought in to take the helm. It took a few years for every ingredient to fall into place, but Adrian Newey's design process began to reap dividends and the cars made steps forward every year.

In 2009, a season in which Brawn GP outflanked its rivals, Red Bull Racing scored its first win, courtesy of Sebastian Vettel in China. However, it was in 2010 that the team truly flowered, going to the final race in Abu Dhabi with both Vettel and Mark Webber in contention in a four-way title shoot-out. Vettel prevailed and started a run of four drivers' and constructors' titles in four years.

Daniel Ricciardo joined the team in 2014 and did well, winning races, but it was the arrival of Max Verstappen, promoted from Red Bull's junior team, Scuderia Toro Rosso, five races into the 2016 campaign that gave the team what it was seeking: a champion elect. Mercedes was the dominant force of the time, but the Dutch ace appeared able to cancel out any performance deficit due to running less effective Renault engines, to be a thorn in Lewis Hamilton's side for the next few years.

Finally, in 2021, he gave Red Bull Racing its fifth drivers' crown, won in a controversial final round in Abu Dhabi when he appeared to be helped to victory over Hamilton by poor officiating.

The next two campaigns were far more straightforward as Newey mastered new aerodynamic rules that were introduced to make it easier for cars to get in a position to overtake; Verstappen was all but unstoppable, winning 34 of the 44 Grands Prix across 2022 and 2023.

Last year will be recalled not only for Red Bull Racing being given a serious challenge for the first time in a few years, but also for the team entering a period of turmoil. The season started with a cloud hanging over team principal Christian Horner due to alleged inappropriate behaviour towards a female team member. He was eventually cleared of that, but the atmosphere within Red Bull Racing had become tense, with Max's father Jos looking for change. More crucially, chief technical officer Newey appeared unhappy and elected to move on, with clear implications for the team's future competitiveness.

Jackie and Paul Stewart congratulate Rubens Barrichello after his second place in Monaco in 1997.

"**Last season was all over the place. We started strong but then had some tough times but we stuck together as a team to get to the bottom of our problems and came back stronger.**"

Max Verstappen

MAX VERSTAPPEN

The Red Bull RB20 might have lost its dominance through last year, but Max never stopped going for gold. If he couldn't be first, then second would do as he chased title number four. This year, he seeks number five.

Max had to dig deep through 2024, but he was able to hold on.

It seems strange now to think that Max did just one year of car racing between the end of his time in karts before he hit Formula 1 when aged just 17. You would never have known, as he was straight on the money, becoming F1's youngest winner when he won in Spain, aged 18.

Wind the clock back to look at his background and you can see that he had a flying start, as father Jos contested 107 Grands Prix and mother Sophie (Kumpen) was a top kart racer. Max followed their guidance and landed title after title, up to claiming the World and European KZ Kart crowns in 2013, the year he turned 16.

So, a single-seater racing career was obviously going to prove fruitful. Yet Max was a driver in a hurry, so he skipped the bottom few rungs of the ladder and went straight into F3. This was in 2014, and he grabbed ten wins in the European series, enough to rank third overall.

F2 is typically next, but Max jumped straight past that when Red Bull offered him an F1 seat with its junior team, Scuderia Toro Rosso. Any doubts that he had arrived too soon were dispelled when Max claimed a couple of fourth places.

His 2016 campaign started with Toro Rosso but, five races in, he took Daniil Kvyat's seat at Red Bull Racing and promptly won on his debut in Spain.

Lewis Hamilton was dominating for Mercedes, but Max chipped away and ranked third overall behind the Mercedes drivers in both 2019 and 2020.

In 2021, though, Max pinched the title from Hamilton in a controversial final round then, with Red Bull Racing building the best car, dominated the next two seasons as he added two more titles.

TRACK NOTES

Nationality:	**DUTCH**
Born:	**30 SEPTEMBER 1997, HASSELT, BELGIUM**
Teams:	**TORO ROSSO 2015–16, RED BULL RACING 2016–25**

CAREER RECORD

First Grand Prix: **2015 AUSTRALIAN GP**

Grand Prix starts: **209**

Grand Prix wins: **63**
2016 Spanish GP, 2017 Malaysian GP, Mexican GP, 2018 Austrian GP, Mexican GP, 2019 Austrian GP, German GP, Brazilian GP, 2020 70th Anniversary GP, Abu Dhabi GP, 2021 Emilia Romagna GP, Monaco GP, French GP, Styrian GP, Austrian GP, Belgian GP, Dutch GP, United States GP, Mexico City GP, Abu Dhabi GP, 2022 Saudi Arabian GP, Emilia Romagna GP, Miami GP, Spanish GP, Azerbaijan GP, Canadian GP, French GP, Hungarian GP, Belgian GP, Dutch GP, Italian GP, Japanese GP, United States GP, Mexico City GP, Abu Dhabi GP, 2023 Bahrain GP, Australian GP, Miami GP, Monaco GP, Spanish GP, Canadian GP, Austrian GP, British GP, Hungarian GP, Belgian GP, Dutch GP, Italian GP, Japanese GP, Qatar GP, United States GP, Mexico City GP, Sao Paulo GP, Las Vegas GP, Abu Dhabi GP, 2024 Bahrain GP, Saudi Arabian GP, Japanese GP, Chinese GP, Emilia Romagna GP, Canadian GP, Spanish GP, Sao Paulo GP, Brazilian GP, Qatar GP

Poles:	**40**
Fastest laps:	**33**
Points:	**3023.5**
Honours:	**2021, 2022, 2023 & 2024 F1 WORLD CHAMPION, 2013 WORLD & EUROPEAN KZ KART CHAMPION, 2012 WSK MASTER SERIES KF2 CHAMPION, 2011 WSK EURO SERIES CHAMPION, 2009 BELGIAN KF5 CHAMPION, 2008 DUTCH CADET KART CHAMPION, 2007 & 2008 DUTCH MINIMAX KART CHAMPION**

DELIVERING THE GOLD STANDARD

Make no bones about this, it was not a happy camp at Red Bull Racing last year as the team was riven with internal politics and yet, even when the atmosphere in camp was toxic, and even as his RB20 was losing its competitive edge, Max still delivered his typical gold standard performances. Team-mate Sergio Perez wasn't even close enough to be running in his shadow. After rattling off seven wins from the first ten rounds, things changed, and Max had to start a defensive action as Ferrari, McLaren and Mercedes all made up ground on Red Bull. As Lando Norris began to put the pressure on, all Max could do was endeavour to finish second and that ought to have been enough to ensure a fourth consecutive title. There was no room for any slip-ups. When he was threatened in September with community service by the FIA for swearing on air, Max suggested that he might walk away from F1. And you felt that this was no idle threat, but then he produced his scintillating drive in Brazil and all was well again.

LIAM LAWSON

Having gone well when standing in at AlphaTauri in 2023, Liam did a similar job when he replaced Daniel Ricciardo at RB for the final six Grands Prix of 2024. This year, the Kiwi steps up to Red Bull's top team.

Liam proved to be a fearless competitor when he stepped in last year.

A double kart champion in his native New Zealand, Liam was immediately on the pace in his first year of single-seaters when he started off in Formula First. However, it was his pace in New Zealand Formula Ford that made his name, as he won 14 of the 15 races in 2016 to become national champion at the age of 14. Liam then contested the 2017 Australian F4 series, and he did well enough to be runner-up.

Realising that it was his best hope of advancing, Liam raced in Europe in 2018 and finished runner-up in the ADAC F4 series. He then went home and won the 2019 Toyota Racing Series before returning to learn about F3 in Euroformula Open. After ranking fifth in the 2020 FIA F3 series, 2021 brought something entirely different: a season in a GT. He took to the DTM series incredibly well, ending the campaign as runner-up after winning three rounds in his Red Bull AF Corse Ferrari.

Having been a member of the Red Bull Junior Team since 2019, thus being looked at with a view to possibly being promoted towards F1, Liam was given his first taste of F1 with a test in an AlphaTauri in late 2021 before having a test for Red Bull Racing at the end of the following season.

Between these, he spent the 2022 campaign in F2. Racing for Carlin, Liam charged to four wins, and this was enough for him to rank third behind Felipe Drugovich and Theo Pourchaire.

Wanting to challenge him more than bringing him back for another shot at F2, Red Bull sent Liam to race in Japan's Super Formula series in 2023. And he really impressed as he took three wins and ended up as runner-up. Even more remarkably, Liam did this despite potentially having his head turned when he was called up to make his F1 debut; he was given the chance to show his skills in five Grands Prix with AlphaTauri in place of Daniel Ricciardo after the Australian broke his hand, finishing ninth in Singapore.

TRACK NOTES

Nationality:	**NEW ZEALANDER**
Born:	**11 FEBRUARY 2002,**
	HASTINGS, NEW ZEALAND
Teams:	**ALPHA TAURI 2023, RB 2024,**
	RED BULL RACING 2025

CAREER RECORD

First Grand Prix:	**2023 DUTCH GP**
Grand Prix starts:	**11**
Grand Prix wins:	**0 (best result: 9th,**
	2023 Singapore GP, 2024 United
	States GP, Sao Paulo GP)
Poles:	**0**
Fastest laps:	**0**
Points:	**6**
Honours:	**2023 JAPANESE**
	SUPER FORMULA RUNNER-UP, 2021 DTM
	RUNNER-UP, 2020 TOYOTA RACING SERIES
	RUNNER-UP, 2019 TOYOTA RACING SERIES
	CHAMPION & EUROFORMULA OPEN
	RUNNER-UP, 2018 ADAC F4 RUNNER-UP,
	2017 AUSTRALIAN F4 RUNNER-UP, 2016
	NEW ZEALAND FORMULA FORD CHAMPION,
	2015 MANFEILD FORMULA FIRST WINTER
	SERIES RUNNER-UP

MOVING IN FROM THE SIDELINES

After much discussion and no little time spent waiting for a decision to be made as to whether Daniel Ricciardo had done enough to continue with RB for the entirety of last season, Liam finally got the nod after considerable urging from Red Bull's motorsport consultant Helmut Marko. He was offered the Australian's seat for the season's final six Grands Prix and was expected to perform well enough to put the heat on Red Bull Racing's second driver Sergio Perez – making the Mexican fear for his future, even though Perez had signed a contract extension. Having had five F1 outings in 2023, Liam was expected to slot in quickly and his most impressive result across those Grands Prix was ninth. One thing that stood out was that Liam made it plain that he would bow to no-one on the track, regardless of their seniority, as shown by a number of times when he was challenged by Perez and reacted robustly, then doing the same to Fernando Alonso.

⫻⫻ MERCEDES

Until Red Bull Racing hit the front in 2021, Mercedes seemed unstoppable. But the last two seasons have shown there is work still to be done to give its drivers the chance to win consistently. Teenage rookie Andrea Kimi Antonelli replaces Lewis Hamilton.

George Russell returned to winning ways at the Red Bull Ring last year, but the team needs to find more lasting form this season.

Mercedes first made an impact on the World Championship when it burst on to the scene just after the start of the 1954 season. This works team brought its cars in the same unpainted silver livery as it had carried when fighting against Auto Union in the late 1930s, when they were known collectively as the Silver Arrows. And the results were just as stunning. Its debut appearance came at the French GP at Reims and its W196s flashed home first and second, with the best of the rest a lap down. Seldom has F1 had to hit the reset button so hard.

Win after win followed as Juan Manuel Fangio wrapped up the title. Then more wins and another title came his way in 1955, with protégé Stirling Moss also getting in on the act.

By season's end, though, they knew that the team was to withdraw, this the result of one of its works cars crashing into a spectator area during the Le Mans 24 Hours, over 80 people.

The next time that Mercedes had any involvement in F1 was in 1993 when it supplied engines to the Sauber team that had entered its works cars in sports car racing, but Mercedes elected to have the V10s badged as Ilmor units before letting them carry the Mercedes badge in 1994. Then it shifted them to McLaren in

KEY PERSONNEL & 2024 ROUND-UP

SIMONE RESTA
One of two former Ferrari technical experts joining the team for 2025 is Simone, a veteran of 19 years with the Italian team from 2001, rising to be chief designer, albeit with a two-year break when he went to Sauber as its technical director. After a brief return to Ferrari, he moved on to Haas as its technical director in 2021. Simone started his career in F1 with Minardi, working in R&D for three years before he moved to Ferrari.

TITLE-WINNING PACE REMAINS ELUSIVE
It was considered likely that Red Bull Racing would dominate again in 2024, especially as Max Verstappen had started at a gallop. However, Mercedes was among a trio of teams that began to challenge it in the second half of the season. George Russell won in Austria and had a win taken away in Belgium (and awarded to team-mate Lewis Hamilton) for his car being underweight; Hamilton also triumphed at Silverstone. Yet, the team's form ebbed and flowed so consistency and reliability will need to be found for 2025.

2024 DRIVERS & RESULTS

Driver	Nationality	Races	Wins	Pts	Pos
Lewis Hamilton	British	24	2	223	7th
George Russell	British	24	2	245	6th

1995 and enjoyed success as an engine supplier, finally taking a first win in the final Grand Prix of 1997, at Jerez. Mika Hakkinen would guide them to drivers' titles in 1998 and 1999.

The Silver Arrows concept finally returned in 2010 when Mercedes GP entered the World Championship. This had no direct bloodline to the works team of 1954 though, having evolved from a British team that broke cover in 1999. This was British American Racing, BAR for short, that had been set up by Craig Pollock to field Jacques Villeneuve. Based in Brackley near Silverstone, it wanted for nothing, except results. These only came in 2004 when its Geoff Willis-designed chassis was good enough to help Jenson Button to ten podium finishes as he was best of the rest behind Ferrari drivers Michael Schumacher and Rubens Barrichello.

In 2006, Honda put more money into the team, and it became Honda Racing and was blessed with an astonishing drive from Button in a wet/dry race at the Hungaroring to give the team its first win. Then, with the world enduring a financial crash in 2008, Honda elected late in the year to withdraw. This seemed as though it might be the end of the team, but technical director Ross Brawn headed up a management buyout. Not only did he save the team, but a clever double-diffuser design turned it into a winner in 2009 until rivals caught on, by which time Button had built enough of a points lead not to be overhauled.

Mercedes had a desire to be seen as more than just an engine supplier and chose that year to step in and bring the team the money it deserved. From 2010, the team would race as Mercedes-AMG, and it brought Michael Schumacher back from retirement to head its attack.

Success wasn't something it could manage initially. Indeed, it took the team's second driver, Nico Rosberg, until the Chinese GP in 2012 to land that. But then came Mercedes' golden years once Lewis Hamilton joined from McLaren. This was in 2013, and success followed success as Hamilton won six titles in seven years, with his record run broken only by team-mate Rosberg in 2016.

FOR THE RECORD

Team base:	**Brackley, England**
Active in Formula One:	**As BAR 1999–2005, Honda Racing 2006–08, Brawn GP 2009, Mercedes 2010 on**
Grands Prix contested:	**492**
Wins:	**129**
Pole positions:	**141**
Fastest laps:	**104**
Constructors' titles:	**9**
Drivers' titles:	**8**

THE TEAM

Head of Mercedes-Benz Motorsport:	**Toto Wolff**
Technical director:	**James Allison**
MD, Mercedes-AMG High Performance powertrains:	**Hywel Thomas**
Chief designer:	**John Owen**
Strategic development director:	**Simone Resta**
Performance director:	**David Nelson**
Sporting director:	**Ron Meadows**
Head of performance software applications:	**Enrico Sampo**
Trackside engineering director:	**Andrew Shovlin**
Chief trackside engineer:	**Simon Cole**
Chassis:	**Mercedes F1 W16**
Engine:	**Mercedes V6**
Tyres:	**Pirelli**

There ought to have been a further title in 2021, but there was some contentious officiating in the Abu Dhabi GP that denied Hamilton that and handed the title to Red Bull Racing's Max Verstappen.

Lewis Hamilton wins in Malaysia in 2014 in the first of six title-winning years with Mercedes.

"Kimi [Antonelli] has been with us since the age of 11. Back in the day, we saw that his karting was exceptional, and maybe the only one who came close to this trajectory through karting was Max Verstappen."

Toto Wolff

GEORGE RUSSELL

The arrival of Andrea Kimi Antonelli at Mercedes creates a new role for George now that he is the old head, not the novice, at the Brackley-based outfit. The speed was there last year, but not the reliability of the car, so George will be hoping for a positive change.

George needs to score more wins in what will be his fourth year with Mercedes.

Kart racing titles seemed to be easy to come by for George in his school days and he peaked in 2012 when he was 14 by winning the European KF3 Kart Championship title.

Two years later, aged 16, he stepped up to single-seaters and raced to the British F4 title. Anxious to keep on moving and with the prestige of having been selected as the recipient of the McLaren Autosport BRDC Young Driver Award after just one year in cars, George moved directly on to F3. The FIA European Championship proved to be a two-year project and George advanced from sixth in 2015 to third in 2016, when Lance Stroll won.

His season in GP3 in 2017 was more successful as George won the title easily, then impressed in his F1 test prize drive. Perhaps inspired by this, George came top of an extremely competitive FIA F2 campaign in 2018, racing to seven wins to beat compatriots Lando Norris and Alex Albon.

So, the door opened to F1 with Williams in 2019 and George went well, but this was with a team that had fallen away from the pace and neither he nor Robert Kubica scored any points. His second year with the team was more of the same, but he was presented with a golden opportunity when Lewis Hamilton was ill at the Sakhir GP and George took his drive. If it hadn't been for a tyre-changing mix-up, George could conceivably have won, but he laid down a marker by outperforming team-mate Valtteri Bottas.

A third year with Williams followed, brightened by second place in a Belgian GP that was so wet that the race began behind the safety car and was abandoned after just one lap.

Timing can be everything and George's eventual move to Mercedes for 2022 was just as the team stopped winning and could only chase Red Bull Racing's Max Verstappen, yet George did make his breakthrough at the Sao Paulo GP to outscore team-mate Lewis Hamilton as he ranked fourth. In 2023, their positions swapped around.

TRACK NOTES

Nationality:	**BRITISH**
Born:	**15 FEBRUARY 1998, KING'S LYNN, ENGLAND**
Teams:	**WILLIAMS 2019–21, MERCEDES 2020 (one race) & 2022–25**

CAREER RECORD

First Grand Prix:	**2019 AUSTRALIAN GP**
Grand Prix starts:	**128**
Grand Prix wins:	**3**
	2022 Sao Paulo GP, 2024 Austrian GP, Las Vegas GP
Poles:	**5**
Fastest laps:	**8**
Points:	**714**
Honours:	**2018 FIA F2 CHAMPION, 2017 GP3 CHAMPION, 2015 F3 MASTERS RUNNER-UP, 2014 BRITISH F4 CHAMPION & McLAREN AUTOSPORT BRDC YOUNG DRIVER AWARD, 2012 EUROPEAN KF3 KART CHAMPION**

PUSHING MERCEDES TO PROGRESS

Life in his first three years at Mercedes has not been what George hoped for, as he joined a winning team that then lost the winning touch. Last year was a case in point, as he finished fifth in the opening round and that remained his best result until he equalled it seven races later. His hopes rose when he qualified on pole in Canada and finished third. One element that George can be proud about when looking back at last year's campaign was his ability, especially in the first half of the year, to outqualify team-mate Lewis Hamilton. He could usually out race him too, but not on Lewis' best days. Victory did come when he inherited the lead in Austria after Lando Norris and Max Verstappen clashed. However, the major frustration of George's season came at Spa-Francorchamps when he was first to the chequered flag in the Belgian GP, but his car was then disqualified for being 3.3lb (1.5kg) underweight. With the F1 W15 working better in cooler conditions, he had a smile back on his face in November when we was dominant in Las Vegas.

ANDREA KIMI ANTONELLI

Mercedes has decided to go for youth for its second seat in 2025, bringing in this 18-year-old Italian prodigy. Andrea Kimi's record is outstanding and his few F1 runs suggest that he could shine after just three full seasons in car racing.

Andrea Kimi is one of 2025's F1 rookies and comes with a winning pedigree from F2.

Andrea Kimi was always likely to try racing, as his father Marco had spent three decades from the early 1990s racing everything with a roof, from touring cars to GTs to Ferraris and in the Lamborghini Super Trofeo too, eventually running his own team.

Young Andrea Kimi – you can guess who inspired his middle name – went kart racing as soon as he was allowed to. This makes him very much the same as all of his rivals. However, he stood out from the crowd as he did it exceptionally well. Andrea Kimi's form was such that he was selected as part of the Mercedes-AMG Petronas Young Driver Programme in 2019, the year that he turned 13. At this age, he was already pitching for glory in the world kart series, racing for the Rosberg family team.

In 2020, he landed the European KF title, then followed it up for good measure with the same title the following year.

Then, at the end of the 2021 season, Andrea Kimi had his first taste of single-seaters, contesting late-season races of the Italian F4 series after he had turned 15, landing three podium finishes.

Back for a full attack in 2022, Andrea Kimi had a phenomenal year, landing the Italian and largely German-based ADAC F4 titles.

This meant that he was more than ready to step up to Formula Regional in 2023 and Andrea Kimi stormed to that European title too, after landing the Middle Eastern series title as a warm-up.

Very much on Mercedes' radar, he had three days of testing F2 and impressed. Indeed, Andrea Kimi was considered talented enough to skip F3 and go straight to F2, the last step beneath F1 on the racing ladder. There might have been concerns that one so young – he was 17 at the start of last season – might not quite be up to this task, but a certain Max Verstappen had proved before him that years spent at the top of the ladder of karting series is all the schooling that the very best require.

TRACK NOTES

Nationality:	**ITALIAN**
Born:	**25 AUGUST 2006,**
	BOLOGNA, ITALY
Teams:	**Mercedes 2025**

CAREER RECORD

First Grand Prix: **2025 AUSTRALIAN GP**

Grand Prix starts:	**0**
Grand Prix wins:	**0**
Poles:	**0**
Fastest laps:	**0**
Points:	**0**
Honours:	**2023 FORMULA REGIONAL EUROPEAN & MIDDLE EAST CHAMPION, 2022 ADAC F4 & ITALIAN F4 & FIA MOTORSPORT GAMES F4 CHAMPION, 2020 & 2021 FIA EUROPEAN KART CHAMPION**

A WINNER IN A STRANGE F2 SEASON

Last year's FIA Formula 2 Championship will go down as one of the most unusual in the F1 feeder formula's history. The reason for an extraordinary tally of 18 drivers taking wins across the 28 races was down to the introduction of a new spec chassis; it put all the teams on a level playing field as they learnt to get the best out of it on top of the unrepresentative results by having a reversed grid for the first race at each meeting. However, although only 17 at the start of the year, Andrea Kimi settled down and began winning after Prema Racing had got a handle on how to set up the car, with wins coming at Silverstone and the Hungaroring in the second half of the season. The highlight of the year, though, was his outing for Mercedes in the first free practice session ahead of his home Grand Prix at Monza. He crashed after only five laps, but his split times were sensational enough to leave team principal Toto Woolf deeply impressed and excited for 2025.

ASTON MARTIN

It was a considerable coup for Aston Martin to land the services of Adrian Newey and the design ace is going to have to weave his magic to coax this team back towards the front of the grid after a slump last season.

After a glorious leap up the F1 rankings in 2023, Aston Martin and Fernando Alonso failed to score a podium finish last year.

This will be the fifth year in which Aston Martin rolls out in its traditional metallic green livery, long enough to make it feel like part of the F1 establishment, but still nowhere near as distinctive as the team was when it raced through the 1990s in a variety of hues as Jordan.

After a semi-successful time racing in Formula 3, then running cars for others in Formula 3000, most notably 1989 champion Jean Alesi, Eddie Jordan's team took the plunge and entered F1 in 1991. It was an instant hit, ranking fifth at its first attempt and always feeling like a wonderfully brash newcomer that was shaking up the show.

The Jordan team was always teetering on the edge financially early on, but a double podium result for Rubens Barrichello and Eddie Irvine in Canada in 1995 helped matters. However, it took backing from Benson & Hedges and Honda engines from Mugen to help the team go for gold. The first win came in a wet/dry race at Spa-Francorchamps, when Damon Hill led home team-mate Ralf Schumacher, a result that both made the team and saved it.

A handful of wins for the team that operates from just outside Silverstone's front gate, came over the following seasons, with Heinz-Harald Frentzen grabbing a pair

KEY PERSONNEL & 2024 ROUND-UP

LAWRENCE STROLL

Although undoubtedly a hugely successful businessman, building his own fortune in the fashion world, this Canadian billionaire is also the owner of the Aston Martin F1 Team, as much of what drives him is his love of motor racing. He brought the Ralph Lauren brand to Europe then invested in Tommy Hilfiger to help it to go global. After racing in Ferrari series, Lawrence bought St Jovite and helped to redevelop the track that hosted the Canadian GP in 1968 and 1970.

NO REPEAT OF ITS SHINING 2023 FORM

Having pushed McLaren hard en route to rank fifth overall in 2023, last year was a shadow of that for Aston Martin. Indeed, instead of starting with a podium result at the first round as it had 12 months earlier, Fernando Alonso and Lance Stroll were soon aware that it was going to be more of a struggle. In fact, there would be no visits to the podium at all across the 24 races, with Alonso's fifth place in the second round at Jeddah being Aston Martin's best result all year and frustratingly it never looked likely to be bettered.

2024 DRIVERS & RESULTS

Driver	Nationality	Races	Wins	Pts	Pos
Fernando Alonso	Spanish	24	0	70	9th
Lance Stroll	Canadian	23	0	24	13th

FOR THE RECORD

Team base: **Silverstone, England**
Active in Formula One: **As Jordan 1991–2005, Midland 2006, Spyker 2006–07, Force India 2008–18, Racing Point 2019–20, Aston Martin 2021 on**
Grands Prix contested: **625**
Wins: **5**
Pole positions: **4**
Fastest laps: **10**
Constructors' titles: **0**
Drivers' titles: **0**

THE TEAM

Aston Martin Executive Chairman: **Lawrence Stroll**
Team principal: **Mike Krack**
Managing technical partner: **Adrian Newey**
Chief executive officer: **Andy Cowell**
Chief technical officer: **Enrico Cardile**
Executive director technical: **Rob Bell**
Sporting director: **Andy Stevenson**
Engineering director: **Luca Furbatto**
Head of trackside engineering: **Bradley Joyce**
Chief designer: **Akio Haga**
Chassis: **Aston Martin AMR25**
Engine: **Mercedes V6**
Tyres: **Pirelli**

in 1999 when he helped the team to end the year third overall. It has never been as good since then, but its lesser years were masked by continual changes of name as new money was brought in and the team became Midland then Spyker as Eddie stepped aside. It took the arrival of Indian drinks mogul Vijay Mallya to give it a long-time name again, and the team ran as Force India in India's sporting colours of white, green and orange from 2008 until 2018. There were periods that yielded the occasional strong results for Giancarlo Fisichella, Paul di Resta, Nico Hulkenberg, Sergio Perez and Esteban Ocon, but there was also a struggle for finance, not helped by Mallya being pursued by the Indian tax authorities.

Then in stepped Canadian billionaire Lawrence Stroll and he eased those financial concerns, renaming the team as Racing Point for 2019. There was no quick fix and the team ranked seventh again before having a way more competitive campaign in 2020 when it ranked fourth, helped by Perez coming home second in the Turkish GP and then winning the Sakhir GP.

Then began the Aston Martin years, with a slump back to seventh in 2021, even with the services of former champion Sebastian Vettel. Fortunately, the 2023 season was a revelation as the AMR23 was instantly a great step forward and Fernando Alonso rattled off five top-three results in the first six rounds en route to ending the year ranked fourth overall.

Once ace designer Adrian Newey had made it known that he was looking for a change from Red Bull Racing, there was a frenzied pursuit of his services. Many thought that he might join Ferrari, but a very lucrative five-year contract and a shareholding in the team was enough to lure him to Aston Martin. Obviously, as he will be on gardening leave until this March, his focus will be on the all-new car required when the rulebook changes in 2026. With the team's new factory and wind tunnel at his disposal, he is expected to move the team up the grid.

There is no change in the driver line-up for 2025, with Alonso and Lance Stroll staying on. However, there is always the accusation that there might be better options for the team's second seat than Stroll, who, despite sometimes displaying his speed, needs to be more consistent if the team is to improve its points tally.

Damon Hill leads Ralf Schumacher in Belgium in 1998 for Jordan's breakthrough victory.

"Once I start with the team, I will be fully in. I need to be. I have to be. This is something different. It is a fresh challenge, new situation, and so I always do what I feel is needed for the best of the team."

Adrian Newey

FERNANDO ALONSO

It has been 11 years since this two-time world champion last won a Grand Prix but, at 43, he is back for more, planning for glory in the years ahead now that Aston Martin has ace designer Adrian Newey on board.

Fernando will be cheered by Adrian Newey's arrival, which will mostly bear fruit from 2026.

A glance through kart racing records reveals that Fernando was at the top of his game, so when he stepped up to single-seaters in 1999 and was immediately on the pace in the Open by Nissan series, Spanish fans became excited. The way that Fernando took to F3000, the level below F1, in his second year gave his fans more cause for optimism as he ranked fourth in a series packed with drivers with more experience.

The Benetton team had seen enough and not only signed him but placed Fernando with the Minardi team for his rookie year in F1. There was no ride available for 2002, so he spent the year testing for the Renault (formerly Benetton) F1 team before landing a seat for 2003. He won in Hungary and ranked sixth. In 2004, he rose to fourth, then grabbed back-to-back titles in 2005 and 2006.

A move to McLaren in 2007 might have helped him to another, but he ended up level with team-mate Lewis Hamilton, a point behind Ferrari's Kimi Raikkonen.

It had been a fractious year, though, and Fernando returned to Renault before moving to Ferrari in 2010. Although this didn't yield another title, he was runner-up in 2010, 2012 and 2013, outscored each time by Red Bull Racing's Sebastian Vettel.

Then the wins stopped flowing and Fernando elected to have a second spell at McLaren, but Honda's second era as the team's engine supplier was woeful. Fernando looked to other branches of motorsport, trying the Indianapolis 500 in 2017 then the Le Mans 24 Hours the following year, which he won for Toyota.

Fernando continued with Toyota, winning the World Endurance Championship but was lured back to F1 by Alpine in 2021, before joining Aston Martin for 2023 and having a great year to rank fourth.

TRACK NOTES

Nationality: **SPANISH**
Born: **29 JULY 1981, OVIEDO, SPAIN**
Teams: **MINARDI 2001, RENAULT 2003–06, McLAREN 2007, RENAULT 2008–09, FERRARI 2010–14, McLAREN 2015–18, ALPINE 2021–22, ASTON MARTIN 2023–25**

CAREER RECORD

First Grand Prix: **2001 AUSTRALIAN GP**
Grand Prix starts: **401**
Grand Prix wins: **32**
2003 Hungarian GP, 2005 Malaysian GP, Bahrain GP, San Marino GP, European GP, French GP, German GP, Chinese GP, 2006 Bahrain GP, Australian GP, Spanish GP, Monaco GP, British GP, Canadian GP, Japanese GP, 2007 Malaysian GP, Monaco GP, European GP, Italian GP, 2008 Singapore GP, Japanese GP, 2010 Bahrain GP, German GP, Italian GP, Singapore GP, Korean GP, 2011 British GP, 2012 Malaysian GP, European GP, German GP, 2013 Chinese GP, Spanish GP
Poles: **22**
Fastest laps: **26**
Points: **2337**
Honours: **2019 DAYTONA 24 HOURS WINNER, 2018/19 WORLD ENDURANCE CHAMPION, 2018 & 2019 LE MANS 24 HOURS WINNER, 2005 & 2006 F1 WORLD CHAMPION, 2010, 2012 & 2013 F1 RUNNER-UP, 1999 FORMULA NISSAN CHAMPION, 1997 ITALIAN & SPANISH KART CHAMPION, 1996 WORLD & SPANISH KART CHAMPION, 1994 & 1995 SPANISH JUNIOR KART CHAMPION**

A YEAR OF DIFFICULT FORM

Not even a multiple world champion could have won in last year's Aston Martin AMR24. It must have been frustrating for Aston Martin's team leader as his glorious 2023 campaign, in which he visited the podium eight times when racing the far superior AMR23, began to feel almost like a dream. Last year was harder for all concerned, the car nowhere near as competitive, and this was clear from the fact that he and team-mate Lance Stroll could finish only ninth and tenth at Sakhir, as opposed to the previous year's third and sixth at the same circuit. There was no quick fix, either, and it was soon clear that it would take a miracle to land a top-three finish. In fact, the highest that this double world champion managed across the 24 Grands Prix was fifth place at the season's second round, the Saudi Arabian GP. However, the team has full confidence in Fernando and despite the fact that he turns 44 this year, have kept him on as the team moves into its Adrian Newey era.

LANCE STROLL

This Canadian driver started last season strongly as Aston Martin had a competitive car, but he couldn't get close to team-mate Fernando Alonso and his form fell away through his eighth year in F1. He needs a big season in 2025.

Lance needs a good season in 2025 to find his way back to better form again.

Inspired by his father's love of motor racing, Lance raced karts and found that he had a rare talent, peaking with sixth in the World KF series in 2013 when he was 14.

At the start of the following year, after he had turned 15, Lance headed south from his native Canada to compete in his first single-seater series. This was the Ferrari-inspired Florida Winter Series, in preparation for heading to Italy to try his hand in their F4 championship and Lance stormed to seven wins and the title.

Lance began 2015 by winning the Toyota Racing Series title in New Zealand, then headed north to contest the FIA F3 Euro series, grabbing a win in a rough-and-tumble year in which he ranked fifth. A less win-or-bust approach was far more fruitful in 2016 and yielded not just 14 wins but the title too, with useful sports car experience being gained when he raced to fifth in the Daytona 24 Hours.

For 2017, it was expected that Lance would step up to F2, but he got a ride in F1. This was with Williams, and he was to spend the year learning from team-mate Felipe Massa. Lance did well, ending the year just three points behind the experienced Brazilian, peaking with third place in an incident-filled Azerbaijan GP. The team was less competitive in 2018 and so it was decided that Lance would join Force India for 2019 – albeit with his father buying a major shareholding in the team, which was renamed Racing Point. Two third-place finishes were the highlight of Lance's second year with the team, but he finished the year down in 11th, seven ranks below team-mate Sergio Perez.

Then the team changed its identity and became Aston Martin Racing from 2021, but it was only in 2023 that Aston Martin ran competitively. That year was Lance's best season to date, ranking in the top ten for the first time, albeit with 74 points to team leader Fernando Alonso's 206.

POINTS ARE HARD-EARNED

If your father owns the team you race for, but you aren't rewarding him with podiums or frequent handfuls of points, there will always be the accusation that you are a protected man. That is the constant charge levelled against Lance, which must be vexing for him. There are still flashes of pace, but the fact that he is usually overshadowed by his team-mate Fernando Alonso suggests that his turn of speed needs to be produced more consistently. Last year was another example of this, when Lance earned less than half of Alonso's points tally. His cause wasn't helped by his self-induced non-start in a wet Brazil. Aston Martin is entering the World Endurance Championship this year and perhaps that might be a new avenue for the next chapter of Lance's career if he doesn't take that all-defining first F1 win, or at least start scoring regularly, in one of the Adrian Newey-designed Aston Martins in the next few campaigns.

TRACK NOTES

Nationality:	**CANADIAN**
Born:	**29 OCTOBER 1998,**
	MONTREAL, CANADA
Teams:	**WILLIAMS**
2017–18, RACING POINT 2019–20,	
ASTON MARTIN 2021–25	

CAREER RECORD

First Grand Prix:	**2017 AUSTRALIAN GP**
Grand Prix starts:	**166**
Grand Prix wins:	**0 (best result: 3rd,**
	2017
Azerbaijan GP, 2020 Italian GP, Sakhir GP)	
Poles:	**1**
Fastest laps:	**0**
Points:	**292**
Honours:	**2016 EUROPEAN**
F3 CHAMPION, 2015 TOYOTA RACING SERIES	
CHAMPION, 2014 ITALIAN F4 CHAMPION	

Fernando Alonso climbs out of his AMR24. The car did not perform as well as its 2023 predecessor.

There was much unrest at Alpine last year, plus a general lack of form, and former team principal Flavio Briatore's return threatened further upheaval, but a late-season run of good results put the team from Enstone back on an even keel.

Alpine's form was up and down last year, and so consistency is sought. This is Pierre Gasly en route to ninth in Montreal.

This England-based, French-themed team has run as Alpine for four years, but its latest identity has yet to inspire the results that the sports car-building arm of Renault would have hoped for to boost its image.

Forty years before it was rebadged as Alpine for 2021, it broke into the World Championship with a different identity, carrying the name of British transport magnate Ted Toleman. This was a team that had won in Formula 2. Alas, it was not for the big time and its cars often failed even to qualify. Indeed, it took until its third year for Rory Byrne to hone the cars into competitive form. In 1984, he was blessed with the arrival of Ayrton Senna. The Brazilian might have been an F1 rookie, but he was soon flying, and he would probably have passed Alain Prost to win at a streaming wet Monaco had the race not been stopped early.

Senna moved on and so did the team name, with its cars being entered as Benettons in 1986, taking the name of its sponsor. Under this guise, and using powerful turbocharged BMW engines, Gerhard Berger brought the team its first win. Then came a few seasons when it gathered enough results and the occasional win to twice end a campaign third overall.

KEY PERSONNEL & 2024 ROUND-UP

OLIVER OAKES

A former single-seater racer then principal of the Hitech team that shone in F2, the 37-year-old Englishman arrives at Alpine with plenty of ambition. He was World Karting champion in 2005 then did well in first Formula BMW in 2006 then Formula Renault in 2007 before trying F3 and rising as high as GP3 before he hung up his helmet. Having formed Hitech GP in 2015, Oliver made a pitch last year, with Kazakh backing, for Hitech to enter F1 but the bid was turned down.

LACKING THE POWER TO GO FORWARD

Being the only team racing with Renault power units made it hard to gauge the team's form, but the fact that it took until the sixth round before it scored a point for tenth place proved that it had fallen back from its 2023 position in the midfield. Three races later, Pierre Gasly grabbed a ninth place, followed by another, but there simply wasn't enough for him or disenchanted team-mate Esteban Ocon to hope for more. Then came their extraordinary two-three finish in the restarted Brazilian GP.

2024 DRIVERS & RESULTS

Driver	Nationality	Races	Wins	Pts	Pos
Pierre Gasly	French	23	0	42	10th
Esteban Ocon	French	23	0	23	14th
Jack Doohan	Australian	1	0	0	24th

FOR THE RECORD

Team base:	**Enstone, England**
Active in Formula One:	**As Toleman 1981–85, Benetton 1986–2001, Renault 2002–11 & 2016–2020, Lotus 2012–15, Alpine 2021 on**
Grands Prix contested:	**761**
Wins:	**50**
Pole positions:	**36**
Fastest laps:	**57**
Constructors' titles:	**3**
Drivers' titles:	**4**

The arrival of Michael Schumacher in late 1991 helped Benetton to start winning more frequently. Then, in 1994, under something of a cloud due to the unproved use of illegal traction control and some robust driving from its German star, Benetton landed its first drivers' title. Things went better still in 1995, when he was champion again and Benetton claimed its first constructors' title.

Having used Renault engines for seven years, the team from near Oxford then eked more backing from the French manufacturer by letting the team be renamed as Renault for 2002. This had no relation to the French-based Renault team that ran in F1 from 1977 to 1985, but it brought greater glory when Fernando Alonso joined and landed the 2005 and 2006 drivers' titles. However, Red Bull Racing was on the rise.

Another name change followed in 2012 when, for marketing reasons, it was renamed as Lotus. As before, this had no connection to the team that had originally run in F1 under that name.

There was a rediscovery of form and Kimi Raikkonen proved that it could win the occasional race.

In 2016, the team reverted to Renault, but there was little chance of glory as Mercedes and its lead driver Lewis Hamilton were dominant. Good only for ninth in the rankings, the team advanced to sixth in 2017 then fourth in 2018 when Nico Hulkenberg and Carlos Sainz scored consistently.

Looking for a change of momentum, the team sought further financial support in ever more expensive F1 and went to Renault for further input. The price of this was to change its name to Alpine in 2021 to help promote Renault's boutique sporting division and a highlight was Esteban Ocon's unexpected win at the Hungaroring. Despite having an admirable continuity in team personnel, there has been no real reason for celebration since then.

Former principal Flavio Briatore returned in 2024 and proposed changing to Mercedes power. However, the desire was there from within the team to keep

THE TEAM

Chief executive officer:	**Philippe Krief**
Executive advisor:	**Flavio Briatore**
Team principal:	**Oliver Oakes**
Technical director:	**David Sanchez**
Chief aerodynamicist:	**Michael Broadhurst**
Sporting director:	**Julian Rouse**
Executive director, Viry-Chatillon:	
	Bruno Famin
Team manager:	**Rob Cherry**
Chassis:	**Renault A525**
Engine:	**Renault V6**
Tyres:	**Pirelli**

using the Viry-Chatillon-built Renault engine, and indeed the Alpine sports car team that competes in the World Endurance Championship plans to do so, as many feel that if the engine-building department is forced to close, then the Renault element of the team will begin to dwindle. However, Alpine will give its cars Mercedes power from 2026, which might also make the team more saleable.

"I was proud of my team last year for securing sixth in the constructors' championship after a very tough start. The lows were very low and the highs were very high after incredible improvement."

Pierre Gasly

The team's most recent title was secured by Fernando Alonso when he won for Renault in 2006.

Last season was another tough one for Alpine, with tension in the team and a marked lack of in-season chassis development. However, Pierre kept his nerve and raced to points in four of the final five races to suggest better times are ahead.

Pierre was easy on his machinery in 2024 but will be praying for a faster car this year.

There was a gang of French drivers right at the front of European kart racing when Pierre was entering his teenage years. And he was one of them, finishing as the runner-up in the European KF3 series in 2010.

He didn't hang around before jumping into single-seaters either, starting in the French F4 series in 2011 when he was just 15. Despite being the youngest driver on the grid, he ranked third and this helped him to find the backing to move up to Formula Renault the following year. He became European champion at his second attempt and Red Bull added him to its list of supported drivers, helping him to make his next move up the racing ladder.

Pierre spent 2014 in Formula Renault 3.5, and he made a push for the title but ended up second behind the more experienced Carlos Sainz Jr. Then came two years in F1's feeder formula of the day, GP2. The first resulted in a handful of podium visits and eighth overall, but a change to Prema Racing helped him to four wins and the 2016 title.

Some years, there are no available seats in F1, so Red Bull decided that the best way for Pierre to develop his talent was to race in Japan's Super Formula. So, he headed east and gave his reputation a big boost by finishing that as runner-up. This meant that he was race-sharp, and this was useful as he was then given his F1 break towards the end of the year when Scuderia Toro Rosso dropped Daniil Kvyat.

Drivers at Toro Rosso know that good results can lead to promotion to Red Bull Racing, and a fourth place finish in the early-season Bahrain GP did the trick. However, midway through Pierre's 2019 campaign, he was dropped unceremoniously back to Toro Rosso as Alex Albon was promoted into his ride.

Pierre's day of days came in 2020, the first year that Toro Rosso was rebranded as AlphaTauri, when he took his only win to date. This happened at Monza with a fortuitously-timed pit stop, but a win is a win.

TRACK NOTES

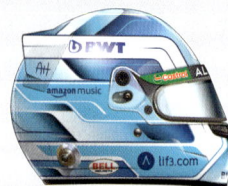

Nationality:	**FRENCH**
Born:	**7 FEBRUARY 1996, ROUEN, FRANCE**
Teams:	**TORO ROSSO 2017–18 & 2019, RED BULL RACING 2019, ALPHATAURI 2020–22, ALPINE 2023–25**

CAREER RECORD

First Grand Prix:	**2017 MALAYSIAN GP**
Grand Prix starts:	**153**
Grand Prix wins:	**1**
	2020 Italian GP
Poles:	**0**
Fastest laps:	**3**
Points:	**436**
Honours:	**2017 JAPANESE SUPER FORMULA RUNNER-UP, 2016 GP2 CHAMPION, 2014 FORMULA RENAULT 3.5 RUNNER-UP, 2013 EUROPEAN FORMULA RENAULT CHAMPION, 2010 EUROPEAN KF3 KART RUNNER-UP**

SCRAPPING FOR THE FINAL POINTS

A trio of ninth-place finishes were perhaps as good as Pierre could expect in 2024, as the Alpine team was in a mess, short of leadership and with a Renault engine that clearly offered them less than their rivals had available. On top of that, most of their rivals made progress through the course of the season and Alpine slipped back. All Pierre could do was to press on and hope to break into the top ten to collect some points. This certainly wasn't helped when he was hit by team-mate Esteban Ocon at Monaco, but he pressed on. Consecutive ninth-place finishes in Canada and Spain, followed by tenth in Austria, were a boost, but the lack of grunt from the Renault engine was a constant disappointment. News that the team will use Mercedes power from 2026 might have offered some cause for optimism, but even a year can seem a very long time in the mind of a racing driver as they all know that they are often seen as being only as good as their last result. Fortunately for Pierre, his surprise third place in Brazil was at the end of the season.

JACK DOOHAN

This son of a motorcycle-racing legend has been determined to forge his own path in the four-wheeled racing world and his seat at Alpine will give him the opportunity to display whether he really has got what it takes.

Jack shadowed the team last year and now wants to deliver in his first year in F1.

Mick Doohan amassed motorbike racing titles seemingly for fun, blazing a trail as he scorched to five consecutive 500cc world titles between 1994 and 1998.

Mick's son Jack opted to race with four wheels rather than two and advanced from karts after competing at World series level in karts and ranking third in the European OK Junior Championship with backing from Red Bull in 2017 to getting into single-seaters as soon as he could. Jack started in F4 at the age of 15 in 2018, ending the season fifth in the British series with three wins.

In 2019, Jack started the year by racing in the Asian F3 series for Hitech Grand Prix and was top rookie, ranking second overall after taking five wins. He then gained more F3 experience by racing in the Euroformula Open Championship.

Jack returned to Asian F3 at the start of 2020, but mechanical failures scuppered his bid to land the title, leaving him second overall again. The main aim of the season, though, was stepping up to the FIA F3 Championship and Jack found it tough, not once finishing in the top ten.

Back to build on the experience that he had gained, Jack joined the Trident team for 2021 and made great strides by winning four races on the way to ending the season as runner-up.

Stepping up to FIA F2 for its final three rounds, Jack showed that these more powerful cars suited him better and qualified second for the final race of the year at Yas Marina, but he spun off on lap 1.

A full F2 campaign was planned for 2022 and he shone for Virtuosi Racing, going to the final round fourth in the championship after pocketing three wins. Then, when leading the feature race, Jack's car had a wheel come loose and this dropped him out of the race and consigned him to sixth in the final reckoning.

After being given his first F1 run by Alpine at the end of 2022, Jack was signed as the team's reserve driver for 2023, to run alongside a second full F2 campaign, again with Virtuosi, in which he ranked third.

TRACK NOTES

Nationality:	**AUSTRALIAN**
Born:	**20 JANUARY 2003, GOLD COAST, AUSTRALIA**
Teams:	**ALPINE 2024–25**

CAREER RECORD

First Grand Prix:	**2024 ABU DHABI GP**
Grand Prix starts:	**1**
Grand Prix wins:	**0 (best result 15th 2024 Abu Dhabi GP)**
Poles:	**0**
Fastest laps:	**0**
Points:	**0**
Honours:	**2021 FIA F3 RUNNER-UP, 2019 & 2019/2020 ASIAN F3 RUNNER-UP, 2016 AUSTRALIAN KA2 JUNIOR KART CHAMPION, 2015 AUSTRALIAN KA JUNIOR KART CHAMPION**

A YEAR SPENT ON THE SIDELINES

No racing driver likes to be told that he won't be racing in the season ahead, but this is what Jack knew that he would have to accept for 2024. He had done probably all that he could do in F1's feeder formula, FIA F2, albeit not landing the championship title that he craved, and it was thought wise for him to accept the role of full-season reserve driver for the Alpine team whose books he had been on for the previous two years. So, Jack settled down to the job of attending Grands Prix, performing invaluable shakedown work on the team SIM and watching and waiting for any opportunity to be sent out in the first practice session on Friday so that he could show his ability. His first free practice session was at the Canadian GP, but Jack got only three laps. Next time, he got more laps in at Silverstone, but largely this was a year of watching, listening and learning, until he was offered the chance to contest the final grand prix when Alpine released Esteban Ocon a round early.

HAAS

Last year was encouraging for the team's first year under Ayao Komatsu's guidance, with Nico Hulkenberg shining. For 2025, Ollie Bearman joins new team leader Esteban Ocon, and Toyota becomes a technical partner.

Nico Hulkenberg was a consistent scorer for Haas last year and the team will be hoping his replacements can do the same.

If there is such a thing as a conventional approach to ascending to F1, this is a team that did things differently. For starters, the cars that it ran before joining the World Championship in 2016 all had a roof and raced principally on oval tracks. This was because Gene Haas wanted to promote his machining tools and thought that NASCAR racing was the way to go. He joined forces with former champion Tony Stewart, and they helped Kevin Harvick to the title in 2014.

With the exposure Haas CNC received from this, Haas then thought about aiming at global publicity and realised that he needed to get into F1 for that. The initial plan was for the new team to be based in North Carolina, alongside the NASCAR team, but sense prevailed, and a British base was set up too. Wisely, a chassis designed by Dallara was selected plus a custom Ferrari engine deal. Then, shocking everyone, Romain Grosjean had an outstanding debut, finishing sixth at the Australian GP and then fifth place next time out in Bahrain. It was unlikely that this would be continued and indeed, only a tenth place followed, yet this was good enough to rank eighth out of the 11 teams.

After showing similar form in its second season, there was a step up in

KEY PERSONNEL & 2024 ROUND-UP

AYAO KOMATSU

Team principal Ayao first came to England when he was 18 to study automotive engineering at Loughborough University. While working on his PhD, he began working in F3 with Japanese compatriot Takuma Sato and then landed a job in F1 via Honda Racing Development with BAR before joining Renault in 2006. In 2016, he joined all-new Haas F1 and so knows the team well.

A SEASON OF PEAKS AND TROUGHS

If the team's year had been made up solely of 11th-place finishes, one place outside the points, of which Nico Hulkenberg grabbed seven and Kevin Magnussen one, then life would have been tough for the squad. However, after the setback of both cars being eliminated on the opening lap of the Monaco GP, there was a wonderful patch midway through the season when Nico raced to consecutive sixth-place finishes at the Red Bull Ring and then Silverstone, with Kevin just two places behind in Austria. Kevin then grabbed a season's best seventh in Mexico. However, Haas was edged back to seventh by Alpine.

2024 DRIVERS & RESULTS

Driver	Nationality	Races	Wins	Pts	Pos
Oliver Bearman	British	2	0	7	18th
Nico Hulkenberg	German	24	0	41	11th
Kevin Magnussen	Danish	22	0	16	15th

FOR THE RECORD

Team bases:	**Annapolis, USA**
	& Banbury, England
Active in Formula One:	**From 2016**
Grands Prix contested:	**190**
Wins:	**0**
Pole positions:	**1**
Fastest laps:	**4**
Constructors' titles:	**0**
Drivers' titles:	**0**

THE TEAM

Team owner:	**Gene Haas**
Team principal:	**Ayao Komatsu**
Chief operating officer:	**Joe Custer**
Technical leader:	**Carlo Mario Motto**
Aerodynamics team leader:	
	Christian Cattaneo
Chief designer:	**Andrea de Zordo**
Operations manager:	**Peter Crolla**
Chassis:	**Haas VF-25**
Engine:	**Ferrari V6**
Tyres:	**Pirelli**

2018 when Haas F1 soared to fifth in the rankings, helped by Kevin Magnussen grabbing two fifth-place finishes and Grosjean coming fourth in Austria.

Reality struck in 2019 as the cost of staying in the hunt in F1 began to weigh heavily on the shoulders of team principal Guenther Steiner and he knew that Magnussen's sixth place in the season's opening race in Australia was a flash in the pan.

Things got no better in 2020, and Steiner was seen berating his drivers as they not only failed to score but also ran into each other. This was great for those watching Netflix's *Drive To Survive* series, but less so for Haas F1. Ironically, the team gained global coverage when Grosjean survived an extraordinary accident at Sakhir when his car split the crash barriers and caught fire.

Seeking vital money ahead of boosting its chance of scoring points, Haas signed two rookies for 2021: Mick Schumacher, who brought the family name and came as part of the deal between Haas and engine supplier Ferrari, and Russian driver Nikita Mazepin, who brought Uralkali money. The outcome was a drop to last in the constructors' championship.

Magnussen returned in place of Mazepin for 2022 and this helped the team to advance two places to eighth overall, much of this down to the Dane coming fifth in the opening round of this year running to new technical regulations and also to a doubly good day at the Austrian GP when they finished sixth and eighth.

For 2023, Nico Hulkenberg was brought in to replace Schumacher who continued to crash too often for the team's liking, but neither the German nor Magnussen could get on with a car that consumed its tyres voraciously. It was competitive in qualifying, with Hulkenberg second fastest in Montreal. Come the races, though, both he and Magnussen would fall back down the order.

With Hulkenberg moving to Sauber for 2025, a year before the team is due to race as Audi's works entry, and Magnussen moving on to other branches of motorsport, Haas F1 will have two new names in its cockpits this year. Esteban Ocon joins after an unhappy time at Alpine and Ollie Bearman, who has knowledge of the team after standing in for Magnussen when he served a one-race ban, and then again at Interlagos.

Kevin Magnussen gave the team a reason to cheer with a fifth place in the 2022 Bahrain GP.

"We were going for sixth overall last year, so it was bittersweet to end up seventh. Everyone understands, though, that if someone said at the start of the year that we would finish seventh, we'd be happy."

Ayao Komatsu

ESTEBAN OCON

Haas F1's new team leader is a one-time Grand Prix winner, but he is starting afresh after leaving Alpine for his new team. Plenty in the F1 paddock think that this French racer can deliver, so all eyes are on him.

Esteban had a tough time at Alpine last year but enjoyed his run to second in Brazil.

After Kimi Raikkonen was talent-spotted in karts and, just 23 car races later, landed an F1 drive, the top teams started to pay attention to the best of the up-and-coming stars. Esteban was one of those who caught the eye and was made part of the Lotus F1 Junior development programme in 2010 when he was 14 and one of the front runners in the European KF3 series.

Armed with this support, Esteban started his single-seater career in Formula Renault in 2012, then ranked third in the European series in 2013. When he really impressed, though, was in 2014, when he graduated to Formula 3 with such style that he raced to nine wins and the European title for the Prema Powerteam, keeping Max Verstappen back in third.

The next step was GP3, and Esteban made it two titles in two years as although he won just once, he was seldom off the podium, finishing in the top three in 14 out of the 18 rounds. The best thing about the title was getting the Mercedes F1 test run that was its main prize. Esteban went very well in that, and Mercedes put him on to its books.

In 2016 Renault used him as its F1 reserve driver, and he went out in a number of Grand Prix practice sessions, but he was also sent by Mercedes to gain experience in something very different. This was the DTM, Germany's touring car series. However, Esteban only did half the season, as he became a full-time F1 driver when he replaced Ryo Haryanto at Manor for the final nine rounds.

Force India signed Esteban for 2017, and he claimed two fifth places in Spain and Mexico, but then Lawrence Stroll took over the team as it changed its name to Racing Point in 2019 and Lance Stroll claimed his drive. Then Renault came to the rescue in 2020, and Esteban stayed on as the team changed its name to Alpine, peaking with his only victory to date when he avoided a first corner melee to win the 2021 Hungarian GP.

TRACK NOTES

Nationality:	**FRENCH**
Born:	**17 SEPTEMBER 1996, EVREUX, FRANCE**
Teams:	**MANOR 2016, FORCE INDIA 2017–18, RENAULT 2020, ALPINE 2021–24, HAAS 2025**

CAREER RECORD

First Grand Prix:	**2016 BELGIAN GP**
Grand Prix starts:	**156**
Grand Prix wins:	**1**
	2021 Hungarian GP
Poles:	**0**
Fastest laps:	**1**
Points:	**445**
Honours:	**2015 GP3 CHAMPION, 2014 EUROPEAN F3 CHAMPION, 2011 EUROPEAN KF3 KART RUNNER-UP, 2008 FRENCH CADET KART CHAMPION**

ALPINE SAYS GOODBYE

Esteban might have thought that he was part of the furniture at Alpine since he was a French driver in a nominally French team. However, he was disabused of that notion midway through last year when, after a few spats with compatriot and team-mate Pierre Gasly, including colliding with him in the Monaco GP, he was told that he was being let go. That was brutal, but irrevocable. The big question to some after that, who thought he was marginally the better racer than Gasly, was whether Esteban would swallow his pride and keep on pushing for the remainder of the year. Impressively, he did, although Alpine's declining form made that difficult to detect at times as they both struggled. Esteban's best result by the middle of the season was ninth in the Belgian GP at Spa-Francorchamps. However, like a bolt from the blue, Alpine's entire season was redeemed when Esteban and Pierre finished in second and third places in the rain-affected and red-flagged Sao Paulo GP.

OLIVER BEARMAN

This British teenager became the sport's third-youngest F1 driver when he was drafted in for one race with Ferrari last year. Then, after impressing on a pair of outings for Haas, his reward is a full season with the American team.

Oliver will be anxious to show his worth in his first full F1 campaign.

A young kart racer's budding career takes a huge degree of management, not just in terms of the logistics required to get them and their karts to races all over their home country and perhaps around their continent, but also in how to fit in their schooling around their racing.

Ollie's early days in karting yielded many race wins in the British cadet championship before he moved up to the junior category in which he peaked in 2019 by winning both the World and European titles.

Naturally, this success was enough to convince his father that Ollie had the ability to go a lot further in the sport and so plans were laid for him to compete in single-seaters in 2020, the year in which he turned 15. He was an instant hit, right on the pace in the German and Italian F4 championships. Back for a full attack in 2021, Ollie took a phenomenal 17 victories to land both titles, and it was at this point that Ferrari signed him up to be a member of its Driving Academy. This meant leaving home to live in Italy, with schooling being done on top of the driving training programme.

A season spent in Formula 3 followed in 2022, with Ferrari placing him with crack Italian team Prema Racing. Ollie did well in his rookie season at this level as he ranked third overall after taking one win from his eight podium visits.

Anxious to keep this momentum going and with Ferrari urging him onwards, Ollie competed in the FIA F2 series for Prema in 2023 and clearly wasn't troubled by the extra power and performance in the last level before F1. He did well enough to grab a pair of race wins on the streets of Baku as well as victories at the Circuit de Catalunya and at Monza to end the year classified sixth in the points table. Even though he went well when he did two Grand Prix practice sessions for Haas F1, it was decided that a second year of F2 would be to his benefit and he stayed on with Prema. Of course, as a member of the Ferrari Driving Academy, he also got to spend grand prix weekends in the Ferrari camp.

TRACK NOTES

Nationality:	**BRITISH**
Born:	**8 MAY 2005, HAVERING, LONDON, ENGLAND**
Teams:	**FERRARI 2024, HAAS 2024–25**

CAREER RECORD

First Grand Prix:	**2024 SAUDI ARABIAN GP**
Grand Prix starts:	**3**
Grand Prix wins:	**0 (best result: 7th, 2024 Saudi Arabian GP)**
Poles:	**0**
Fastest laps:	**0**
Points:	**7**
Honours:	**2021 ADAC F4 & ITALIAN F4 CHAMPION, 2020 WORLD & EUROPEAN JUNIOR X30 KART CHAMPION & INTERNATIONAL JUNIOR X30 KART CHAMPION, 2017 BRITISH CADET KART RUNNER-UP**

STEPPING UP TO F1 & SHINING

Very few drivers can say that they made their F1 debut with Ferrari, but Ollie can. He was just settling down to his second year in F2 when Carlos Sainz Jr was sidelined with suspected appendicitis at the Saudi Arabian GP and Ollie was asked to stand in. With no chance to acclimatise, he simply got in and got on, qualifying 11th and finishing in seventh place, just behind George Russell's Mercedes but ahead of Lando Norris' McLaren. Then it was back to F2, and it was a season of highs and lows that gradually became more competitive as he and the Prema Racing team got to grips with the new-for-2024 car; it was a car that kept all the team engineers guessing as they learnt its foibles, and he raced to wins at the Red Bull Ring, Monza and Lusail. The year kept getting better for Ollie and he had another F1 ride, this time with Haas F1, when Kevin Magnussen was serving a one-race ban. This was in Baku and Ollie scored again, coming home tenth ahead of team-mate Nico Hulkenberg. He also raced in Brazil.

RB

Changing a driver during the course of a season is not something that teams tend to do, but RB dropped Daniel Ricciardo in 2024. The team now needs a strong run with both Yuki Tsunoda and rookie Isack Hadjar.

Yuki Tsunoda pressed on and claimed points whenever his car was competitive last year, such as here in the Miami GP.

There was something wonderfully old-fashioned in the way that this team of many names ascended to F1. Certainly, this was back when things in motor racing were more organic, but there was a purity to the way in which Giancarlo Minardi tried F2. His cars did well in the hands of Michele Alboreto and Alessandro Nannini, and he thought that he ought to make the final step just when F2 was to be replaced by F3000. There was no raft of corporate finance behind this in 1985, just a desire to race in F1 and a degree of hope.

Minardi didn't make much of an impression in its early outings, held back by a lack of money and, in turn, heavy Motori Moderni engines. A change to Ford power in 1988 brought its first point, when Pierluigi Martini finished sixth in Detroit and a pair of fifth places in 1989 marked further progress. Martini shocked everyone by qualifying on the outside of the front row for 1990's season-opening race on the streets of Phoenix thanks to Pirelli's superior qualifying tyre. In races, though, his tyres were no match for his rivals' Goodyears and he fell to seventh and failed to score a point all year.

Where Minardi did shine, though, was in giving young drivers their F1 break, including future world champion Fernando Alonso, allowing them to get

KEY PERSONNEL & 2024 ROUND-UP

TIM GOSS

A graduate of Imperial College London, the team's new chief technical officer had his first involvement with motor racing when he joined Cosworth in 1986. He moved to McLaren in 1990 and stayed for decades, rising from being in charge of engine installation design to being Mika Hakkinen's race engineer, then chief powertrain engineer and kept on rising to become the team's technical director after Paddy Lowe left. Moving on after 28 years, Tim then worked for the FIA as its technical director before joining RB.

EASING ITS WAY UP THE F1 ORDER

From eighth overall in 2023, this newly renamed team fought it out in 2024 with Alpine and Haas F1 for sixth place, but ended up finishing eighth again despite a better points haul. The camp wasn't an entirely happy one though, as Daniel Ricciardo was brought back for a full season so that his speed would put pressure on Sergio Perez at Red Bull Racing, but the results weren't sufficient, and Liam Lawson was given his seat for the final six Grands Prix.

2024 DRIVERS & RESULTS

Driver	Nationality	Races	Wins	Pts	Pos
Liam Lawson	New Zealander	6	0	4	21st
Daniel Ricciardo	Australian	18	0	12	17th
Yuki Tsunoda	Japanese	24	0	30	12th

FOR THE RECORD

Team base:	**Faenza, Italy**
Active in Formula One:	**As Minardi 1985–2005, Toro Rosso 2006–19, AlphaTauri 2020–2023, RB 2024 on**
Grands Prix contested:	**715**
Wins:	**2**
Pole positions:	**1**
Fastest laps:	**4**
Constructors' titles:	**0**
Drivers' titles:	**0**

THE TEAM

Team principal:	**Laurent Mekies**
Chief executive:	**Peter Bayer**
Chief technical officer:	**Tim Goss**
Technical director:	**Jody Egginton**
Deputy technical director:	**Guillaume Cattelani**
Chief designer:	**Paolo Marabini**
Head of vehicle performance:	**Guillaume Dezoteux**
Racing director:	**Alan Permane**
Sporting director:	**Marco Perrone**
Chassis:	**RB V-CARB02**
Engine:	**Honda RBPT V6**
Tyres:	**Pirelli**

used to F1 away from the glare as few expected much of Minardi's underdogs.

The Red Bull drinks company had been attracted increasingly by F1. It bought Jaguar Racing and turned that into Red Bull Racing for 2005, then took over Minardi for the following year, changing its name to Scuderia Toro Rosso. The team continued to operate from Minardi's base in Faenza, and its aim wasn't wins but to bring on the pick of the drivers rising through Red Bull's scholarship scheme that signed the best kart racers and junior formulae drivers and helped them up the single-seater ladder. If they proved good enough at Toro Rosso, then they might be promoted to Red Bull Racing.

This policy was thrown into focus when Sebastian Vettel dominated a wet 2008 Italian GP and gave the team its first win, rather embarrassingly before Red Bull Racing struck gold itself. Promotion followed for the German ace and he would go on to win four titles in a row from 2010.

With Red Bull's motorsport consultant Helmut Marko keeping an eye on young talent, drivers at Toro Rosso knew that promotion to Red Bull Racing wasn't always lasting, as Daniil Kvyat discovered when he was demoted to Toro Rosso. Notably, one driver advancing from Toro Rosso had no such fears as he won on his debut. That was Max Verstappen, who took Kvyat's seat at the 2016 Spanish GP and the rest is history.

The team's name was changed to Scuderia AlphaTauri for marketing reasons in 2020 and gained more presence by running in a livery of its own rather than a 'mini me' version of Red Bull Racing's. Every F1 fan used to have a space in their heart for plucky Minardi, perhaps less so for Toro Rosso and AlphaTauri, but there was delight at Monza when Pierre Gasly took victory.

For 2024, there was another new name, and it was revealed only after a close season of debate that the chassis would be known as VCARB, short for

Visa Card App Red Bull. Even the sport's insiders ignored that, and it was known in the paddock as RB.

The team's intent to progress was made clear last year when it snapped up the services of Tim Goss from McLaren via the FIA, Guillaume Cattelani from Red Bull Racing and Alan Permane from Alpine.

Pierre Gasly celebrates taking this team's second-ever win, at the 2020 Italian GP.

"**Last year was a mega-intense year from day one. We had our highs and lows along the way but we have started to build stronger foundations together for the future of the team.**"

Laurent Mekies

YUKI TSUNODA

This could prove to be Yuki's final year with the only team for which he has raced in F1, first as AlphaTauri and then RB, because a host of drivers are queuing up in F2 looking to show that they can do better.

Yuki continues to race for RB but didn't get his promotion to a Red Bull Racing seat.

Motor racing has always been popular in Japan, with incredibly strong national championships for single-seaters and GTs, plus annual visits from the top international series. However, the list of Japanese drivers who have made it to F1, let alone shone in it, is surprisingly short.

Yuki realised that it might be possible to become one of those when he was only 12 years old after coming second in the World FP junior kart championship.

His first step in single-seaters was in Japanese F4 after he had been made to focus on his academic studies. Yuki ranked third at the conclusion of his second year in the category but then rattled off seven wins in 2018 to become champion.

Next stop was Europe, leaping straight into the FIA European series but also gaining extra track time in the Euroformula Open series that used F3 machinery, winning a race in each.

Helped by being one of Red Bull's academy drivers, he had the funds to start his 2020 season in New Zealand where he finished the Toyota Racing Series in fourth, then return to Europe to step up to F2. This was a huge success as Yuki grabbed three wins to end the year third, as Mick Schumacher landed the title.

No doubt anxious to have a Japanese driver in F1 again, Yuki was then offered a ride with Red Bull's second team, Scuderia AlphaTauri (now rebranded RB), and there he has remained ever since. Teams rise and fall in F1 and, as yet, his 2021 F1 season remains his best points haul, as Yuki gathered 32 of them, with his fourth place in the season-closing Abu Dhabi GP still the best result that Yuki has ever achieved.

Yuki's speed and clear aggression when in the cockpit was clear to see as the Japanese driver learnt from Pierre Gasly, but the number of early accidents soon dwindled as he calmed down a little. In 2023, though, Yuki became team leader when he outperformed Nyck de Vries then matched his replacements Daniel Ricciardo and Liam Lawson.

TRACK NOTES

Nationality:	**JAPANESE**
Born:	**11 MAY 2000, KANAGAWA, JAPAN**
Teams:	**ALPHATAURI 2021–23, RB 2024-25**

CAREER RECORD

First Grand Prix:	**2021 BAHRAIN GP**
Grand Prix starts:	**87**
Grand Prix wins:	**0 (best result: 4th, 2021 Abu Dhabi GP)**
Poles:	**0**
Fastest laps:	**1**
Points:	**91**

Honours: **2018 JAPANESE F4 CHAMPION, 2017 EAST JAPAN F4 CHAMPION, 2012 WORLD FP KART RUNNER-UP, 2011 & 2010 NEW TOKYO NTC KART CHAMPION, 2006 JAPANESE KID KARTS CHAMPION**

BEATING RICCIARDO SAVED SEAT

The Red Bull driver scholarship has brought a handful of drivers to F1 across the years, but none, with the exception of world champions Sebastian Vettel and Max Verstappen, can ever feel secure. Fail to perform to the level that Helmut Marko expects, either for Red Bull Racing or its junior team, RB, and you're out. This was the sword of Damocles held over both Yuki and Daniel Ricciardo last year and it was the Japanese driver who scored more points. Neither had done enough to merit promotion to Red Bull Racing for 2025, but at least Yuki kept his ride at RB. The high points of his season were his pair of seventh-place finishes in Australia and Miami early in the year, followed by a third seventh-place finish in the streaming wet Sao Paulo GP. Point-scoring positions became harder to come by as the top teams became more competitive as the season progressed, but Yuki kept on attacking and gathered some useful points in a couple of late-season races.

ISACK HADJAR

When Sergio Perez was dropped by Red Bull Racing after last season, it opened a door into F1 for this promising French driver, a star last year in F2 who had otherwise been hoping for, at most, a reserve F1 driver role.

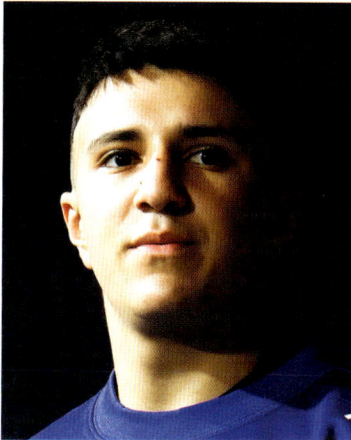

Isack ended up as the F2 driver with the most wins last year.

After racing impressively in European and World karting circles, Isack contested six rounds of the French Formula 4 series towards the end of the 2019 season when he was just 15. He showed his talent by winning one of these, then built on this experience by racing in the United Arab Emirates series at the start of 2020, then contested a full season of French F4, winning three times to rank third overall.

After having a crack at the Asian Formula 3 series at the start of 2021, Isack raced to a pair of wins and fifth place overall in the more hotly contested Formula Regional European Championship.

Then, after keeping himself race sharp by starting his 2022 campaign with two victories in the Formula Regional Asian series, Isack stepped up to the FIA Formula 3 Championship for 2022. He settled in quickly with the Hitech GP team to score the first of his three wins early in the year against many more experienced competitors – eventually losing out in a four-way title battle with Victor Martins, Zane Maloney and Oliver Bearman.

Instead of returning to try and land the title, he tested a Formula 2 car for Hitech and decided that this was what he wanted to race in 2023. Isack first demonstrated his pace at this final level beneath F1 by qualifying on pole for F2's support race in Monaco, but retired from that. However, a win came Isack's way when he triumphed at Zandvoort. Yet, a final ranking of only 14th meant that he would need to return to try to do better in 2024.

So, after moving across to Campos Racing last year, Isack really stepped up to the plate and ranked second overall. Before the year was out, Isack made the most of being one of Red Bull's young drivers by trying F1 too. He had a run with both Scuderia AlphaTauri and Red Bull Racing and it was his speed that put him in a position to move up to F1 should Sergio Perez leave Red Bull Racing, which he did in December 2024.

SHINING AT SECOND TIME OF ASKING

The battle for honours in last year's FIA Formula 2 Championship was incredibly tight, with Isack heading to the final two races at Abu Dhabi's Yas Marina Circuit just half a point behind Gabriel Bortoleto after he outscored the Brazilian across the pair of races at the penultimate round at Lusail. Driving for the Campos Racing team, the 20-year-old Parisian had made clear progress during his second season in F1's feeder formula. Four retirements in the first seven races didn't suggest that he would be a title challenger, even though that run of races included a win. It was a famously difficult season as the teams all struggled to become accustomed to the new F2 car, but Isack then added a second win in the eighth race, at Imola, and things picked up from there as he began a flow of points. A third win followed at Silverstone and another at Spa, and then Isack chipped away at Bortoleto's points margin, seeking the consistency that would be key. With Perez out of sorts at Red Bull, he knew that an F1 seat might be his prize and seized his chance.

TRACK NOTES

Nationality:	**FRENCH**
Born:	**28 SEPTEMBER 2004,**
	PARIS, FRANCE
Teams:	**RB 2025**

CAREER RECORD

First Grand Prix:	**2025 AUSTRALIAN GP**
Grand Prix starts:	0
Grand Prix wins:	0
Poles:	0
Fastest laps:	0
Points:	0
Honours:	**2024 FIA FORMULA 2 RUNNER-UP**

WILLIAMS

There was a drop from seventh place in 2023 to ninth last year but expect progress this season as Carlos Sainz Jr arrives to join Alex Albon in a team that is benefitting from the restructuring work carried out by principal James Vowles.

Alex Albon came home with points in last year's British GP but Williams struggled to score often enough to feature strongly.

Sir Frank Williams was a remarkable man. Firstly, he was a racing driver, reaching F3 when there were races pretty much every weekend somewhere around Europe. He was one of the racing gypsies who travelled around hoping equally for the glory of wins but also the prize money too. A lack of funds was always a problem, though, and he came to the conclusion that he might go higher up racing's ladder if he ran cars for those who did have the funds.

Frank duly took Piers Courage under his wing and ran him in F3 then F2. He then bought a Brabham for 1969 when they stepped up to F1, with a pair of second place finishes in Monaco and the US GP at Watkins Glen standing out. For 1970, life was expected to be easier as he landed backing from the de Tomaso sports car company and had a car built to carry its name. Sadly, Courage crashed and burned to death in the Dutch GP. Understandably, this hit Frank hard, but

he came back all the more determined and spent the middle part of the decade trying every trick he could think of to keep his team going. Second place for Jacques Laffite in the 1975 German GP stood out and was perhaps why Austrian oil baron Walter Wolf asked Frank to run a team for him. It was not a marriage

KEY PERSONNEL & 2024 ROUND-UP

JAMES VOWLES

This British engineer, who is leading the reshaping of the way Williams is run, qualified with a masters' degree in motorsport engineering from Cranfield University and went straight into F1 with BAR. That was in 2001 and he stayed with the team as it changed to be first Honda Racing, Brawn GP then Mercedes, focusing on strategy. The titles flowed as James rose to become motorsport strategy director. He then moved to Williams to be team principal at the start of 2023 after Jost Capito moved on.

STARTING TO SHOW SIGNS OF REBIRTH

Everyone who watched F1 in the 1980s and 1990s can only respect Williams, so it was with some pleasure that the sport's insiders got to watch signs of the first shoots of recovery last year. Logan Sargeant wasn't doing much to back up Alex Albon, crashing too often and failing to score a single point, so he was replaced by rookie Franco Colapinto and immediately things began to change, with a double points finish in Baku.

2024 DRIVERS & RESULTS

Driver	Nationality	Races	Wins	Pts	Pos
Alex Albon	British/Thai	23	0	12	16th
Franco Colapinto	Argentinian	9	0	5	19th
Logan Sargeant	American	14	0	0	23rd

FOR THE RECORD

Team base:	**Grove, England**
Active in Formula One:	**From 1971**
Grands Prix contested:	**839**
Wins:	**114**
Pole positions:	**128**
Fastest laps:	**133**
Constructors' titles:	**9**
Drivers' titles:	**7**

THE TEAM

Chairman:	**Matthew Savage**
Team principal:	**James Vowles**
Chief technical officer	**Pat Fry**
Chief operating officer:	
	Frederic Brousseau
Sporting director:	**Sven Smeets**
Chief aerodynamicist:	**Adam Kenyon**
Design director:	**Dave Worner**
Head of design:	**Jonathan Carter**
Chief engineer:	**Dave Robson**
Team manager:	**David Redding**
Chassis	**Williams FW47**
Engine:	**Mercedes V6**
Tyres:	**Pirelli**

made in heaven and the pair parted company. Wolf went on to finance his own team that would win on its debut in 1977 and Frank forged a partnership with engineer Patrick Head that would wholly exceed that.

Victory was finally earned in the 1979 British GP when Clay Regazzoni won at Silverstone. However it was Alan Jones who was the team's standard-bearer, and he raced to the 1980 drivers' title as Williams scored almost double the points of second-ranked Ligier. Another title followed in 1982 when Keke Rosberg came out on top in a really tight title battle.

There was a huge setback just before the start of the 1986 World Championship when Frank crashed his car after leaving a pre-season test and was paralysed from the neck down, leaving him wheelchair-bound for the rest of his life.

It took a combination of Honda engines and the FW11 chassis to put the team back on track. In 1986, Nigel Mansell would have won the title but for a blow-out late in the final round in Adelaide. His team-mate Nelson Piquet got the job done in 1987.

V10 engines have a special place in the affections of older F1 fans and the Renault V10 was the pick of these and gave the team its greatest purple patch. This started in 1992 when Mansell had the supreme FW14B at his disposal and he steamrollered the opposition with it. Frank and Patrick then replaced him with Alain Prost and he made it two titles in a row. Prost was then also moved on, to be replaced by Ayrton Senna who was expected to make it three in a row. But tragically, after finding a stern challenge from Benetton's Michael Schumacher, he crashed fatally in the third round at Imola.

Damon Hill stepped up to be team leader and was a serious title contender over the next few years before taking the crown in 1996. This was matched by Jacques Villeneuve in 1997.

Williams went well with BMW engines in the early 21st century but lost works engine deals and slipped down the constructors' table. Then, in 2020, the team was sold.

The arrival of Carlos Sainz from Ferrari will bolster its likelihood of gathering the points to help guide it up the constructors' championship table, in which positions mean dollars at the end of the season.

"Success is being at the sharp end of the grid and everything that we have gone through has built a set of foundations that mean that we won't return to the tail of the grid again."

James Vowles

Nigel Mansell enjoyed Williams' strongest run, winning nine times in 1992, including at Silverstone.

ALEX ALBON

🇬🇧 🇹🇭

Times in F1 are changing and Alex has as much confidence in Williams as the team has in him. However, it might take until the arrival of new technical rules in 2026 for the teams to make a move up the grid.

Alex deserves a better car in 2025 after years working miracles to help Williams score points.

Like so many of his rivals, there was a strong racing backbone in Alex's family, with his father Nigel competing in the British Touring Car Championship and then racing Ferraris and Porsches across South-East Asia. So, it was only natural that Alex would be introduced to kart racing.

Alex was runner-up in the World KF1 series in 2011 when he was 15.

From there, it was a simple hop into single-seaters, starting with Formula Renault the following year, already with the assistance of Red Bull's driver search programme. The key with this programme is to keep winning, but Alex didn't and lost the backing at the end of his second year in the category.

A third year in Formula Renault followed, this time with support from the Lotus F1 junior team, and Alex ranked third overall. This was his redemption, and he then performed well but not spectacularly in the 2015 European F3 series. Following this, a move to GP3 for 2016 was a bit of a risk, but Alex got back up to speed and ended the series as runner-up to Charles Leclerc.

Staying on with ART Grand Prix, Alex advanced to FIA F2 in 2017 and ranked tenth. So, a second attempt was going to be required, moving to DAMS for 2018. And what a year it turned out to be as a three-way fight ensued between Alex and fellow British drivers George Russell and Lando Norris, with Alex ending up third with four wins.

This got him back into Red Bull's young driver programme and he was rewarded with his F1 break with Scuderia Toro Rosso for 2019 and the season became better still when he moved up to Red Bull Racing during the season when Pierre Gasly was dropped in the other direction after disappointing results.

Despite taking two third-placed finishes in 2020, he was overshadowed by Max Verstappen and dropped. This meant a year racing touring cars in the DTM, but Alex returned to F1 in 2022 with Williams and his form has helped the troubled team move forward again.

TRACK NOTES

Nationality:	**BRITISH/THAI**
Born:	**23 MARCH 1996, LONDON, ENGLAND**
Teams:	**TORO ROSSO 2019, RED BULL RACING 2019–2020, WILLIAMS 2022–25**

CAREER RECORD

First Grand Prix:	**2019 AUSTRALIAN GP**
Grand Prix starts:	**104**
Grand Prix wins:	**0 (best result: 3rd, 2020 Tuscan GP & Bahrain GP)**
Poles:	**0**
Fastest laps:	**0**
Points:	**240**
Honours:	**2016 GP3 RUNNER-UP, 2011 WORLD KF1 KART RUNNER-UP, 2010 EUROPEAN KF3 KART CHAMPION, 2009 SUPER 1 HONDA KART CHAMPION**

COLLECTING POINTS WHERE POSSIBLE

While the management has been changed at Williams since the take-over at the end of 2020, most recently with team principal James Vowles arriving from Mercedes at the start of 2023, the desired move up the constructors' table didn't happen in 2024. In fact, Williams fell from seventh in the rankings in 2023 to ninth overall last year. None of this decline could be blamed on Alex, who was as competitive as ever, but Haas F1 had a superior chassis-engine package and so did a better job. Any time a Williams driver got into the top ten last year, either in qualifying or in a race, was cause for celebration and a highlight was Alex's drive to seventh place in the Azerbaijan GP. A pair of retirements in Singapore and Mexico and a non-start in Brazil rather spoiled his late-season results. Knowing that he will have Carlos Sainz Jr as a team-mate in 2025 will certainly have given Alex reason to focus extra hard over the close season and their rivalry will be a feature of the year ahead, very much to the benefit of everybody at Williams.

CARLOS SAINZ JR

When Lewis Hamilton looked to Ferrari for a ride in 2025, one driver was going to have to move, and it was decided that it would be Carlos. He considered his options, didn't get a Mercedes ride, and opted for Williams, hoping they would find form.

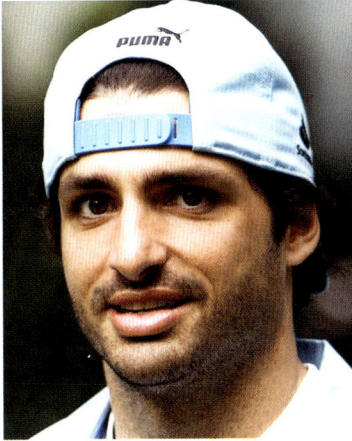

Carlos' arrival has given Williams its strongest driver line-up in years.

Racing and rallying don't often go together, being seen as the opposite ends of motorsport. Yet, in the Sainz household, they most certainly do. Carlos Sainz Sr tried both, but it was in the latter specialisation that he made his fame and fortune, becoming World Rally Champion for Toyota in both 1990 and 1992.

His son, Carlos Jr, was only ever interested in competing on circuits.

Karting came first and Carlos was right at the top of the European scene, finishing as runner-up in the KF3 category in 2009 and winning the Monaco Kart Cup.

Then came single-seaters, starting with Formula BMW in 2010, the year in which Carlos turned 16. He moved up to Formula Renault and was second in the European series. Fifth place in the European F3 Championship in 2012 was a good way to follow that, and continued support from being one of Red Bull's young drivers took him into GP3 in 2013. However, the year didn't go well and only showing speed in a Formula Renault 3.5 test kept him on their payroll.

Carlos then stepped up in 2014 and stormed the Formula Renault 3.5 series, beating Pierre Gasly to the title. And so, the door to F1 swung open, with Carlos racing for Scuderia Toro Rosso for the next two and a half seasons. He then switched to Renault midway through 2017 when Jolyon Palmer was dropped from its line-up, and he ended the season ranked ninth overall.

In 2019, Carlos joined McLaren and then was ranked sixth in each of the next two seasons, coming within 0.4 seconds of winning the Italian GP in 2020.

Then came a move to Ferrari and Carlos achieved career-high end-of-season rankings of fifth in both 2021 and then 2022 as well as grabbing his first win at Silverstone in 2022 and his second at Marina Bay in 2023, picking up the scraps when Red Bull Racing's Max Verstappen faltered.

TRACK NOTES

Nationality:	SPANISH
Born:	1 SEPTEMBER 1994, MADRID, SPAIN
Teams:	TORO ROSSO 2015–17, RENAULT 2017–18, McLAREN 2019–20, FERRARI 2021–24, WILLIAMS 2025

CAREER RECORD

First Grand Prix: **2015 AUSTRALIAN GP**

Grand Prix starts: **206**

Grand Prix wins: **4**
2022 British GP, 2023 Singapore GP, 2024 Australian GP, Mexico City GP

Poles: **6**

Fastest laps: **4**

Points: **1272.5**

Honours: **2014 FORMULA RENAULT 3.5 CHAMPION, 2011 EUROPEAN FORMULA RENAULT RUNNER-UP & NORTHERN EUROPE FORMULA RENAULT CHAMPION, 2009 MONACO KART CUP WINNER & EUROPEAN KF3 RUNNER-UP, 2008 ASIA PACIFIC JUNIOR KART CHAMPION, 2006 MADRID CADET KART CHAMPION**

BOUNCING BACK FROM ILLNESS

This was Carlos' fourth season with Ferrari and, as he was made aware of early in the year, it was to be his last. A third-place finish in the opening round between the two Red Bulls was as good a start as he could have hoped for. Then, suspected appendicitis meant that Carlos had to miss the second round of the season in Jeddah, but he bounced back with a fabulous win in the third round, in Melbourne. This was the first sign that Red Bull Racing's Max Verstappen might not have everything go his way in 2024. However, further wins were to prove hard to come by as first McLaren and then Mercedes raised their games. Suddenly, the front of the field was as competitive as it had been for years, and every podium result was hard fought. Impressively, as Carlos came to terms with the fact that neither Mercedes nor Red Bull Racing were going after his signature and he had to settle for lesser Williams instead, he continued to race with his cool style, even though Ferrari gradually lost ground to their rivals.

SAUBER

This Swiss team will spend its final season racing as Sauber before being renamed as Audi for 2026. It really does need something special to shake it out of its poor form so at the very least it can start scoring points regularly again.

There is an all-new driver line-up at Sauber for the first year in which Audi is involved, with Valtteri Bottas one of those dropped.

Over the years since it made its F1 debut in 1993, the team founded by one-time sports car entrant Peter Sauber has been connected with Mercedes, BMW and nominally Alfa Romeo as well as being used by Ferrari to bring on its young driver Charles Leclerc. Next year, it will take the name of another manufacturer: Audi. Hopefully for all involved the manufacturer's money will be enough to start turning this team around and driving it out of its slump. Don't expect miracles straight away, though.

Peter Sauber built cars initially to compete in hill climbs then in sports car racing, with the Le Mans 24 Hours his primary aim. In fact, his prototypes went so well that Mercedes started paying attention and, in time, financing his project. The Silver Arrows won at Le Mans in 1989, with Jochen Mass, Manuel Reuter and Stanley Dickens in the winning line-up. That same year, Jean-Louis Schlesser was crowned World Sportscar Champion for the team, then added another title in 1990,

partnered by Mauro Baldi, while a young Michael Schumacher gained valuable experience paired with Jochen Mass.

Then, sure that he had Mercedes support to try F1, Sauber gained a place in the 1993 World Championship. Plans for this to be backed by Mercedes collapsed but Sauber went ahead anyway and did

KEY PERSONNEL & 2024 ROUND-UP

JONATHAN WHEATLEY

Starting as a mechanic with Benetton in the 1990s, Jonathan crossed over to Red Bull Racing when it morphed out of Jaguar Racing in 2005. He rose through the ranks from chief mechanic to become sporting director, a role that he filled for many years as the team first became Grand Prix winners and then world champions, with Sebastian Vettel its first title winner and then Max Verstappen in recent years. This degree of expertise ought to help Sauber as it waits for Audi's arrival.

TAKING A STEP INTO OBSCURITY

The 2024 season was one of Sauber's toughest in its 32-year existence as its drivers Valtteri Bottas and Zhou Guanyu looked set to score not a single championship point between them. Fortunately, albeit in the 23rd of the 24 rounds, Zhou saved Sauber from embarrassment by coming home eighth in the Qatar GP. But despite Sauber's best efforts, it was clear that Haas had vaulted past them in F1's order and there was no avoiding last place in the constructors' table.

2024 DRIVERS & RESULTS

Driver	Nationality	Races	Wins	Pts	Pos
Valtteri Bottas	Finnish	24	0	0	22nd
Zhou Guanyu	Chinese	24	0	4	20th

FOR THE RECORD

Team base:	**Hinwil, Switzerland**
Active in Formula One:	**As Sauber 1993–2018 & 2024 (as BMW Sauber 2006–10), Alfa Romeo 2019–23)**
Grands Prix contested:	**590**
Wins:	**1**
Pole positions:	**1**
Fastest laps:	**7**
Constructors' titles:	**0**
Drivers' titles:	**0**

THE TEAM

Owner:	**Finn Rausing**
Chairman:	**Gernot Dollner**
Chief technical officer:	**Mattia Binotto**
Team principal:	**Jonathan Wheatley**
Technical director:	**James Key**
Head of aerodynamics:	**Alessandro Cinelli**
Racing director:	**Xevi Pujolar**
Chief designer:	**Eric Gandelin**
Head of race engineering:	
	Giampaolo Dall'Ara
Sporting director:	**Ignacio Rueda**
Chassis:	**Sauber C45**
Engine:	**Ferrari V6**
Tyres:	**Pirelli**

well enough to rank above four other teams, with JJ Lehto finishing fifth on its debut in South Africa.

A works engine deal followed for 1994, and Karl Wendlinger came fourth at Imola, a result matched by Heinz-Harald Frentzen at Magny-Cours. However, McLaren spoiled things by taking the Mercedes engine deal and Sauber lost momentum over the next few campaigns with Ford power. Yet, every now and again, this lean team produced a podium result, starting with Frentzen at the 1995 Italian GP and being emulated by similar results achieved by Jean Alesi, Johnny Herbert and Nick Heidfeld.

It was only when BMW offered its backing in 2006 that things began to improve and, finally, after two second places in the first two races of 2008, its first win came. This was in Canada when not only did Robert Kubica win, but Heidfeld finished second. Sauber ranked third that year, a career best.

When the deal with BMW ended, Sauber chose to use customer Ferrari engines from 2011 on, and the team's only decent result since then was Sergio Perez chasing Fernando Alonso's Ferrari home in the 2012 Malaysian GP. In 2018, Sauber was given a boost when Ferrari placed Leclerc with the team and he shone, particularly in qualifying.

Then, in 2019, a year after Peter Sauber stepped back as the Rausing family bought a major shareholding, the team became associated with Alfa Romeo. As with other teams before it, this had no bloodline that connected it with that manufacturer's previous involvement in F1, but was a badging exercise. No Alfa Romeo engines were used, as there were none available, so the team raced on with Ferrari power.

The team continued to operate from its base in Switzerland – a location that still limits the signing of F1's top technical brains, who prefer to remain in Britain – and the results didn't improve, even when Kimi Raikkonen led its attack in 2019. There was improved form in 2022 when the team ranked sixth, thanks to strong early-season form from Valtteri Bottas, but it dropped back to ninth in 2023.

Mattia Binotto was brought in last year to be chief technical officer following Frederic Vasseur's departure to run Ferrari's F1 attack. However, once he has served his gardening leave, former Red Bull Racing sporting director Jonathan Wheatley will relieve Binotto of some of his workload when he assumes the role of team principal.

BMW backing boosted Sauber in 2008, with Robert Kubica winning in Canada.

> **"I am proud to have been part of the Red Bull journey for 18 years. However, the opportunity to play an active part in Audi's entry into Formula 1 as head of a factory team is a uniquely exciting prospect."**
>
> Jonathan Wheatley

NICO HULKENBERG

This looks like a shrewd signing for the team that will become Audi in 2026, as this experienced German racer showed last year that he knows how to wring the maximum out of underperforming cars.

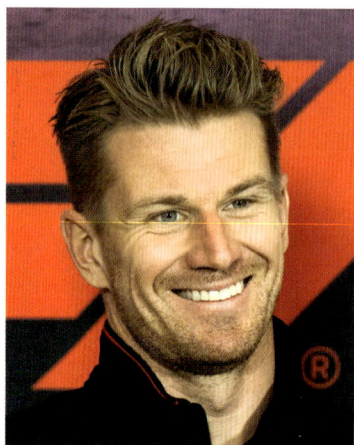

Nico is a good choice, bringing speed and experience to help the team rediscover its form.

Very few Grand Prix drivers have managed to shine in F1 without racing for one of the top teams and this is why the driver who looked to be the next German F1 star after Sebastian Vettel is still without a win.

Nico won a pair of German karting titles as he advanced through the age groups, then he made an instant impression in single-seaters by romping to the Formula BMW ADAC title at his first attempt.

This marked Nico out as one to watch but he only had the budget to graduate to F3 with a less competitive car, a Ligier rather than a Dallara. Still, he did well enough to be given a test for the country's A1GP team. This was a series for more powerful single-seaters in which drivers were chosen to race for their country. He got the German seat and dominated the 2006/07 series.

This set up Nico for a ride in the European F3 Championship and he ranked third in 2007, then landed the 2008 title. Then came GP2, the level below F1, where even some future Grand Prix winners spend at least two years. But not Nico, who won it at his first attempt, outpacing his much more experienced team-mate Pastor Maldonado.

This earned Nico his F1 break, alongside Rubens Barrichello at Williams in 2010, and he rounded out the year by taking pole in Brazil. Unfortunately for him, Maldonado arrived with a large budget, and he lost his drive. For 2012, though, Nico was back, with Force India. There was even talk of a move to Ferrari but that didn't

occur, and he soldiered on, gathering a trio of fourth-place finishes. Winning the Le Mans 24 Hours for Porsche in 2015 was a rare highlight.

A move to Renault in 2017 didn't get him clear of the midfield and so it continued with Racing Point then Aston Martin.

A move to Haas F1 in 2023 was seen as a last roll of the dice, but Nico's dogged form has kept him in demand.

TRACK NOTES

Nationality:	**GERMAN**
Born:	**19 AUGUST 1987, EMMERICH, GERMANY**
Teams:	**WILLIAMS 2010, FORCE INDIA 2012 & 2014–16, SAUBER 2013 & 2025, RENAULT 2017–19, RACING POINT 2020, ASTON MARTIN 2022, HAAS 2023–4**

CAREER RECORD

First Grand Prix:	**2010 BAHRAIN GP**
Grand Prix starts:	**227**
Grand Prix wins:	**0 (best result: 4th, 2012 Belgian GP, 2013 Korean GP, 2016 Belgian GP)**
Poles:	**1**
Fastest laps:	**2**
Points:	**571**
Honours:	**2015 LE MANS 24 HOURS WINNER, 2009 GP2 CHAMPION, 2008 EUROPEAN F3 CHAMPION, 2007 F3 MASTERS WINNER, 2006/07 A1GP CHAMPION, 2005 GERMAN FORMULA BMW ADAC CHAMPION, 2003 GERMAN KART CHAMPION, 2002 GERMAN JUNIOR KART CHAMPION**

QUALIFYING WAS ONLY REWARD

Both Haas F1 drivers knew last year that the VF-24 certainly wasn't going to win any races. They did know, though, that there was a chance of gathering a point or two here and there if they could qualify far enough up the grid and then resist attacks from faster rivals for as much of the Grand Prix as they could. Qualifying was an area in which Nico excelled, embarrassing many of the drivers from the top teams over the course of the year as he harnessed the power of his car's Ferrari engine to the full and hung on for the ride. His best grid position was a really impressive sixth, at both the British and Singapore GPs, and he raced to one of his two sixth-place finishes at the first of these. Knowing that Audi will be taking over the team in 2026 no doubt gave Nico cause to be optimistic, but he has been around F1 long enough to know that nothing happens overnight and that he will have to be in it for the long haul to reap the benefits of their increased budget.

GABRIEL BORTOLETO

After being one of the very quickest drivers in the FIA F3 and F2 series for the past two years, Gabriel is one of a new crop of F1 drivers and will be a vital asset for Sauber as it morphs into Audi. He will learn his trade from Nico Hulkenberg.

Gabriel has moved from under McLaren's wing as his F1 racing experience begins.

Gabriel followed his older brother Enzo by moving abroad from his native Brazil to try his hand racing single-seaters in Europe. His karting career had come to an end a year after he had shown his talents by ranking third at both World and European level in the OK-Junior category in 2018.

His maiden season in cars was in 2020, when he was still only 15, and came after his brother had returned home to race in touring cars. Gabriel spent It In the Itallan F4 serles and won once to rank fifth overall.

The Formula Regional European series was more of a challenge for him in 2021, and Gabriel achieved just one podium finish, a second place at the Red Bull Ring. This left him ranked outside the top 10 at the end of the season. However, he did at least get to enjoy a quartet of races in the Brazilian Stock Light series, ranking third in the rookie class.

Back for a second shot in 2022, this time with R-ace GP and with better knowledge of the circuits, the season went better, as he improved to rank sixth overall thanks to wins at Spa-Francorchamps and Barcelona.

Up to this point, Gabriel was one watch but was not considered championship-winning material. But then came 2023, when he climbed the racing ladder to the FIA F3 Championship with the Trident team, winning two of the first four races, at Sakhir then Melbourne. No further wins followed, but Gabriel impressed with outstandingly consistent form, adding four second-place finishes to a stream of point-scoring drives. He duly romped to the champlonshlp tltle, outscoring runner-up Zak O'Sullivan 164 points to 119, with Williams' stand-in driver, Franco Colapinto, ending up fourth overall.

Managed by F1's most experienced driver, Fernando Alonso, Gabriel has a great mentor in the shape of the double World Champion. He also been on McLaren's books as part of its driver development programme since the end of the 2023 season, learning invaluable skills at one of the sports top teams. However, as the McLaren didn't have a race seat available for him for the year ahead, they agreed to let him go when Sauber chief operating officer Mattia Binotto came calling.

A STAR OF THE FIA'S RACING SERIES

This has been an extraordinary season for the FIA Formula 2 Championship as new regulations meant a learning curve for all the teams. Not all of them understood their new designs straight away and this resulted in a higher number of different winners than usual, with 18 in 2024 as opposed to 13 in 2023. In F2, there are a large number of races, 28, with the top eight finishers in each of the pair of races starting the second race in reverse order. Gabriel (and Invicta Racing) made consistent progress in his first season in this category, taking a first win in the 14th race, at the Red Bull Ring, as well as a second place at Monza. His team-mate, Indian racer Kush Maini, proved that Invicta was doing something right when he became a winner too. It was consistent scoring though that took the 19-year-old to the top of the points table. It was very tight at the top, with Campos Racing's Isack Hadjar hot on his heels, but he held on to be champion.

TRACK NOTES

Nationality:	**BRAZILIAN**
Born:	**14 OCTOBER 2004,**
	SAO PAULO, BRAZIL
Teams:	**SAUBER 2025**

CAREER RECORD

First Grand Prix: **2025 AUSTRALIAN GP**

Grand Prix starts:	0
Grand Prix wins:	0
Poles:	0
Fastest laps:	0
Points:	0

Honours: **2024 FIA F2 CHAMPION, 2023 FIA F3 CHAMPION**

TOP DESIGNER ADRIAN NEWEY SEEKS A NEW CHALLENGE

Adrian Newey, the fertile brain behind more F1-winning cars than any other designer, decided last year to move on from Red Bull Racing to take on new challenges. The news triggered a bidding war for his services before he settled on joining Aston Martin. We look back at the high points of his illustrious career that spans fully 37 F1 campaigns.

There was a point midway through 2024 when it was a case of 'forget the drivers, get Newey', as Ferrari and Aston Martin went after the 65-year-old British designer's signature. His Midas touch in designing winning cars is unparalleled and thought to be more important than the input of even the best drivers.

Adrian studied aeronautical engineering at the University of Southampton, but it was his love of racing that drew him to focus on cars rather than aeroplanes. His first job was with the Fittipaldi F1 team in 1980. The following year, Adrian joined March and worked first as an engineer for its Formula 2 team; then he was allowed to start designing and he helped to produce a GTP sports car that won the IMSA series in 1983 and 1984. Next up was a spell designing March's IndyCars that won the 1985 title for Al Unser and that year's Indianapolis 500 for Danny Sullivan, with Bobby Rahal winning both the following year in Adrian's next IndyCar design. Designing cars for these different disciplines gave Adrian a broad base for all that followed.

Adrian was given his second F1 break by March when it asked him to design its 1988 challenger, and this was the first sign that he could crack F1 as one of his 881s helped Ivan Capelli finish second in the Portuguese GP. He was the team's technical director when it changed its name to Leyton House and Capelli came close to winning the French GP. Then he got fired and Adrian's move to Williams was the making of him as it provided him with the environment in which to thrive.

Working with Patrick Head, the team produced cars competitive enough to help Nigel Mansell to the crown in 1992 when he made the most of the FW14B's active-ride system to win nine of the 16 rounds. Alain Prost then did a similar job in the FW15C in 1993 and then Damon Hill added a third title in 1996 to make Williams the team of the decade.

Adrian then decided that it was time to move on, as he wanted control of the design side and knew that Head would never allow him that at Williams. So he joined McLaren as technical director in 1997, with the first car that he was involved in being the MP4-13 that dominated the 1998 season to help Mika Hakkinen to the first of two titles. But then the combined forces of Ferrari and Michael Schumacher took over and dominated the start of the 21st century and Adrian began to look for a new challenge. He was encouraged by David Coulthard to join him in moving across to Red Bull Racing for 2006, a team that had evolved from Jaguar Racing for 2005.

Red Bull Racing was not a team that knew how to win, but it became more competitive with every year, claiming its first wins in 2009 then a run of four titles in a row with Sebastian Vettel from 2010 to 2013 before Lewis Hamilton and Mercedes assumed control.

Max Verstappen took his first win with Red Bull Racing in 2016, but it took until he got his hands on the RB16B in 2021 for him to mount a title challenge that was settled in his favour at the final round.

The next two seasons put this success in the shade as he and, occasionally, Sergio Perez guided Adrian's creations to 17 wins in 2022 and then set a staggering record as the RB19 won 21 of 2023's 22 Grands Prix, with Verstappen claiming all but two of these in that second season.

Of course, such is the vast expansion in the size of F1 teams that by now Adrian was leading a huge design department, so is far from solely responsible for all this success. Yet, it's Adrian's concepts that are finessed to create the end product.

By the end of 2024 his cars had won more than 200 Grands Prix and a dozen constructors' titles, as well as helping seven different drivers land 14 drivers' titles.

Adrian wants to take on projects beyond F1 and his last four years with Red Bull Racing included leading a 140-strong design team in creating the RB17 hypercar. Don't expect that this will be the last such project, as he enjoys working without the strictures of a rule book.

Opposite top left: Sebastian Vettel and Adrian Newey celebrate victory with Red Bull Racing in 2013.

Opposite top right: Ivan Capelli led the field during the 1990 French GP.

Opposite middle: Adrian transformed Williams. This is Nigel Mansell in 1992.

Opposite bottom left: Moving on to McLaren, Adrian helped the team to win consistently in 1998.

Opposite bottom right: Fireworks fly at Yas Marina in 2023, rounding out another Verstappen title year.

NORRIS VICTORY BOOSTS BRITAIN TO 21 F1 WINNERS

When the World Championship powered into life at Silverstone in 1950, Italian teams dominated. However, British drivers soon began to show their skill and in 1953 Mike Hawthorn became the first one to win a Grand Prix, and was then crowned as Britain's first champion in 1958. Since then, no other country has produced as many winners.

In the early 1950s, Alfa Romeo led the way before Ferrari took over, then Maserati came on song. British drivers could only look on with envy, but rose to the challenge, predominantly when racing for Ferrari. But then British teams pioneered technology in the 1960s that would propel them ahead of the established teams.

Mike Hawthorn became the first British driver to win a round of the World Championship when he edged his Ferrari ahead of Juan Manuel Fangio's Maserati to win the 1953 French GP. Five years later, with Stirling Moss, Peter Collins and Tony Brooks also having become winners (in 1955 for Mercedes, 1956 for Ferrari and 1957 for Vanwall respectively), Hawthorn became Britain's first world champion.

The 1960s were a boom time for British wins. Cooper, BRM and Lotus shone, and Brabham and McLaren would follow, both owned by Antipodean drivers who based their teams in England, which had become the centre of the motor racing industry.

Ferrari remained a constant threat, but the start of the 1960s marked the blossoming of Jim Clark, Graham Hill, motorbike great John Surtees and Jackie Stewart, with all of these becoming world champions; while Innes Ireland won just once, as did Peter Gethin when he got the nose of his BRM just in front of a five-car pack to win the 1971 Italian GP.

James Hunt was the rising star when he won for Hesketh in 1975, then followed this up by coming out on top of a classic tussle with Ferrari's Niki Lauda in 1976. John Watson was also a frontrunner into the 1980s, scoring a couple of remarkable wins when charging from the back of the grid. This was also when Nigel Mansell came good and had a fabulous run to the world title in his second spell with Williams.

Williams was in a rich vein of form in the early 1990s and Damon Hill came on strong in 1996 to become the first second-generation world champion at a time when fellow British drivers Johnny Herbert and Eddie Irvine occasionally took wins.

David Coulthard became Britain's next prolific winner with McLaren in the 1990s, followed by the start of the Lewis Hamilton age, as he almost won the world title at his first attempt in 2007, but then got the job done in 2008. Jenson Button became Britain's tenth driver to be crowned world champion when he enjoyed Brawn GP's extraordinary aerodynamic advantage in 2009.

It took a move to Mercedes for Hamilton's next title in 2014, followed by five more by 2020 before he took his tally of GP victories past 100 during his 2021 campaign.

Since then, the new brigade of drivers has started to shine, with George Russell taking his first win in 2022 before McLaren's Lando Norris became Britain's 21st GP winner in Miami last year.

In terms of ranking nations, the next most successful producer of winners is Italy, with 15, while France has 14. That said, France's winners have claimed 81 victories, largely thanks to Alain Prost's 51, almost double Italy's 43. Although only seven Germans have won, Michael Schumacher (91 wins) and Sebastian Vettel (53) pushed their total to 179.

Holland is among the six nations ranked 18th on the list with one winner, but Max Verstappen's Red Bull Racing years have produced 63 wins, enough for the Dutch to rank fifth on the list for the number of wins.

British teams, including foreign-owned teams based in Britain, are also the most successful, with 19 of them (27 if team name changes are taken into account) having won 804 of the 1,111 Grands Prix up to the end of the 2024 season. Ferrari is still the most successful team with its tally of 248 victories and McLaren the best of the rest on 189.

WINNING DRIVERS BY COUNTRY

1	Great Britain – 21 winners/316 wins		7	Australia – 5 winners/45 wins
2	Italy – 15 winners/43 wins		8	USA – 5 winners/22 wins
3	France – 14 winners/81 wins		9	Argentina – 3 winners/38 wins
4	Germany – 7 winners/179 wins		10	Austria – 3 winners/41 wins
5	Brazil – 6 winners/101 wins		11	Sweden – 3 winners/12 wins
6	Finland – 5 winners/57 wins			

Opposite top left: Mike Hawthorn was the first British winner, at the 1953 French GP.

Opposite top right: It's a thumbs up from Jim Clark after winning the 1964 British GP.

Opposite middle: Jenson Button enjoyed a golden streak for Brawn GP in 2009.

Opposite bottom: Lewis Hamilton, celebrating at Silverstone, is F1's record winner.

TALKING POINT:
THE FERRARI DRIVER ACADEMY BEARS SOME FRESH FRUIT

Haas F1 signing Ollie Bearman is a fresh boost for the Ferrari Driver Academy, as he is the latest of its graduates to make the final step up to a ride in F1. The 19-year-old British driver, who shone during stand-in drives for Ferrari and Haas, follows in the tracks of Jules Bianchi, Sergio Perez, Lance Stroll, Zhou Guanyu and Charles Leclerc.

It was always said that Enzo Ferrari cared solely for his cars, with drivers coming some way further down in his reckoning. That was part of the team founder's bluff, though, to keep his drivers at arm's length back in the days when death might be just around the corner. He certainly had his favourites, from Peter Collins in the 1950s to Gilles Villeneuve in the 1980s, both of whom would be killed when racing for the Scuderia.

However, Enzo once commented 'I love to think that Ferrari can create drivers as well as cars.' And, although he had been dead for 21 years when the Ferrari Driver Academy was created in 2009, the team had already shown that it was prepared to help the best up-and-coming drivers. This was shown when it placed Euro Formula 3000 champion Felipe Massa in F1 with Sauber in 2002 to see whether the 20-year-old Brazilian could advance enough to race for Ferrari. In 2006, he made that ultimate step and never looked back.

Three years after that, the Ferrari Driver Academy opened its doors to help Jules Bianchi advance from F3 after winning the European title. The promising and popular French ace would make it to F1 four years later with the Marussia team, as part of the package in its engine deal, only to die a year after sustaining a head injury at the 2014 Japanese GP.

The Ferrari Driver Academy took on Mirko Bortolotti and Daniel Zampieri in 2010. Neither of these would go on to reach F1 but competed in GT racing with a good deal of success. Two of the following

year's intake did make it to F1, though, with Sergio Perez reaching the big time that year with Ferrari-powered Sauber and Lance Stroll, aged just 12 at the time, taking a further six years as he worked his way through the junior single-seater formulae before he became a Grand Prix driver with Williams in 2017.

The academy's 2013 intake included Antonio Fuoco, who went on to compete in endurance racing, winning the Le Mans 24 Hours for Ferrari last year. Then, with an eye on drivers starring in karting, the academy signed rising Chinese star Zhou Guanyu in 2014 just before he took his step into single-seaters. His arrival in F1 came in 2022 with Alfa Romeo, another team using Ferrari powerplants.

The greatest success story so far was the signing in 2016 of current Ferrari F1 driver Charles Leclerc who Ferrari then helped to ease into F1 for 2018 with Sauber – to whom it supplied engines. The academy's hunch that the FIA F2 champion would be competitive was proved right when he shone in qualifying. In fact, he did so well with the unfancied Swiss team that he was promoted to Ferrari for 2019 and became a winner before the year was out.

The latest success, Ollie Bearman, made the major decision to leave his school friends behind after winning world and European karting titles and starting to make an impression in junior single-seaters to join the Ferrari Driver Academy in 2022. This meant moving from England to base himself in Italy while he competed in first the FIA Formula 3 series, in which

he ranked third, and then FIA Formula 2, again with success at the last stop before F1. When Ollie was called up by Ferrari to replace an unwell Carlos Sainz Jr in Jeddah, he seized the opportunity and raced to an impressive seventh place.

Being a member of the Ferrari Driver Academy is not just about learning to race, though, as it includes a study of the sport's rules, legal matters related to racing and, of course, the history of the team.

Bearman's fellow 2024 academicians included Swedish racer Dino Beganovic, a 20-year-old race winner in the FIA F3 Championship. One level below him, both 19-year-old Brazilian, Rafael Camara and 18-year-old Finn, Tuuka Taponen were pacesetters in Formula Regional European.

The Ferrari Driver Academy also backed two racers in the all-female F1 Academy that supported most World Championship rounds, with 20-year-old Spaniard, Maya Weug, being chased by 18-year-old American-born Aurelia Nobels.

The big question is which of the 2025 intake might become the seventh member of the Ferrari Driver Academy to go on to make it to F1.

Opposite top left: Ferrari academy racer Jules Bianchi starred in Formula 3 in 2009.

Opposite top right: Current Ferrari F1 star Charles Leclerc won the 2017 FIA F2 title as a Ferrari Academy driver.

Opposite middle: There was more Ferrari Driver Academy success when Fuoco, Nielsen and Molina won Le Mans in 2024.

Opposite bottom: Oliver Bearman impressed when he made his F1 debut in 2024.

// KNOW THE TRACKS 2025

Having 24 Grands Prix in a World Championship season appears to have become the norm, but a shuffling of the race dates makes this year's championship look slightly more manageable than it was in 2024. In a welcome move, the Australian GP has been reinstated as the opening race and, with an extra two weeks of pre-season testing, the teams ought to be more ready for the off.

In the days when there were 16 Grands Prix each season, it was easier to arrange them in a logical pattern, usually with a weekend off in between. Also, with the majority of races being held in Europe, F1 was less of a logistical competition and one that gave the personnel a chance to get home. The addition of a further eight Grands Prix per year since Liberty Media bought the sport has led to understandable concerns of burn-out. But although there will be the same number of runs of three Grand Prix weekends in a row in 2025, they have been reorganised to make them less of a stress for all concerned.

The first change for this year's World Championship calendar is the Australian GP being returned to its long-standing slot as the home for the first race of the year, regaining the spot from Bahrain. This will ensure that the season is launched in the best possible style as the race is always incredibly well attended. It also makes sense to get the race that involves the longest journey from the team bases in Europe out of the way from the outset when the teams are fresh. In fact, the 2025 season is set to kick off a fortnight later than last year, offering the teams two more weeks of valuable time to get their new cars ready.

The moving of the Bahrain and Saudi Arabian GPs back to April is also down to Ramadan being held in March in 2025.

After Melbourne, F1 stops off for the Chinese GP and, a fortnight later, goes to Japan in the blossom season. The next two weekends are spent continuing to head back towards Europe via Sakhir and Jeddah in the year's first triple-header.

Ideally from a travel point-of-view, the Miami GP would be paired with the Canadian, but that still won't happen until 2026, so it's then back to Europe for a triple-header comprising visits to Imola, Monaco and Barcelona for the final Spanish GP before its move to a street circuit in capital city Madrid.

Another transatlantic hop takes the F1 circus to Montreal in June before returning to Europe for the Austrian and British GPs.

After a welcome gap of three weeks, races in Belgium and Hungary, in the reverse order to 2024, complete the run up to the much-needed summer break. This is now stipulated in the championship regulations, with all teams being forced to close their factories for a fortnight, something that has been mandated in a bid to prevent personnel burn-out.

The season then kicks back into action at the end of August with the favourite race for Max Verstappen fans, the Dutch GP at Zandvoort, then it's straight on to Monza for the Italian GP before a week's break and on again to Baku for the Azerbaijan GP.

The races at the tail-end of the season are better spaced this year, without the four-week break that was included between the Singapore and United States GPs last year. This time, the race on Singapore's Marina Bay Circuit is on 5 October, a fortnight before the cars go into battle at the Circuit of the Americas and, straight after that, in Mexico City.

There is a further week's gap as the teams continue on down through the Americas to get to Interlagos for the Brazilian GP. Then comes the same heavy-duty end to the season, with a triple-header taking in Las Vegas, Qatar and Abu Dhabi. At least the Las Vegas GP is held on Saturday night to give American F1 fans more of a chance to travel back across their giant country in time to make it to work on the Monday morning. This also allows for an extra day's travel for the teams to get to Lusail, with the final hop to Yas Marina a short one.

Sprint races will be held at the Chinese, Miami, Belgian, United States, Sao Paulo and Qatar GPs.

MELBOURNE

Now that it has been moved back to its traditional season-opening slot, the Albert Park circuit will be the setting once more for hopes realized and ambitions dashed as the teams go head-to-head.

Something just feels right about the Australian GP opening the season, getting the show on the road. Whether it is the setting, the circuit or the sheer passion for all things sporting from the fans, the event has great energy. In all honesty, the circuit would not be considered one of the greats if it was located out in the country, but its city setting really boosts its appeal and visitors can step out on to a tram to take them downtown or the short hop to Melbourne Bay to keep the fun rolling.

Recent tweaks have helped the flow of the past few races, with the opening two-corner combination now less staccato. The first real test for the drivers comes when they power down the wall-bound avenue of trees to turn 3. It's wider than it used to be and where passing moves can be made, or front wings bent.

Accelerating through turns 4 and 5, the drivers steer right at turn 6 and then build up speed around the far side of the park's lake as they hit eighth gear and reach 185mph (300kph). They are now able to keep more speed through the more open esse entered at turn 9 before braking heavily and dropping to fourth gear for the 90-degree right at turn 11. The run to the end of the lap is more enclosed and provides next to no chance of overtaking through the final three corners. In fact, a driver's focus will be on getting the best possible exit from the final corner so that they can get close enough to the car in front to line up a passing move into turn 1.

INSIDE TRACK

AUSTRALIAN GRAND PRIX

Date:	**16 March**
Circuit name:	**Albert Park**
Circuit length:	**3.280 miles/5.278km**
Number of laps:	**58**

PREVIOUS WINNERS

2013	**Kimi Raikkonen** LOTUS
2014	**Nico Rosberg** MERCEDES
2015	**Lewis Hamilton** MERCEDES
2016	**Nico Rosberg** MERCEDES
2017	**Sebastian Vettel** FERRARI
2018	**Sebastian Vettel** FERRARI
2019	**Valtteri Bottas** MERCEDES
2022	**Charles Leclerc** FERRARI
2023	**Max Verstappen** RED BULL
2024	**Carlos Sainz Jr** FERRARI

Location: Melbourne is a bustling city, with bars, restaurants and casinos lining the River Yarra and the circuit just a 1.5-mile (2.4km) tram ride to the south.

Toughest corner: Turn 6 is the one that drivers need to nail, as this right-hander feeds the cars on to the longest high-speed stretch of the circuit.

Best passing spot: This is a pick between turns 1 and 3, both tight right-handers that now offer a little more space in which to squeeze past a rival than they did before the recent modifications.

Melbourne's first Grand Prix: Having taken over from Adelaide in 1996, Melbourne's first Grand Prix was won by Damon Hill for Williams to kick off the season in which he would become world champion. However, rookie team-mate Jacques Villeneuve led until his engine suffered an oil leak, but still finished second.

Rising Australian star: With Oscar Piastri rising towards the top, the country is well set, and now Jack Doohan has landed a seat with Alpine for 2025. This 22-year-old son of legendary bike racer Mick, five-time World 500cc champion, has been gaining F1 seat time as reserve driver for Alpine after ranking second in FIA F3 in 2021, then third in F2 in 2023.

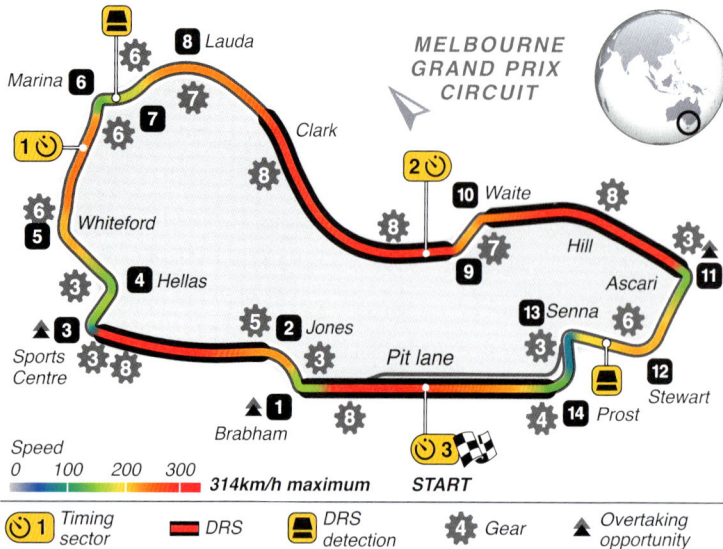

MELBOURNE GRAND PRIX CIRCUIT

Speed
0 100 200 300
314km/h maximum
START

| Timing sector | DRS | DRS detection | Gear | Overtaking opportunity |

2024 POLE TIME: **VERSTAPPEN (RED BULL), 1M15.915S, 155.523MPH/250.290KPH**
2024 WINNER'S AVERAGE SPEED: **141.869MPH/228.316KPH**
2024 FASTEST LAP: **LECLERC (FERRARI), 1M19.813S, 147.896MPH/238.066KPH**
LAP RECORD: **LECLERC (FERRARI), 1M19.813S, 147.896MPH/238.066KPH, 2024**

SHANGHAI

This circuit, with its giant facilities, raised the bar for other nations hoping to join F1 when it became part of the World Championship schedule in 2004, and it still provides the space for the drivers to really race.

INSIDE TRACK

CHINESE GRAND PRIX

Date:	23 March
Circuit name:	Shanghai International Circuit
Circuit length	3.387 miles/5.451km
Number of laps:	56

PREVIOUS WINNERS

2011	**Lewis Hamilton**	McLAREN
2012	**Nico Rosberg**	MERCEDES
2013	**Fernando Alonso**	FERRARI
2014	**Lewis Hamilton**	MERCEDES
2015	**Lewis Hamilton**	MERCEDES
2016	**Nico Rosberg**	MERCEDES
2017	**Lewis Hamilton**	MERCEDES
2018	**Daniel Ricciardo**	RED BULL
2019	**Lewis Hamilton**	MERCEDES
2024	**Max Verstappen**	RED BULL

The Shanghai International Circuit could only have been built as it was with considerable government assistance. However, that it had, as China wanted F1 and F1's sponsors really wanted to promote their brands there.

The site provided was challenging, as it was swampy, but the nation's engineering skills were put on show by the sinking of enormous polystyrene blocks to stabilize the land. The Hermann Tilke-designed circuit immediately earned plaudits for the challenge and flow that it offered. In addition, the grandstand opposite the pits was huge and the space in the paddock considerable, making life easy for the teams, all of whom could use individual villas in a park behind as their bases.

The first corner complex of four turns is a masterpiece, with a wide right-hander taking the cars up to a crest at turn 2 before diving down and turning left at turn 3, and then left again at turn 4.

Then comes the infield section, with a series of sweeping corners broken only by the broad hairpin at turn 6 and slower lefts at turns 9 and 10. After a short straight, the cars reach a section which closely mirrors the opening complex. The key part of this is the exit on to the back straight.

The straight runs for a full kilometre before the cars reach turn 14, with drivers reaching a top speed of 200mph (322kph) before having to brake for the hairpin. There is ample space for slipstreaming and the width of the track on corner entry gives drivers the chance to try several different lines as they either attack or defend.

Location: The circuit was built in countryside 20 miles (32km) north of Shanghai, but the urban spread of the past two decades has brought the city out to meet it.

Toughest corner: Turn 16 is a tricky left that can help a driver catch a tow if executed right.

Best passing spot: The long back straight makes the turn 14 hairpin the best place to make a move.

China's first Grand Prix: Rubens Barrichello was the driver who left with the widest smile, after F1's first visit, as he won for Ferrari. What made the race extraordinary was how team leader Michael Schumacher was out of sorts, failing even to set a time in qualifying. Luckily for the Tifosi, Barrichello resisted BAR's Jenson Button and McLaren's Kimi Raikkonen.

China's greatest Grand Prix: F1's 2007 visit was a stage set for rookie Lewis Hamilton to be crowned as champion at the penultimate race. However, he made an error when he stayed out too long in changeable conditions and his intermediate tyres were almost through to the canvas when he slid his McLaren into a gravel trap at pit entry and got stuck. Kimi Raikkonen, who had just passed him for the lead, then raced to victory for Ferrari.

63

SHANGHAI INTERNATIONAL CIRCUIT

START

Pit lane

Speed
0   100   200   300   348km/h maximum

⏱1 Timing sector	DRS	DRS detection
4 Gear		▲ Overtaking opportunity

2024 POLE TIME: **VERSTAPPEN (RED BULL)**, 1M33.660S, 130.189MPH/209.519KPH
2024 WINNER'S AVERAGE SPEED: **112.748MPH/181.450KPH**
2024 FASTEST LAP: **ALONSO (ASTON MARTIN)**, 1M37.810S, 124.665MPH/200.629KPH
LAP RECORD: **M SCHUMACHER (FERRARI)**, 1M32.238S, 132.202MPH/212.759KPH, 2004

SUZUKA

For the second year in succession the Japanese GP will be held in spring rather than its traditional autumn slot, when the new season is still shaping up rather than in full flow.

INSIDE TRACK ●

JAPANESE GRAND PRIX
Date:	**6 April**
Circuit name:	**Suzuka International Racing Course**
Circuit length:	**3.609 miles/5.807km**
Number of laps:	**53**

Financed by Honda and opened for racing in 1962, the Suzuka circuit had to wait on the sidelines as the Fuji Speedway became the first Japanese circuit to host a round of the World Championship. That was in 1976 and again in 1977, but it took until 1987 before Suzuka was awarded the race and it has been a near constant ever since.

The changes introduced here, as ever more modern circuits have been built in the following decades, give Suzuka an old-school feel, as the run-off areas are small and the barriers sometimes not far from the circuit's edge. However, every driver sees it as one of the year's major challenges.

What makes Suzuka so great is its flow, taking drivers at first down the hillside to the fairly open first couple of corners before doubling back, running through the fearsome Esses then flattening out at turn 7, and kinking twice to the right through the two Degners. Then, unusually, the track goes under a bridge carrying its return leg before the cars have to drop to second gear for the hairpin.

The track then opens out again through a lengthy right to its highest point at the entry to Spoon Curve, with an open, dipping left-hand entry to the homeward straight. It's flat-out from here, with its fastest point just after eighth-gear 130R, where the cars hit 195mph (315kph) after crossing over the outward leg of the lap after the Degners.

The lap ends with a tight right/left chicane complex before a dipping exit takes the cars on to the pit straight. The final corner is overlooked by the giant Ferris wheel in the amusement park across the road.

PREVIOUS WINNERS
2013	**Sebastian Vettel**	RED BULL
2014	**Lewis Hamilton**	MERCEDES
2015	**Lewis Hamilton**	MERCEDES
2016	**Nico Rosberg**	MERCEDES
2017	**Lewis Hamilton**	MERCEDES
2018	**Lewis Hamilton**	MERCEDES
2019	**Valtteri Bottas**	MERCEDES
2022	**Max Verstappen**	RED BULL
2023	**Max Verstappen**	RED BULL
2024	**Max Verstappen**	RED BULL

Location: The circuit is in rolling hills 90 miles (145km) west of Osaka, around 30 miles (48km) to the southwest of Nagoya.

Toughest corner: The Esses, an uphill, four-corner sequence of twists, stands out.

Best passing spot: The entry to the hairpin always offers an opportunity.

Suzuka's greatest Grand Prix: For sheer drama, the 1998 title shoot-out between McLaren's Mika Hakkinen and Ferrari's Michael Schumacher takes some beating. Schumacher knew that he had to win and get help from team-mate Eddie Irvine to keep Hakkinen back, but then the German wasted his pole position by stalling at the start. Forced to take the restart from the back of the grid, when Irvine failed to get ahead of Hakkinen, Schumacher soon climbed the order. But then, having got to third, his car hit debris on the track and suffered a blow-out, ensuring that Hakkinen became champion.

Rising Japanese star: Ritomo Miyata is looking to be the next Japanese F1 driver. He was champion in Japan's Super Formula single-seater series and Super GT in 2023 before competing in FIA F2 last year and recording a best finish of fifth as he learned the European circuits that make up much of the calendar.

64

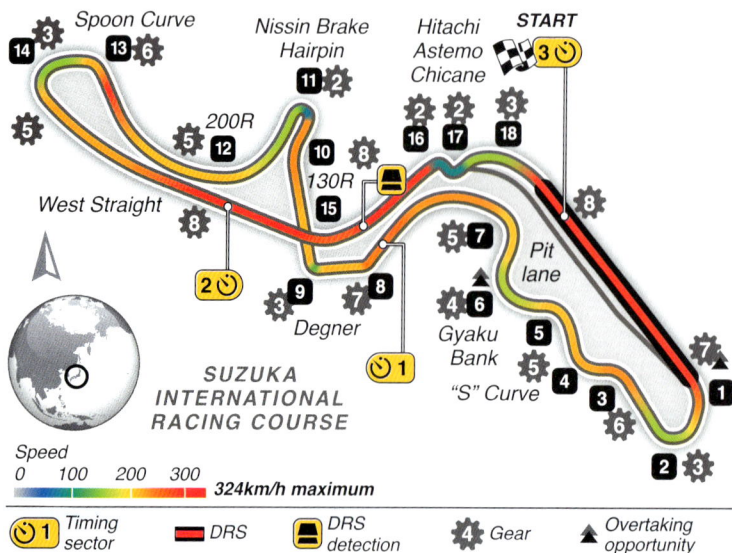

Spoon Curve — Nissin Brake Hairpin — Hitachi Astemo Chicane — START — 200R — 130R — West Straight — Degner — Gyaku Bank "S" Curve — Pit lane

SUZUKA INTERNATIONAL RACING COURSE

Speed
0 100 200 300   324km/h maximum

🕐1 Timing sector   ▬ DRS   ▣ DRS detection   ⚙4 Gear   ▲ Overtaking opportunity

2024 POLE TIME: **VERSTAPPEN (RED BULL)**, 1M28.197S, 147.282MPH/237.028KPH
2024 WINNER'S AVERAGE SPEED: **100.209MPH/161.271KPH**
2024 FASTEST LAP: **VERSTAPPEN (RED BULL)**, 1M33.706S, 138.623MPH/223.093KPH
LAP RECORD: **HAMILTON (MERCEDES)**, 1M30.983S, 142.772MPH/229.770KPH, 2019

SAKHIR

The engineers will need to match their car set-ups to hotter conditions now that the Bahrain GP has been pushed back by six weeks from being the season-opener to mid-April.

INSIDE TRACK

BAHRAIN GRAND PRIX

Date:	**13 April**
Circuit name:	**Bahrain International Circuit**
Circuit length:	**3.363 miles/5.412km**
Number of laps:	**57**

The Bahrain International Circuit desert circuit broke the mould when it was opened in 2004. But the main comment was about the sand that blew across the circuit, making the track surface treacherous and changeable from lap to lap. The spraying of glue over the surrounding areas was a sensible plan.

With pit buildings and paddock offices on either side of a palm-shaded avenue and a ten-storey control tower with VIP observation balconies, BIC made a good impression. However, the track itself was worthy of consideration for the way that architect Hermann Tilke highlighted its desert setting by effectively splitting the track into distinct parts, with grass verges making the area around the pits the 'oasis' section and all else from turn 3 being the 'desert' part.

The first corner is classic Tilke as it turns through 140 degrees then feeds almost immediately into an easier left, quite like the first two corners at Sepang. It's then flat-out into the 'desert' section, up an incline to a hairpin where it's possible to attack.

Then comes a three-turn esse on the descent, followed by a tight right. The track goes over a light brow at turn 9 then drops into a left-hand hairpin at turn 10. From here, there's a short straight behind the paddock before an uphill left at turn 11. Then the track sweeps up to turn 13 at which point the drivers turn right and accelerate back down the slope. It's a shame turn 14 isn't more open to give a chance for a driver to make a challenge on the 185mph (298kph) approach to turn 1.

PREVIOUS WINNERS

2016	**Nico Rosberg**	MERCEDES
2017	**Sebastian Vettel**	FERRARI
2018	**Sebastian Vettel**	FERRARI
2019	**Lewis Hamilton**	MERCEDES
2020	**Lewis Hamilton**	MERCEDES
2020*	**Sergio Perez**	RACING POINT
2021	**Lewis Hamilton**	MERCEDES
2022	**Charles Leclerc**	FERRARI
2023	**Max Verstappen**	RED BULL
2024	**Max Verstappen**	RED BULL

* As the Sakhir GP

Location: The Bahrain International Circuit occupies an arid and rocky site 20 miles (32km) to the south of the capital Manama.

Toughest corner: Getting it right through the esses (turns 5 to 7) is always a challenge, as drivers are accelerating hard down the hill out of the turn 4 hairpin and to find the ultimate line through is far from easy on an often slippery surface.

Best passing spot: The first corner is always the best place to mount an overtaking bid, thanks to drivers being able to catch a tow along the pit straight and then try to dive up the inside into this tight right.

Bahrain's first Grand Prix: Ferrari loved F1's first visit in 2004 as Michael Schumacher and team-mate Rubens Barrichello started on the front row and dominated proceedings, with Jenson Button a distant third for BAR.

Bahrain's greatest Grand Prix: It looked as though Charles Leclerc was going to have a fairytale result in only his second race for Ferrari here in 2019. The Monegasque had just stepped up from Sauber and was immediately on the pace. He was leading when an engine glitch dropped him to an eventual third.

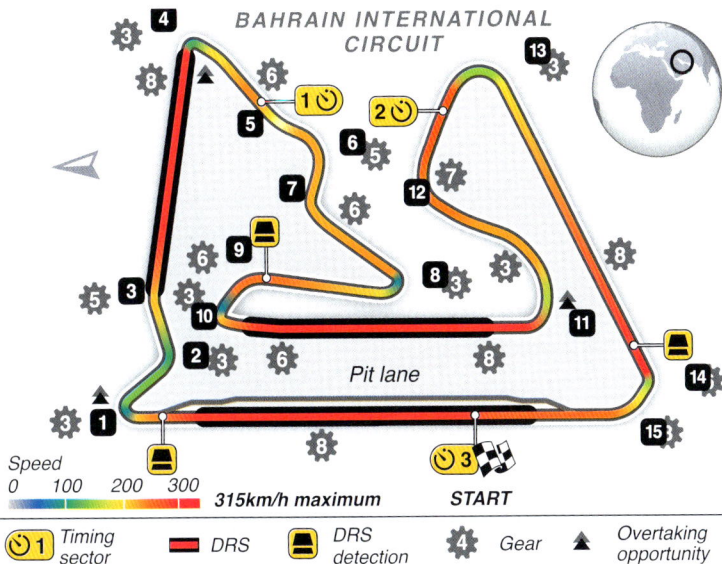

BAHRAIN INTERNATIONAL CIRCUIT

Speed
0   100   200   300
315km/h maximum   START

⏱1 Timing sector	▬ DRS	🅿 DRS detection	⚙4 Gear	▲ Overtaking opportunity

2024 POLE TIME: **VERSTAPPEN (RED BULL)**, 1M29.179S, 135.752MPH/218.472KPH
2024 WINNER'S AVERAGE SPEED: **125.256MPH/201.581KPH**
2024 FASTEST LAP: **VERSTAPPEN (MERCEDES)**, 1M32.608S, 130.726MPH/210.383KPH
LAP RECORD: **DE LA ROSA (MCLAREN)**, 1M31.447S, 132.392MPH/213.018KPH, 2005

JEDDAH

While Bahrain offers a track in a desert setting, Saudi Arabia's F1 circuit is more urban, with high-speed sweepers a feature of this circuit built on a cliff above a lagoon.

The most striking feature of the Jeddah Corniche Circuit is just how many high-speed corners it contains in its busy 27-turn lap. More than that, what makes it so entirely different to all other street circuits is how these come in long sequences of fast corner after fast corner, with the flow seldom broken by a slower corner. It could not be further from the stop/start flow of F1's original street circuit in Monaco.

The first corner is a 90-degree left into an even tighter right, both tricky on the opening lap of the race, but the true nature of the lap becomes apparent after turn 4 as open corner follows open corner, taken mostly in sixth and seventh gear, all the way to the hairpin at turn 13. The drivers said initially that it was like nothing that they had seen before.

The return leg on the circuit's narrow site is very close to the outward leg and has an even more open flow to it, all the way to the second hairpin at turn 27 that turns the cars back on to the start/finish straight.

The fastest point of the lap comes on the approach to turn 22, with cars accelerating through five easy corners after turn 16 and hitting 205mph (330kph) before the drivers have to slow for a tighter left flick.

It is expected that this circuit will be used just once more next year before the Saudi Arabian GP is relocated in 2027, moving on to the revolutionary Speed Park Track near the new city of Qiddiya not far from capital Riyadh. This promises a track design which blends racing circuit with rollercoaster as it nestles into a theme park.

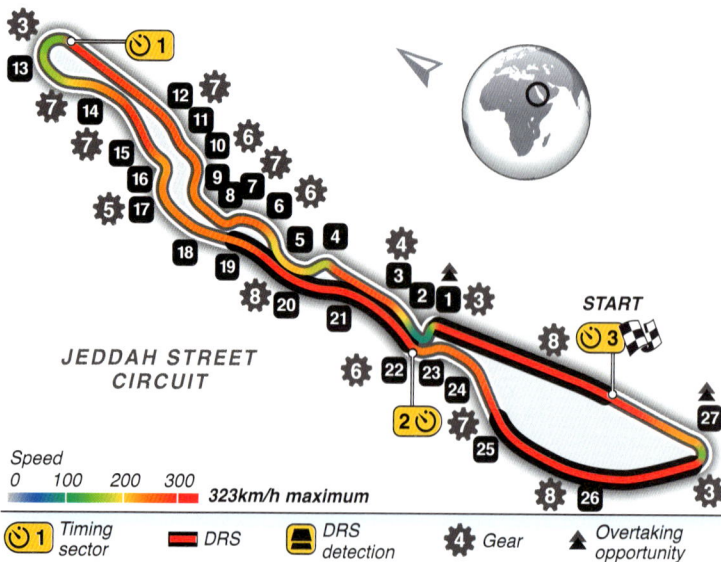

JEDDAH STREET CIRCUIT

Speed
0   100   200   300   323km/h maximum

Timing sector · DRS · DRS detection · Gear · Overtaking opportunity

---

2024 POLE TIME: **VERSTAPPEN (RED BULL)**, 1M27.472S, 158.888MPH/254.097KPH
2024 WINNER'S AVERAGE SPEED: 142.462MPH/229.270KPH
2024 FASTEST LAP: **LECLERC (FERRARI)**, 1M31.632S, 150.720MPH/242.561KPH
LAP RECORD: **HAMILTON (MERCEDES)**, 1M30.734S, 152.212MPH/244.962KPH, 2021

INSIDE TRACK

SAUDI ARABIAN GRAND PRIX

Date:	**20 April**
Circuit name:	**Jeddah Corniche Circuit**
Circuit length:	**3.837 miles/6.174km**
Number of laps:	**50**

PREVIOUS WINNERS

2021	**Lewis Hamilton**	MERCEDES
2022	**Max Verstappen**	RED BULL
2023	**Sergio Perez**	RED BULL
2024	**Max Verstappen**	RED BULL

Location: This circuit, always intended as a stop-gap until a permanent venue could be built at Qiddiya near Riyadh, is set on a corniche overlooking a lagoon on the northern outskirts of Jeddah.

Toughest corner: The sheer speed at almost all points is a challenge, with near constant twists making it hard for drivers to see far ahead. Turn 6 is a key example.

Best passing spot: Turn 1 is a sharp left and is always a possible passing place, but drivers can be forced wide and many told to hand back any advantage that they might have gained.

Saudi Arabia's first Grand Prix: Lewis Hamilton and Max Verstappen battled here in the penultimate round in 2021. The Dutch ace gained an advantage when his Red Bull was changed on to harder tyres for a restart after Mick Schumacher triggered a stoppage. Hamilton, still on his old rubber, was angry. Then came a second red flag, but their furious place-swapping continued until Hamilton won.

Saudi Arabia's greatest Grand Prix: Max Verstappen's car failed qualifying in 2023 and he had to forge forward from 15th. The Red Bull RB19 was the class of the field, but he still had to make the passing moves and climbed to second, but team-mate Sergio Perez held on to win by five seconds.

Rising Saudi star: There are still no up-and-coming Saudi Arabian drivers in the junior single-seater scene, with GT racing continuing to be a greater draw.

MIAMI

The three Grands Prix per year that F1 owners Liberty Media have scheduled in the USA could hardly be more different to one another. But Miami is the least exciting of the trio.

The US has a long history of taking F1 to the people by running Grands Prix on temporary street circuits, holding rounds of the World Championship in Long Beach, Las Vegas, Detroit, Dallas and Phoenix. Miami was long expected to be added to that list and finally, after the COVID pandemic, the Floridian city was awarded a race in 2022. The Miami International Autodrome is laid out in temporary fashion in the parking lot of the stadium where the Miami Dolphins NFL team plays.

The circuit is nothing like the street venues listed above as its layout is not dictated to by a grid-shape pattern of urban streets, instead enjoying a greater freedom for the lap to be given some sweeping corners and the sort of flow more usually found on a tailor-made circuit.

The early part of the lap is through a series of mid-speed corners before the cars get up to more F1-like speed, before reaching a three-corner esse entered at turn 4.

Out of turn 7, the drivers double back and run through three sweepers and can top 200mph (320kph) just before having to brake hard for the 120-degree left-hander at turn 11. The track then runs through a low-speed sequence of corners, including a chicane at turns 14 and 15 before a 90-degree left on to the back straight.

The blast from turn 16 is the longest of the lap, as the straight that follows down to the hairpin at turn 17 is long enough for the cars to reach almost 200mph (320kph). Then, with a run through a pair of open bends, the drivers arrive back at the pit straight to do it all again.

INSIDE TRACK 🇺🇸

MIAMI GRAND PRIX

Date:	**4 May**
Circuit name:	**Miami International Autodrome**
Circuit length:	**3.364 miles/5.412km**
Number of laps:	**57**

PREVIOUS WINNERS

2022	**Max Verstappen**	RED BULL
2023	**Max Verstappen**	RED BULL
2024	**Lando Norris**	McLAREN

Location: The Miami Gardens suburb, on the northern edge of the city, is home to the Hard Rock Stadium, and the circuit is laid out each year in its car park.

Toughest corner: Getting a clean exit from turn 16 is tricky but essential to carry speed down the lap's longest straight.

Best passing spot: The run from turn 7 is a long and twisting one to turn 11, but heavy braking into this tight left offers a chance for overtaking.

Miami's first Grand Prix: The circuit's debut in 2022 is sadly remembered as much for the disinterested celebrities on the grid as the racing but should be recalled for Max Verstappen passing Charles Leclerc to win for Red Bull.

Miami's greatest Grand Prix: Max Verstappen was very much in the swing of winning with two wins from the first two rounds when the F1 circus arrived in Miami in 2023. However, an interrupted second qualifying run left him only ninth on the grid. With passing places limited in Miami, he had to be patient, but still the Dutch ace advanced to second place behind Sergio Perez and then pounced with ten laps to go.

Rising American star: Jak Crawford continues to lead the way in the quest to find the next American F1 driver. He has just completed his second year in the FIA Formula 2 Championship and he added to his one victory from his 2023 campaign and bolstered that with five podium visits to prove that he is truly ready.

MIAMI INTERNATIONAL AUTODROME

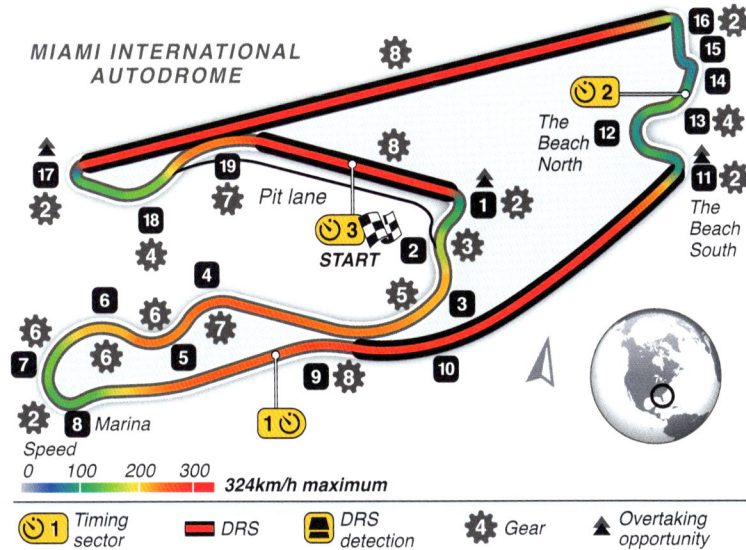

The Beach North

The Beach South

Pit lane

START

Marina

Speed
0   100   200   300   **324km/h maximum**

Symbol	Meaning
⏱ 1	Timing sector
▬	DRS
⏱	DRS detection
⚙ 4	Gear
▲	Overtaking opportunity

2024 POLE TIME: VERSTAPPEN (RED BULL), 1M27.241S, 138.768MPH/223.326KPH
2024 WINNER'S AVERAGE SPEED: 126.572MPH/203.699KPH
2024 FASTEST LAP: PIASTRI (MCLAREN), 1M30.634S, 133.573MPH/214.965KPH
LAP RECORD: VERSTAPPEN (RED BULL), 1M29.708S, 134.952MPH/217.184KPH, 2023

// IMOLA

This circuit looks fantastic, properly old school with its narrow confines, but the drivers were vocal last year that it is hard to race on, with passing opportunities rare.

INSIDE TRACK

EMILIA ROMAGNA GRAND PRIX

Date:	**18 May**
Circuit name:	**Autodromo Enzo e Dino Ferrari**
Circuit length:	**3.051 miles/4.909km**
Number of laps:	**63**

The differences between an old circuit and the ones built in the past few decades specifically to host F1 races is to be found in every element of venues like Autodromo Enzo e Dino Ferrari. The pit infrastructure is outdated and the paddock behind cramped as it is hemmed in by the River Santerno. Access for fans is awful, and yet the place oozes charm, with palpable history in the air and a setting that is stunning in spring, when the fields and orchards in the sloping infield are in full bloom.

The circuit itself, named in tribute to Enzo Ferrari and his son Dino, who died of muscular dystrophy at the age of 24, follows an undulating and twisting course up and down the hillside; the banks along its flanks are far closer than at modern circuits, giving the place an intimate feel.

The first seven corners are all on the flat, from the flat-out first kink to Tosa. The approach to the second corner, Variante Tamburello, is the fastest point of the lap, with cars exceeding 205mph (330kph) before having to slow for the left/right esse. This was inserted following Ayrton Senna's fatal accident at Tamburello in 1994, as was a more open chicane that was then named Variante Villeneuve.

At Tosa, the track turns hard left and begins to rise to a crest at Piratella before diving steeply down the slope to bottom out at Acque Minerali, with its rising exit. The track then seems very contained as drivers negotiate the Variante Alta chicane and run between the trees to the first of the Rivazza left-handers. That leaves just the blast along the level to the end of the lap.

PREVIOUS WINNERS

2001*	**Ralf Schumacher**	WILLIAMS
2002*	**Michael Schumacher**	FERRARI
2003*	**Michael Schumacher**	FERRARI
2004*	**Michael Schumacher**	FERRARI
2005*	**Fernando Alonso**	RENAULT
2006*	**Michael Schumacher**	FERRARI
2020	**Lewis Hamilton**	MERCEDES
2021	**Max Verstappen**	RED BULL
2022	**Max Verstappen**	RED BULL
2024	**Max Verstappen**	RED BULL

* Run as the San Marino GP

Location: The circuit lies between a riverbank and a rising slope on the edge of the town of Imola which is 20 miles (32km) south-east of Bologna.

Toughest corner: Turn 11, Acque Minerali, is really tricky, as it's in a compression at the foot of a descent, before the track then flips back up the slope again.

Best passing spot: Overtaking is far from easy on this narrow old-school track, but the most likely place for drivers to make a move is after getting a tow from a rival past the pits before reaching Tamburello.

Imola's first Grand Prix: The first World Championship race held at Imola was in 1980 when Monza was out of favour after Ronnie Peterson's death there in 1978. It was won by Nelson Piquet for Brabham after usurping the Renaults.

Imola's greatest Grand Prix: There have been some great scraps over the decades, but the emotional release in 2006 was intense as Michael Schumacher won for Ferrari. What made it so exciting was the fact that he had to pass reigning world champion Fernando Alonso's Renault. There was to be no repeat visit for 14 years, as the circuit lost its place until 2020 when COVID restricted travel, giving Italian fans two home races each year.

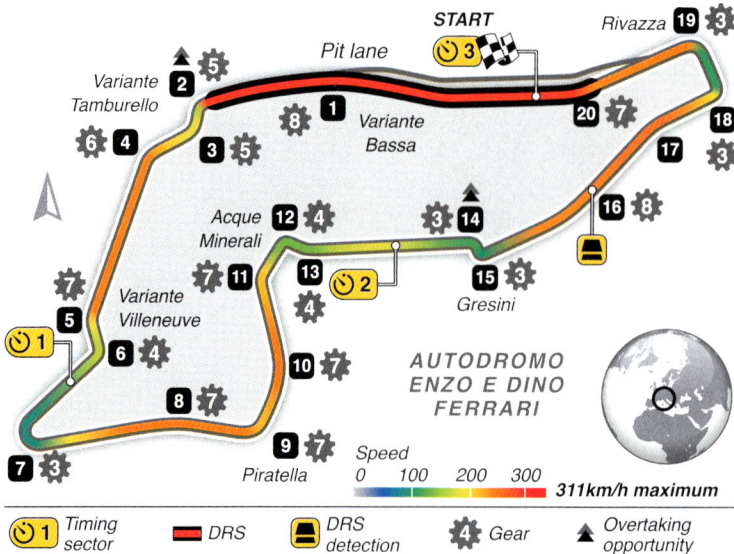

AUTODROMO ENZO E DINO FERRARI

| Timing sector | DRS | DRS detection | Gear | Overtaking opportunity |

311km/h maximum
Speed 0 100 200 300

2024 POLE TIME: **VERSTAPPEN (RED BULL), 1M14.746S, 146.930MPH/236.462KPH**
2024 WINNER'S AVERAGE SPEED: **134.879MPH/217.077KPH**
2024 FASTEST LAP: **RUSSELL (MERCEDES), 1M18.589S, 139.728MPH/224.871KPH**
LAP RECORD: **HAMILTON (MERCEDES), 1M15.484S, 145.476MPH/234.121KPH, 2020**

MONACO

This fabled street circuit is undoubtedly an anachronism and is clearly too narrow to offer much hope of overtaking for today's big F1 cars, but it remains a jewel that F1 simply can't afford to discard.

MONACO GRAND PRIX

Date:	**25 May**
Circuit name:	**Monte Carlo**
Circuit length:	**2.074 miles/3.337km**
Number of laps:	**78**

PREVIOUS WINNERS

2013	**Nico Rosberg** MERCEDES
2014	**Nico Rosberg** MERCEDES
2015	**Nico Rosberg** MERCEDES
2016	**Lewis Hamilton** MERCEDES
2017	**Sebastian Vettel** FERRARI
2018	**Daniel Ricciardo** RED BULL
2019	**Lewis Hamilton** MERCEDES
2021	**Max Verstappen** RED BULL
2022	**Sergio Perez** RED BULL
2023	**Max Verstappen** RED BULL
2024	**Charles Leclerc** FERRARI

The streets of Monte Carlo are narrow, steep and, for most of the year, packed with extravagance at every turn. Then, in almost every spring since 1929, the streets have been cleared and turned into a motor racing venue.

The world's most famous street circuit starts on a straight that isn't even straight, followed by a constricted entry to Sainte Devote. A good exit from this tight right is almost as important as not having had your car's wings reshaped in a jostling first lap. The track rises steeply until it reaches a crest as it turns through the long, third gear left at Massenet.

Then comes the blast through Casino Square, down the narrow bumpy descent to Mirabeau, dropping further to the hairpin and on down through the right-handers of Mirabeau Bas and Portier on to the seafront.

High walls stop the drivers seeing the sea, then they are plunged into a curving tunnel. The lap's fastest part is when the cars emerge from the tunnel and incredibly hit 180mph (290kph) before drivers brake heavily and drop to second gear for the left/right/left Nouvelle Chicane.

Running around two sides of the harbour, the cars have to take a sharp right at La Rascasse before a flick through slow Virage Anthony Noghes on to the pit straight.

There was much uproar after last year's Monaco GP, with not one of the top ten cars on the grid changing position during the race. The fix suggested by most of the frustrated fans was for F1 to revert to the more nimble and dynamic cars of the late 1980s, which were considerably shorter and lighter. Obviously, this can't happen in the immediate future, but it's a thought...

Location: The circuit snakes its way along the harbour front and up through the streets of Monte Carlo.

Toughest corner: Sainte Devote, the tight first corner of the lap is always tricky, as a clean exit from this bumpy right-hander is vital for carrying speed all the way up the hill towards Casino Square.

Best passing spot: Overtaking is at a premium on this circuit that still has more than a passing resemblance to the one first used in 1929. A good run out of Portier and through the tunnel can provide an opportunity into the Nouvelle Chicane.

Monaco's greatest Grand Prix: Jochen Rindt's pursuit of Jack Brabham in 1970 was legendary. The Lotus driver got closer and closer, but the Australian resisted all the pressure, until the 80th and final lap when he slid his Brabham into the straw bales at Gasworks Hairpin. He reversed out and was still able to finish second.

Rising Monegasque star: Charles Leclerc's younger brother, Arthur, stepped away from single-seaters after racing in F2 in 2023 and is now focusing on sports car racing, racing in the European Le Mans Series, no doubt with the aim of landing a ride with one of the predominantly manufacturer-entered teams in the World Endurance Championship.

69

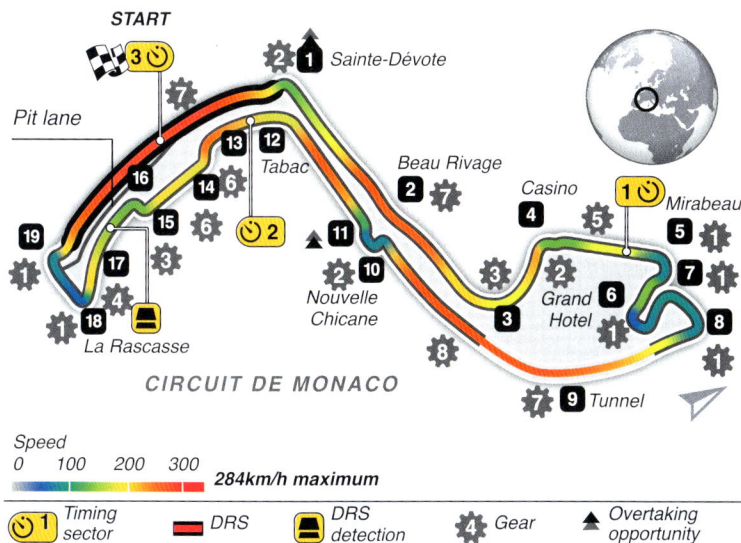

CIRCUIT DE MONACO

Speed
0 100 200 300
284km/h maximum

🕐1 Timing sector   ▬ DRS   ⬛ DRS detection   ⚙4 Gear   ▲ Overtaking opportunity

2024 POLE TIME: **LECLERC (FERRARI), 1M10.270S, 106.228MPH/170.957KPH**
2024 WINNER'S AVERAGE SPEED: **67.737MPH/109.013KPH**
2024 FASTEST LAP: **HAMILTON (MERCEDES), 1M14.165S, 100.649MPH/161.979KPH**
LAP RECORD: **HAMILTON (MERCEDES), 1M12.909S, 102.383MPH/164.769KPH, 2021**

BARCELONA

This year will be the final time, for now at least, that the Circuit de Barcelona-Catalunya hosts the Spanish GP as the race will be held on a street circuit in Madrid from 2026.

In 1991, after moving from Jarama and Jerez de la Frontera, Barcelona regained the rights to host the Spanish GP for the first time since 1975. The all-new Circuit de Catalunya was a breath of fresh air and, with its mixture of corner types and usually fine weather, it would be the venue of choice when testing was carried out in most weeks that didn't host a Grand Prix.

The lap starts with a downhill straight to the open right then left sweepers where so many drivers fancy their chances on the opening lap, with a large gravel trap to catch any fallers.

A long, slightly uphill right-hander follows before a short straight to another long right-hander. Turn 5, Seat, a left-hander, then feeds the cars back down the slope towards the paddock. At third-gear turn 7, the track then tilts up again until it reaches a crest at tricky Campsa, through which drivers need to carry as much momentum as possible on to the downhill infield straight.

The ascent from tight turn 10 takes the cars up to turn 12, Banc Sabadell, after which two open rights take the drivers back to the pit straight. The fastest point comes at the end of the straight, where speeds of 200mph (320kph) can be hit before drivers have to brake down to 100mph (160kph) before turning into turn 1.

The move to a street circuit in Madrid will be a welcome change and offer F1 fans in the capital the first chance to have the Spanish GP on their doorstep since it quit Jarama after Gilles Villeneuve won for Ferrari in 1981.

INSIDE TRACK

SPANISH GRAND PRIX

Date:	1 June
Circuit name:	Circuit de Barcelona-Catalunya
Circuit length:	2.894 miles/4.657km
Number of laps:	66

PREVIOUS WINNERS

2014	**Lewis Hamilton**	MERCEDES
2015	**Nico Rosberg**	MERCEDES
2016	**Max Verstappen**	RED BULL
2017	**Lewis Hamilton**	MERCEDES
2018	**Lewis Hamilton**	MERCEDES
2019	**Lewis Hamilton**	MERCEDES
2020	**Lewis Hamilton**	MERCEDES
2021	**Lewis Hamilton**	MERCEDES
2022	**Max Verstappen**	RED BULL
2023	**Max Verstappen**	RED BULL
2024	**Max Verstappen**	RED BULL

Location: The Circuit de Barcelona-Catalunya lies in what was once rolling agricultural land 15 miles (24km) north of Barcelona but is now increasingly dotted with industrial buildings.

Toughest corner: Turn 10, La Caixa, the left-hander at the end of the infield straight, is difficult as drivers have to brake heavily on the downhill approach, fend off attacks from behind and get a clean exit for the uphill run through Banc Sabadell.

Best passing spot: Now that the chicane before the final corner has been removed, the longer run on to the main straight now offers more chance to make a passing bid into turn 1.

Barcelona's greatest Grand Prix: Many a Grand Prix here has been processional, but no one predicted the most unlikely of wins here. This came in 2012 when Pastor Maldonado, whose previous best finish was eighth place, triumphed for Williams after starting from pole. He let Ferrari's Fernando Alonso past but moved ahead after his second pit stop when the Spaniard was blocked in traffic, then didn't put a foot wrong.

Rising Spanish star: Pepe Marti demonstrated strong form last year in the FIA Formula 2 Championship, peaking with victory for Campos Racing in the first race at the final round in Abu Dhabi.

CIRCUIT DE BARCELONA-CATALUNYA

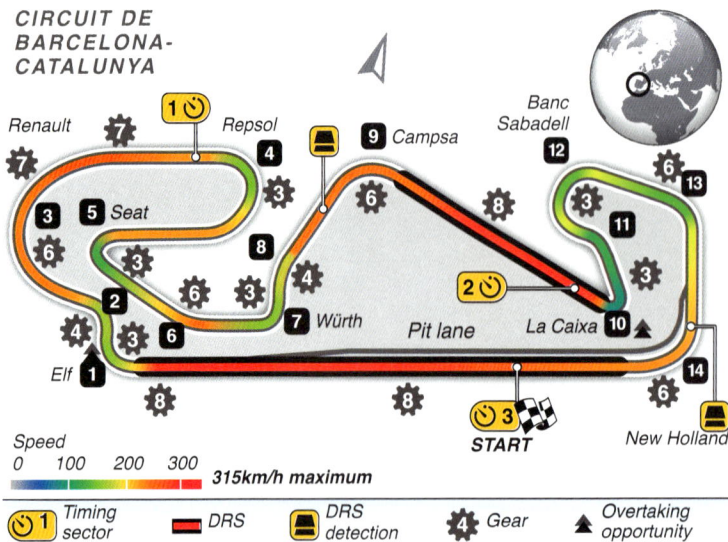

Speed
0   100   200   300
315km/h maximum

Symbol	Meaning
🕐1	Timing sector
▬	DRS
DRS detection	DRS detection
⚙4	Gear
▲	Overtaking opportunity

2024 POLE TIME: NORRIS (MCLAREN), 1M11.383S, 145.936MPH/234.862KPH
2024 WINNER'S AVERAGE SPEED: 129.667MPH/208.679KPH
2024 FASTEST LAP: NORRIS (MCLAREN), 1M17.115S, 135.089MPH/217.405KPH
LAP RECORD: VERSTAPPEN (RED BULL), 1M16.330S, 136.478MPH/219.641KPH, 2023

MONTREAL

This metropolitan circuit is one that ought not to provide such interesting races, but rain has enlivened more than a few Canadian GPs, with last year's being a good example.

Several heavy accidents at Mosport Park in upstate Ontario in 1977 convinced the Canadian motorsport authorities that the circuit was no longer safe enough to host F1. Furthermore, they reckoned a track closer to a major centre of population would serve them well, and the Labatt's brewery picked up much of the bill. This led to the creation of this circuit on the site of the Expo global trade fair of 1967 on an island just across the river from Montreal.

The plot was long and thin, with the river on one side and the 1976 Olympic rowing lake on the other.

The blast to the first real corner is through a kink to the right, with the sharpish left followed almost immediately by a long right, the Island Hairpin, often with drivers still jockeying for position as they arrive there on the opening lap.

The track then leaves the grandstands behind and runs through a series of twists through the trees until it reaches turn 7. There it opens out on to a high-speed but curving run to a right/left esse at turns 8 and 9, out of which drivers need to carry as much speed as possible for the run all the way to the lap's tightest corner, the L'Epingle hairpin.

From here, it is flat-out acceleration alongside the rowing lake and the fastest point of the lap is reached just before the drivers must brake heavily for the final chicane, shaving their speed from 195mph (315kph) to 85mph (135kph) for the right/left flick. Many drivers have had accidents there, with the concrete wall on its exit known locally as 'Champions' Wall' after even the best have whacked into it with car-wrecking consequences.

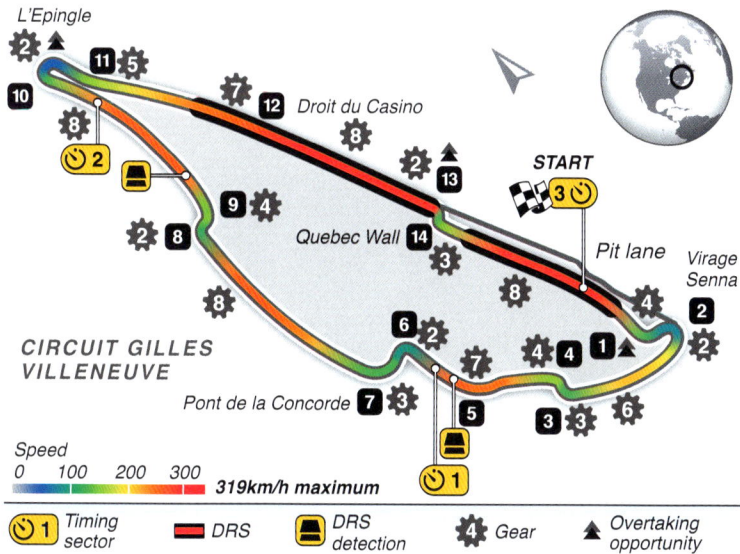

CIRCUIT GILLES VILLENEUVE

L'Epingle · Droit du Casino · Quebec Wall · Pont de la Concorde · START · Pit lane · Virage Senna

Speed
0 100 200 300
319km/h maximum

Timing sector · DRS · DRS detection · Gear · Overtaking opportunity

2024 POLE TIME: **RUSSELL (MERCEDES), 1M12.000S, 135.490MPH/218.050KPH**
2024 WINNER'S AVERAGE SPEED: **107.573MPH/173.122KPH**
2024 FASTEST LAP: **HAMILTON (MERCEDES), 1M14.856S, 130.320MPH/209.730KPH**
LAP RECORD: **BOTTAS (MERCEDES), 1M13.078S, 133.491MPH/214.833KPH, 2019**

INSIDE TRACK 🍁

CANADIAN GRAND PRIX

Date:	**15 June**
Circuit name:	**Circuit Gilles Villeneuve**
Circuit length:	**2.710 miles/4.361km**
Number of laps:	**70**

PREVIOUS WINNERS

2013	**Sebastian Vettel**	RED BULL
2014	**Daniel Ricciardo**	RED BULL
2015	**Lewis Hamilton**	MERCEDES
2016	**Lewis Hamilton**	MERCEDES
2017	**Lewis Hamilton**	MERCEDES
2018	**Sebastian Vettel**	FERRARI
2019	**Lewis Hamilton**	MERCEDES
2022	**Max Verstappen**	RED BULL
2023	**Max Verstappen**	RED BULL
2024	**Max Verstappen**	RED BULL

Location: The Circuit Gilles Villeneuve is on the Ile Notre-Dame, an island in the St Lawrence Seaway that is connected to the city of Montreal by a bridge and by a metro link.

Toughest corner: Turn 6 is difficult as drivers need to get their cars balanced for this 90-degree left-hander as it leads on to a high-speed run towards the far hairpin, L'Epingle. Mess up the exit, and the chance to outrun a rival is lost.

Best passing spot: Passing moves are attempted occasionally into the final chicane, but the more likely place for a passing move to be achieved is under heavy braking into L'Epingle hairpin.

Montreal's greatest Grand Prix: For sheer joy, nothing has yet beaten the patriotic fervour when Gilles Villeneuve won in front of his home crowd as Montreal hosted the Canadian GP for the first time in 1978, after its move from Mosport Park. He triumphed for Ferrari after Jean-Pierre Jarier's Lotus broke down.

Rising Canadian star: Aspiring Canadian single-seater drivers are thin on the ground. Patrick Woods-Toth followed his success in winning the 2023 USA F4 series with a promising campaign in Formula Regional Americas last year, dominating the series with eight wins.

RED BULL RING

If points were awarded for GP venues having a scenic setting, the Red Bull Ring would be placed at the top of the list, but unfortunately it doesn't rank as highly for its overtaking opportunities.

This circuit was opened in 1969 when it was known as the Osterreichring and hosted the Austrian GP for the first time in 1970. It offered an infinitely superior home for the Austrian GP than the Zeltweg circuit had on a military airfield at the foot of the valley. The Osterreichring was famous for its sweeping corners that allowed drivers to hit impressive average speeds as they traversed the hillside over which the 3.673-mile (5.911km) circuit was laid out. After 1987, the venue was dropped and it was only after it had much of the first third of the lap removed, its lap length cut to 2.684 miles (4.318km) and been renamed the A1 Ring, that it returned in 1997. More recently, it became the Red Bull Ring.

The start of the lap is an incredibly steep ascent from the start line up to the first corner. This is an 80-degree right-hander with enough width for assorted overtaking bids. A good exit is vital, though, as it's a lengthy run up the hillside to the second real corner: Remus. The lap's highest speeds of almost 205mph (327kph) are recorded on the approach to this tight right and it's a magnet for passing attempts.

The run from here to Schlossgold is over a brow before the track dips for the approach to the right-hand hairpin. The track then snakes one way and then the other across the face of the hillside, doubling back on itself out of turn 7 and running through an uphill esse before dipping again for a downhill right, named after the nation's first world champion Jochen Rindt. A good exit is key to a good run through the last corner.

INSIDE TRACK 🔴

AUSTRIAN GRAND PRIX

Date:	**29 June**
Circuit name:	**Red Bull Ring**
Circuit length:	**2.684 miles/4.318km**
Number of laps:	**71**

PREVIOUS WINNERS

2017	**Valtteri Bottas**	MERCEDES
2018	**Max Verstappen**	RED BULL
2019	**Max Verstappen**	RED BULL
2020	**Valtteri Bottas**	MERCEDES
2020*	**Lewis Hamilto**n	MERCEDES
2021	**Max Verstappen**	RED BULL
2021*	**Max Verstappen**	RED BULL
2022	**Charles Leclerc**	FERRARI
2023	**Max Verstappen**	RED BULL
2024	**George Russell**	MERCEDES

*As the Styrian GP

Location: This hillside circuit near Zeltweg is remote, with the closest city, Graz, being 45 miles (72km) away to the south-east.

Toughest corner: The first corner is the toughest as its approach is up such a steep incline that drivers can't see the apex until they are almost on it. A mistake here will cost the drivers momentum all the way up the hill to Remus (turn 3).

Best passing spot: It's risky to try diving up the inside into Remus, as wings can get bent, but it remains the best place to overtake.

Red Bull Ring's greatest Grand Prix: The 1982 season was extraordinary. By the time the teams arrived for its 13th round, it had had eight winners. Going into the final laps, just after Alain Prost's Renault had retired from the lead, two drivers who had yet to win, Lotus driver Elio de Angelis and Williams racer Keke Rosberg, were nose to tail, but the Italian held on to win by just 0.05 seconds.

Rising Austrian star: Charlie Wurz, son of former Benetton, McLaren and Williams F1 driver Alex Wurz, is leading the next generation of Austrian talent, but will need a second year in the FIA Formula 3 series and aim to be frequently in the points and to start challenging for podium results.

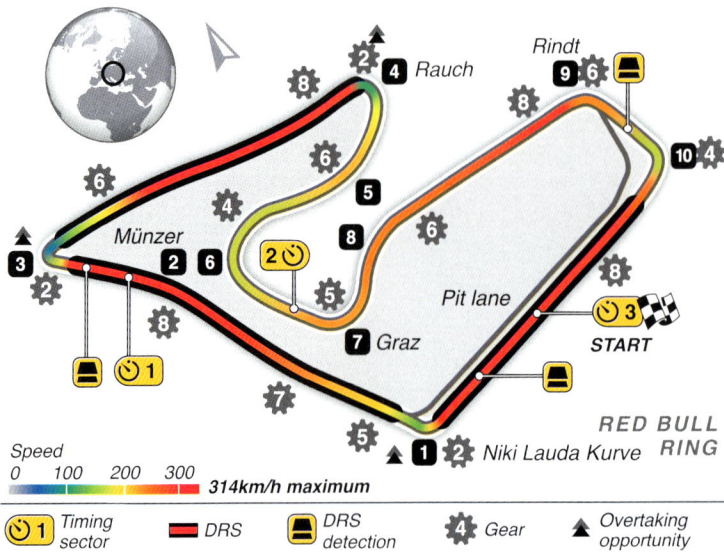

Speed
0   100   200   300
314km/h maximum

🕐1 Timing sector   ▬ DRS   🅳 DRS detection   ⚙4 Gear   ▲ Overtaking opportunity

2024 POLE TIME: **VERSTAPPEN (RED BULL), 1M04.314S, 150.186MPH/241.701KPH**
2024 WINNER'S AVERAGE SPEED: **135.401MPH/217.908KPH**
2024 FASTEST LAP: **ALONSO (ASTON MARTIN), 1M07.694S, 142.687MPH/229.633KPH**
LAP RECORD: **SAINZ JR (MCLAREN), 1M05.619S, 147.199MPH/236.894KPH, 2020**

SILVERSTONE

It's Silverstone's proud boast that it staged the opening round of the inaugural World Championship back in 1950, and this high-speed circuit remains one of F1's cornerstone tracks to this day.

INSIDE TRACK

BRITISH GRAND PRIX

Date:	**6 July**
Circuit name:	**Silverstone Circuit**
Circuit length:	**3.661 miles/5.891km**
Number of laps:	**52**

PREVIOUS WINNERS

2016	**Lewis Hamilton**	MERCEDES
2017	**Lewis Hamilton**	MERCEDES
2018	**Sebastian Vettel**	FERRARI
2019	**Lewis Hamilton**	MERCEDES
2020	**Lewis Hamilton**	MERCEDES
2020*	**Max Verstappen**	RED BULL
2021	**Lewis Hamilton**	MERCEDES
2022	**Carlos Sainz Jr**	FERRARI
2023	**Max Verstappen**	RED BULL
2024	**Lewis Hamilton**	MERCEDES

* Run as 70th Anniversary GP

Silverstone was one of many airfields that had been operational during World War Two. After it was all over, they were largely obsolete, but Silverstone was saved when it was decided in 1948 that a combination of its runways and perimeter roads might be a good place to go racing. Two years later, it kicked off the World Championship. Since then, it has evolved through many configurations, with all offering a high-speed layout. Other British circuits have hosted the British GP – with Aintree and Brands Hatch sometimes alternately – but Silverstone has kept the race to itself since 1987.

The most recent track reconfiguration followed the old pits between Woodcote and Copse being replaced by the far larger Wing complex between Club and Abbey. The fast right-hander at Abbey is followed by a gentle left at full speed before drivers have to brake heavily for Village and then keep turning left through The Loop to reach the infield Wellington Straight. This offers an overtaking opportunity at its conclusion at Brooklands. From here, there's the long right at Luffield, a fast kink and then Copse.

The cars twice hit 188mph (303kph). The first time comes at the entrance to the Becketts esses, just before the drivers have to flick their cars right then left, dropping to sixth gear and then down to fifth for the tighter right that follows.

Then, accelerating hard through the left kink at Chapel, the cars reach a similar speed at the far end of the Hangar Straight before having to slow for Stowe. Then drivers drop into the Vale before negotiating the lengthy final corner.

Location: Silverstone is near the centre of England, situated 40 miles (64km) north-east of Oxford on the Buckinghamshire/Northamptonshire border near Towcester.

Toughest corner: The Becketts esse is not only the hardest corner here but one of the toughest at any F1 venue. Approached in seventh gear, this right, left, right combination tests the cars' grip to the maximum as they change direction.

Best passing spot: When braking hard into the third corner of the lap, Village, drivers have their best shot at an overtake, particularly on the opening lap, with many moves not completed until the drivers accelerate out of The Loop.

Silverstone's greatest Grand Prix: When it comes to putting on a masterclass performance, Lewis Hamilton's run to victory in 2008 stands out. This was his second year in F1, and he was under pressure after two non-scores, but he atoned by being the outstanding driver in the British GP, mastering wet/dry conditions.

Rising British star: Although Ollie Bearman was given a one-off F1 shot with Ferrari and impressed enough to get an F1 ride for 2025, his F2 rivals Taylor Barnard and Zak O'Sullivan are also proving fast by winning several races.

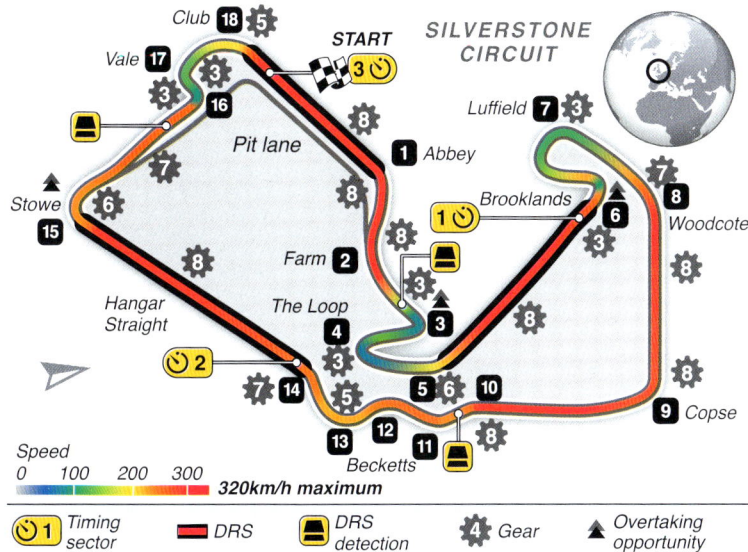

SILVERSTONE CIRCUIT

Speed
0 100 200 300
320km/h maximum

Timing sector | DRS | DRS detection | Gear | Overtaking opportunity

2024 POLE TIME: **RUSSELL (MERCEDES), 1M25.819S, 153.553MPH/247.120KPH**
2024 WINNER'S AVERAGE SPEED: **138.454MPH/222.821KPH**
2024 FASTEST LAP: **SAINZ JR (FERRARI), 1M28.293S, 149.250MPH/240.195KPH**
LAP RECORD: **VERSTAPPEN (RED BULL), 1M27.097S, 151.300MPH/243.494KPH, 2020**

SPA-FRANCORCHAMPS

This is a circuit with a true link to the past, having hosted a Belgian GP in 1925, but although it's now shorter and safer, it still provides drivers with one of their greatest challenges.

This year marks the centenary of this fabulous, classic circuit. The original was considerably longer, its lap measuring 9.236 miles (14.864km) as it ventured into the next valley before returning up a tree-lined ascent to the current pit and paddock area at La Source.

As it is, the circuit nestles in a wooded area of the Ardennes, the track rising and falling as it traverses a largely triangular course. The start offers one of the shortest dashes to the first corner used by F1, with many an incident occurring either in or out of the La Source hairpin. Then the track turns sharply downhill and bottoms out in a compression at Eau Rouge, where the drivers have to steer swiftly left then right and hang on as the track ahead rises steeply and turns left through Raidillon.

What follows is the long, uphill Kemmel Straight, a great place to line up a slipstream to assist a possible pass before Les Combes. On the approach, the cars can hit 200mph (320kph) before drivers have to haul them down to third gear before turning into the right/left combination.

The track then dips downwards again, through the Rivage hairpin, the left-hand kink at Speaker's Corner, then the angle becomes less steep through the double-apex Pouhon corner at its foot. After the Fagnes esses and Campus corner, drivers then accelerate hard through Curve Paul Frere so that they can carry as much speed as possible up the climb back towards the pits, with flat-out Blanchimont an exhilarating sweeper. The final twist is a sharp right then a sharp left on to the start/finish straight.

INSIDE TRACK

BELGIAN GRAND PRIX

Date:	**27 July**
Circuit name:	**Spa-Francorchamps**
Circuit length:	**4.352 miles/7.004km**
Number of laps:	**44**

PREVIOUS WINNERS

2015	**Lewis Hamilton** MERCEDES
2016	**Nico Rosberg** MERCEDES
2017	**Lewis Hamilton** MERCEDES
2018	**Sebastian Vettel** FERRARI
2019	**Charles Leclerc** FERRARI
2020	**Lewis Hamilton** MERCEDES
2021	**Max Verstappen** RED BULL
2022	**Max Verstappen** RED BULL
2023	**Max Verstappen** RED BULL
2024	**Lewis Hamilton** MERCEDES

Location: The circuit starts its lap on a wooded hillside just below the village of Francorchamps, 30 miles (48km) to the south-east of Liege.

Toughest corner: The Eau Rouge and Raidillon combination was long considered the greatest challenge, but modern F1 cars can take it fairly easily in seventh gear, making the flat-out blast through Blanchimont more daunting.

Best passing spot: La Source sees passing moves on lap 1, but most moves are made at the right/left Les Combes chicane after a driver has caught a tow up the Kemmel Straight from Raidillon.

Spa-Francorchamps' greatest Grand Prix: Jordan not only made its F1 breakthrough here when Damon Hill won in changeable conditions in 1998, but he was followed home by team-mate Ralf Schumacher to trigger yet more euphoric celebrations after a race that started with a pile-up out of the first corner that involved 13 of the 22 starters. Michael Schumacher passed Hill on the restart, but his Ferrari clattered into David Coulthard's delayed McLaren, leaving Hill out front.

Rising Belgian star: F2 racer Amaury Cordeel is at the head of Belgium's pack as the country seeks its first F1 driver since Stoffel Vandoorne raced for McLaren in 2018 and one who might emulate 1960s' star Jacky Ickx.

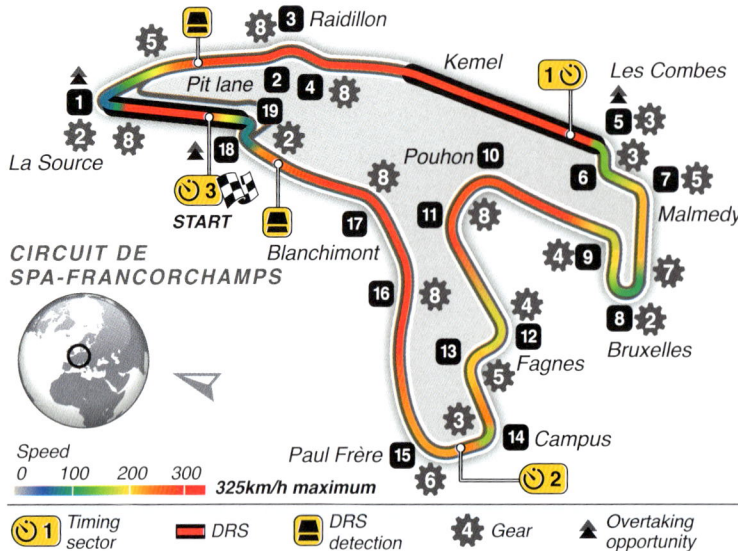

CIRCUIT DE SPA-FRANCORCHAMPS

Speed
0 100 200 300
325km/h maximum

🕐1 Timing sector   DRS   DRS detection   Gear   Overtaking opportunity

2024 POLE TIME: **LECLERC (FERRARI), 1M53.754S, 137.731MPH/221.657KPH**

2024 WINNER'S AVERAGE SPEED: **143.633MPH/231.156KPH**

2024 FASTEST LAP: **PEREZ (RED BULL), 1M44.701S, 149.640MPH/240.822KPH**

LAP RECORD: **PEREZ (RED BULL), 1M44.701S, 149.640/237.240.822KPH, 2024**

HUNGARORING

When this circuit burst onto the scene in 1986, few thought that it would still be part of the World Championship four decades later, but it remains, albeit as a twisty circuit.

HUNGARIAN GRAND PRIX

Date:	**3 August**
Circuit name:	**Hungaroring**
Circuit length:	**2.722 miles/4.381km**
Number of laps:	**70**

PREVIOUS WINNERS

2015	**Sebastian Vettel**	FERRARI
2016	**Lewis Hamilton**	MERCEDES
2017	**Sebastian Vettel**	FERRARI
2018	**Lewis Hamilton**	MERCEDES
2019	**Lewis Hamilton**	MERCEDES
2020	**Lewis Hamilton**	MERCEDES
2021	**Esteban Ocon**	ALPINE
2022	**Max Verstappen**	RED BULL
2023	**Max Verstappen**	RED BULL
2024	**Oscar Piastri**	McLAREN

There wasn't a great deal of change in the World Championship calendar through the 1970s, with a few new street circuits popping up in the USA in the 1980s. Then came an announcement that shocked the establishment: that most capitalist of sports, F1, would be heading to a communist country in 1986. Hungary had held a Grand Prix once before, but that was in 1936, before it turned into a communist country after World War Two.

F1 recognised a deal was to be done and a new circuit was built to host the new race, the Hungaroring. Apart from the removal of a chicane just after what is turn 3 and the reshaping of the third last corner, turn 11, nothing has changed.

The circuit basically starts on one side of a valley, drops into the valley, runs across the far side of the valley and then returns. Turn 1 is one of the few places where overtaking happens, with this hairpin dropping from entry to exit and continuing to fall through turn 2, where cars still sort themselves out on lap 1, and on down out of turn 3.

Then the climb begins, through the kink at turn 4 and up until the exit of turn 5, where it flattens out. The run along to turn 10 is a series of twists, then the track drops back into the valley, only climbing again from turn 11, with a clean exit from the final corner key to having a chance to pass into turn 1.

As there are very few points on the lap that run straight for long, the highest speed achieved is, not surprisingly, just 185mph (295kph), at the end of the start/finish straight.

Location: The circuit is spread across a valley in rolling hills a dozen miles to the north-east of capital city Budapest.

Toughest corner: Turn 4 is difficult as it's a rare high-speed corner on this generally twisting circuit. Its challenge is made greater as this left kink is taken somewhat unsighted as the track flattens after the uphill approach.

Best passing spot: This is a circuit at which every passing move is hard earned, with turn 1 the most likely spot as it is approached down the lap's longest straight.

Hungaroring's first Grand Prix: Watched by a crowd of 200,000, Nelson Piquet won Hungary's first World Championship round in 1986 for Williams. Ayrton Senna led away from pole in his Lotus and Piquet was demoted to third by team-mate Nigel Mansell but bounced back and went on to win.

Hungaroring's greatest Grand Prix: Perhaps the finest of Jenson Button's wet weather performances came in Hungary in 2006 when he took his first F1 win at his 114th attempt. The Honda driver started 14th due to a ten-place grid penalty. He soon advanced on a wet track as Renault's Fernando Alonso hit the front, only to lose a wheel after a pit stop. Button then took the win.

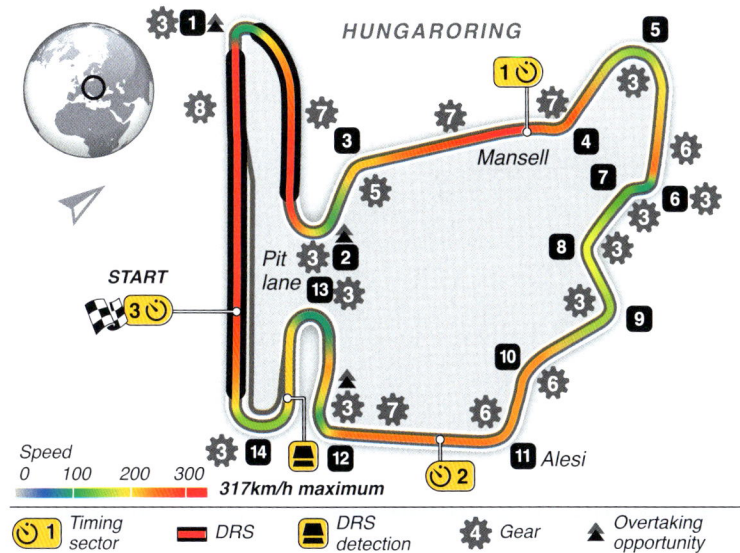

HUNGARORING

Mansell

Alesi

START

Pit lane

Speed
0   100   200   300
317km/h maximum

Timing sector · DRS · DRS detection · Gear · Overtaking opportunity

2024 POLE TIME: **NORRIS (MCLAREN), 1M15.227S, 130.272MPH/209.653KPH**
2024 WINNER'S AVERAGE SPEED: **116.612MPH/187.669KPH**
2024 FASTEST LAP: **RUSSELL (MERCEDES), 1M20.305S, 122.035MPH/196.396KPH**
LAP RECORD: **HAMILTON (MERCEDES), 1M16.627S, 127.892MPH/205.823KPH, 2020**

ZANDVOORT

This seaside circuit has clear links with earlier F1 days, but it has evolved to stay relevant and is now home to the army of Max Verstappen fans.

Zandvoort was built out of access roads in the sand dunes on the North Sea coastline and it was granted a round of the World Championship in 1952. It was a near-permanent F1 fixture until 1985.

The circuit was immediately popular because of the flow it offered as the lap rose and fell in a largely high-speed route through the dunes.

The lap starts with a short blast to Tarzan, a long and lightly banked right-hander that offers great potential for overtaking, especially on the opening lap.

The twisting stretch of track behind the cramped paddock rises slightly through Gerlachbocht, then drops into the first of the modifications that were required for F1's return here in 2021. This is the Hugenholzbocht left-hander, now not only wider but banked too.

From here, it's flat-out for the drivers as they rise and fall all the way to daunting Scheivlak where the drivers have to commit before they reach the crest at the entry to the corner. The track then drops between the dunes down to the tight right of Mastersbocht that takes the cars on to a run of slower corners before they reach an infield straight. This concludes at a tight right, another possible passing place, and this feeds straight into a long left, Hans Ernst Bocht.

The end of the lap is all about drivers getting the best run through the penultimate corner to build speed through steeply banked Arie Luyendyk Bocht and then accelerating down the main straight, catching a rival's tow if possible and hitting a top speed of around 195mph (310kph) before having to brake for Tarzan.

INSIDE TRACK

DUTCH GRAND PRIX

Date:	**31 August**
Circuit name:	**Circuit Zandvoort**
Circuit length:	**2.647 miles/4.259km**
Number of laps:	**72**

PREVIOUS WINNERS

1980	**Nelson Piquet**	BRABHAM
1981	**Alain Prost**	RENAULT
1982	**Didier Pironi**	FERRARI
1983	**Rene Arnoux**	FERRARI
1984	**Alain Prost**	McLAREN
1985	**Niki Lauda**	McLAREN
2021	**Max Verstappen**	RED BULL
2022	**Max Verstappen**	RED BULL
2023	**Max Verstappen**	RED BULL
2024	**Lando Norris**	McLAREN

Location: The circuit lies in among the sand dunes only metres from the North Sea at the northern end of this seaside resort, 15 miles (24km) west of Amsterdam.

Toughest corner: For sheer thrill, Scheivlak takes the prize, as it's fast, taken at 150mph (241kph) in sixth, and the drivers are unsighted as the apex is over a brow.

Best passing spot: The modern Zandvoort was reshaped with a banked final corner to offer more chance of passing into Tarzan, and the first corner is still the main place to pass.

Zandvoort's most noteworthy Grand Prix: There have been some tremendously exciting races at Zandvoort, and the race in 1967 was not one of these, with only four cars finishing on the lead lap. However, there was considerable relevance to F1 as it was a winning debut for the Ford Cosworth DFV engine – backbone of F1 for the next two decades, with Jim Clark 23 seconds clear of Jack Brabham. DFVs would take a further 155 wins.

Rising Dutch star: Richard Verschoor remains the highest-ranked Dutch racer outside F1, but the fact that last year was his fourth campaign in the FIA F2 Championship suggests that he might not make the grade.

CIRCUIT ZANDVOORT

Scheivlak · Mastersbocht · Slotemakerbocht · Hunserug · Gerlachbocht · Tarzanbocht · Pit lane · Hans Ernst Chicane · Arie Luyendykbocht · START

Speed
0   100   200   300
321km/h maximum

Timing sector · DRS · DRS detection · Gear · Overtaking opportunity

2024 POLE TIME: **NORRIS (McLAREN)**, 1M09.673S, 136.740MPH/220.062KPH
2024 WINNER'S AVERAGE SPEED: **125.941MPH/202.682KPH**
2024 FASTEST LAP: **NORRIS (McLAREN)**, 1M13.817S, 129.064MPH/207.708KPH
LAP RECORD: **HAMILTON (MERCEDES)**, 1M11.097S, 134.031KPH/215.656KPH, 2021

MONZA

This is a circuit that comes alive when there is hope of Ferrari success and the grandstands are packed with fervent partisan support for Italian teams and drivers.

INSIDE TRACK

ITALIAN GRAND PRIX

Date:	**7 September**
Circuit name:	**Autodromo Nazionale Monza**
Circuit length:	**3.600 miles/5.793km**
Number of laps:	**53**

Now more than 100 years old, this classic Italian parkland circuit has had incredibly few changes since it opened for racing in 1922. Certainly, the banked oval is no longer part of its lap, last used by F1 in 1961, and chicanes have been inserted to stem the flow, when once there were none. Yet the general rhythm is as it was intended, meaning that it's fast and a great place for drivers to go hunting.

The lap is simple once the first chicane has been negotiated. It's then hard on the throttle through the long right of Curva Biassono, better known as Curva Grande. Although the first chicane is the key place for overtaking moves, particularly on the opening lap, the left/right combination of the second chicane also offers scope for trying to get past a rival.

What follows is the two Lesmo right-handers as the circuit runs through a wooded section. Exit speed from the second Lesmo is critical for a quick lap, as that speed can be built on, all the way into the dip beneath the bridge carrying a section of the old, banked circuit, then rises to the Ascari chicane. With a hard left on entry, then a right and another left, passing is possible, but collision more likely.

All that remains after this is the final corner, the Curva Parabolica (now Alboreto), a long right that brings the cars back onto the pit straight. It is at the end of this that the cars hit their highest speed on this very fast track, 204mph (327kph), just before the drivers have to get hard on the brakes to slow for the first chicane.

PREVIOUS WINNERS

2015	**Lewis Hamilton**	MERCEDES
2016	**Nico Rosberg**	MERCEDES
2017	**Lewis Hamilton**	MERCEDES
2018	**Lewis Hamilton**	MERCEDES
2019	**Charles Leclerc**	FERRARI
2020	**Pierre Gasly**	ALPHATAURI
2021	**Daniel Ricciardo**	McLAREN
2022	**Max Verstappen**	RED BULL
2023	**Max Verstappen**	RED BULL
2024	**Charles Leclerc**	FERRARI

Location: The circuit is located within a walled park in the town of Monza which lies 10 miles (16km) to the north-west of Milan.

Toughest corner: The Lesmos are tricky, but the final corner, Parabolica (now Alboreto), is vital to get right as it feeds the cars on to the main straight.

Best passing spot: Monza has tried many permutations of chicane since inserting them in 1972, and the current first chicane, a right/left combination, is always tempting drivers to have a go, not always successfully.

Monza's greatest Grand Prix: Nothing in F1 history has ever come close to the final lap sort-out in 1971, the last year before chicanes interrupted the circuit's flow. There was a five-car pack going for victory and the outcome was not likely to be resolved until the final corner, or even on the finish line if one of the challengers could get a tow. Right on the line, Peter Gethin edged the nose of his BRM just ahead of Ronnie Peterson's March, with the top five covered by 0.61 seconds.

Rising Italian star: With 18-year-old Andrea Kimi Antonelli having been promoted to the brink of F1 by Mercedes, the next Italian rising star is F3 pace-setter Gabriele Mini, who ended the year ranked second overall.

79

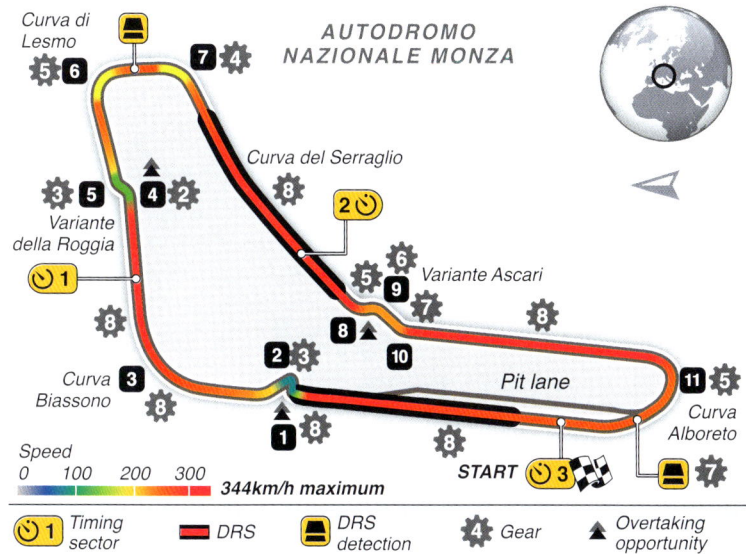

AUTODROMO NAZIONALE MONZA

Curva di Lesmo
Curva del Serraglio
Variante della Roggia
Variante Ascari
Curva Biassono
Pit lane
Curva Alboreto
START

Speed
0 100 200 300
344km/h maximum

⏱1	Timing sector	DRS	DRS detection	Gear	Overtaking opportunity

2024 POLE TIME: **NORRIS (MCLAREN), 1M19.327S, 163.356MPH/262.896KPH**
2024 WINNER'S AVERAGE SPEED: **153.125MPH/246.431KPH**
2024 FASTEST LAP: **NORRIS (MCLAREN), 1M21.432S, 159.133MPH/256.100KPH**
LAP RECORD: **BARRICHELLO (FERRARI), 1M21.046S, 159.909KPH/257.349KPH, 2004**

BAKU

Nobody had any expectations when F1 headed to Azerbaijan in 2016, but this street circuit around capital city Baku has become a distinctive fixture in the World Championship season.

Oil-rich Azerbaijan craved global recognition as it entered the 21st century and, after having a trial run by hosting a couple of GT races to attract international interest, the country was granted a place on the World Championship calendar starting from 2016.

The lap starts with a pit straight laid out along a broad street that flanks a park next to Baku's seafront. The first corner is a 90-degree left and it is followed by three more 90-degree corners as it tracks a rectangular route around several blocks of smart apartments in the new town district. These standard turns are followed by a left/right chicane and then a short blast towards the old citadel.

After a sharp right-hander, turn 7, and another short straight, the nature of the lap changes entirely and becomes tighter

and narrower as it climbs alongside the old city wall and then gains light and space again as it bursts in front of temporary grandstands across a park to reach turn 12. From here, the track is then a series of fast left kinks as it runs past grand buildings, with tighter corners at turns 15 and 16.

After dropping back to sea level, the run through turns 17 to 20 is flat-out, with the cars hitting their highest speed as they pass the pits, touching 200mph (322kph) before having to slow for turn 1. Here the track is at least wide enough to offer drivers the chance to use various lines into the left-hander and thus, at least, an opportunity to try an overtaking move.

Baku's street circuit is one like no other.

INSIDE TRACK

AZERBAIJAN GRAND PRIX

Date:	**21 September**
Circuit name:	**Baku City Circuit**
Circuit length:	**3.731 miles/6.003km**
Number of laps:	**51**

PREVIOUS WINNERS

2016	**Nico Rosberg** MERCEDES
2017	**Daniel Ricciardo** RED BULL
2018	**Lewis Hamilton** MERCEDES
2019	**Valtteri Bottas** MERCEDES
2021	**Sergio Perez** RED BULL
2022	**Max Verstappen** RED BULL
2023	**Sergio Perez** RED BULL
2024	**Oscar Piastri** McLAREN

Location: This is one of only a handful of F1 circuits in the heart of a capital city, with its start line next to a park that fronts the Caspian Sea.

Toughest corner: Turn 16 is really testing. Approached down the slope from turn 15, it's a 110-degree right-hander taken in third and a clean exit is imperative to build speed for the run all the way to turn 1.

Best passing spot: The first corner is by far the most likely place for an overtaking move, as drivers have plenty of time on the flat-out blast from turn 16 to catch and use a tow from a rival.

Baku's first Grand Prix: There was a fast-developing battle between the Mercedes drivers in 2016 as Nico Rosberg had found form and took the fight to Lewis Hamilton like never before. He raced to victory here with Hamilton helping the German's cause by qualifying only tenth after clipping a wall and then progressing only to fifth place as Sebastian Vettel and Sergio Perez completed the podium.

Baku's greatest Grand Prix: With overtaking always hard to achieve on this street circuit, sometimes it takes a great strategy call to get to the front, and this was the case in 2019 when Mercedes out-thought Ferrari to put Valtteri Bottas into the lead as Charles Leclerc struggled on old tyres.

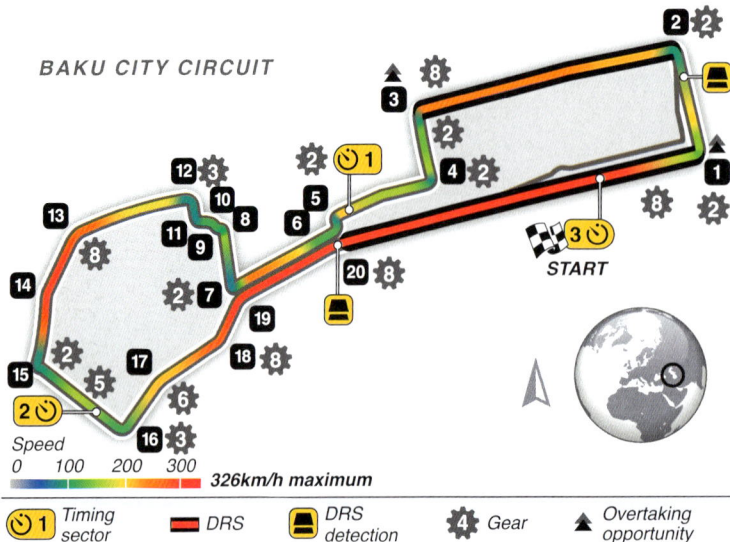

BAKU CITY CIRCUIT

Speed
0   100   200   300
326km/h maximum

Timing sector | DRS | DRS detection | Gear | Overtaking opportunity

2024 POLE TIME: **LECLERC (FERRARI)**, 1M41.365S, 132.474MPH/213.197KPH
2024 WINNER'S AVERAGE SPEED: 122.734MPH/197.521KPH
2024 FASTEST LAP: **NORRIS (MCLAREN)**, 1M45.255S, 128.200MPH/206.318KPH
LAP RECORD: **LECLERC (FERRARI)**, 1M43.009S, 130.360MPH/209.795KPH, 2019

MARINA BAY

It's always hot and humid in Singapore but these discomforts for the drivers and crews are countered by the fabulous images offered as the race is held after dark against a stunning backdrop.

It took years of planning before Singapore landed a Grand Prix in 2008, but the efforts by the race promoters have been a gift to F1 as the sight of F1 cars powering under floodlights past the city's smart central blocks is something unique. It also boosted support for F1 in South-East Asia, welcome as the World Championship looked to increase its global reach.

The race often starts with a bang, as the first three corners come in quick succession, a left, right then tight left combination that is often the scene of a flurry of passing moves on the opening lap.

The reason for this desperation to make moves that can often be to the detriment of front wings is that the majority of corners around the lap are 90-degree bends, thus making it difficult to overtake.

Despite a third gear right-hander, turn 5, the run from turn 3 to turn 7 is rapid, with the lap's fastest point coming at the end of this run, with the fastest cars hitting around 185mph (300kph) before braking hard for turn 7.

The tall office blocks in the backdrop are then replaced by hotels and less corporate buildings as the track goes right at turn 8 and starts its run around three flanks of a park filled with the grounds of the Singapore Cricket Club.

After a chicane at turn 11, the track then runs across the distinctive Anderson Bridge and then opens out for a broader blast up to turn 14.

The homeward run is through a sequence of five corners, with a quick exit through the last two key for carrying momentum onto the start/finish straight.

INSIDE TRACK

SINGAPORE GRAND PRIX

Date:	**5 October**
Circuit name:	**Marina Bay Street Circuit**
Circuit length:	**3.070 miles/4.940km**
Number of laps:	**62**

PREVIOUS WINNERS

2013	**Sebastian Vettel**	RED BULL
2014	**Lewis Hamilton**	MERCEDES
2015	**Sebastian Vettel**	FERRARI
2016	**Nico Rosberg**	MERCEDES
2017	**Lewis Hamilton**	MERCEDES
2018	**Lewis Hamilton**	MERCEDES
2019	**Sebastian Vettel**	FERRARI
2022	**Sergio Perez**	RED BULL
2023	**Carlos Sainz Jr**	FERRARI
2024	**Lando Norris**	McLAREN

Location: Like the Baku circuit, this is another circuit in the heart of a capital, running past Singapore's central business district and over the Esplanade Bridge.

Toughest corner: Turn 10 is difficult as drivers must carry as much momentum as possible towards and over the Anderson Bridge.

Best passing spot: The run from turn 17 to the first corner enables drivers to catch a tow and make a move.

Marina Bay's first Grand Prix: Singapore's first Grand Prix in 2008 was also F1's first night race. Then there was the moment that handed Fernando Alonso victory when his Renault team-mate Nelson Piquet Jr had a timely accident that brought out the safety car. Alonso had just pitted from 11th and took the lead as his rivals pitted. Piquet would later admit that he had been told to crash.

Marina Bay's greatest Grand Prix: The 2023 Singapore GP had one of the most exciting finishes of any of the 15 Grands Prix held here as there was a great battle between Ferrari's Carlos Sainz Jr, McLaren's Lando Norris and the Mercedes duo of George Russell and Lewis Hamilton. Sainz triumphed to break Red Bull's extraordinary sequence of taking victory in the season's first 14 races.

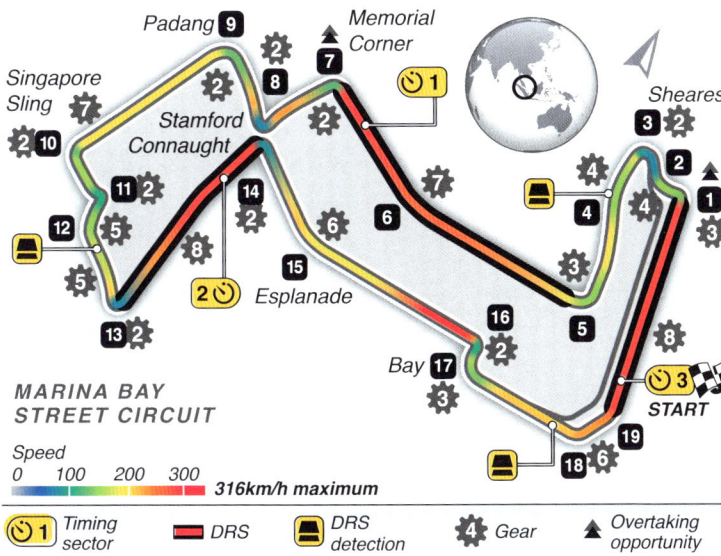

MARINA BAY STREET CIRCUIT

Speed
0   100   200   300   **316km/h maximum**

⏱1 Timing sector	▬ DRS	🔲 DRS detection
⚙4 Gear	▲ Overtaking opportunity	

2024 POLE TIME: NORRIS (McLAREN), 1M29.525S, 123.434MPH/198.648KPH
2024 WINNER'S AVERAGE SPEED: 113.145MPH/182.090KPH
2024 FASTEST LAP: RICCIARDO (RB), 1M34.486S, 116.953MPH/188.218KPH
LAP RECORD: RICCIARDO (RB), 1M34.486S, 116.953MPH/188.218KPH, 2024

CIRCUIT OF THE AMERICAS

This rare anti-clockwise circuit was built with corners inspired by the best of other F1 circuits from around the world, and its distinctive topography helps it provide a unique challenge.

INSIDE TRACK 🇺🇸

UNITED STATES GRAND PRIX

Date:	19 October
Circuit name:	Circuit of the Americas
Circuit length:	3.426 miles/5.513km
Number of laps:	56

PREVIOUS WINNERS

2014	Lewis Hamilton	MERCEDES
2015	Lewis Hamilton	MERCEDES
2016	Lewis Hamilton	MERCEDES
2017	Lewis Hamilton	MERCEDES
2018	Kimi Raikkonen	FERRARI
2019	Valtteri Bottas	MERCEDES
2021	Max Verstappen	RED BULL
2022	Max Verstappen	RED BULL
2023	Max Verstappen	RED BULL
2024	Charles Leclerc	FERRARI

With the United States now being allocated three Grands Prix per year, this is the one for classical fans, as it's a tailor-made road circuit built for purpose rather than one built with the compromises faced by the USA's temporary street circuits in Miami and Las Vegas.

The US GP has moved around a lot over the decades and it wasn't until 2012 that the Circuit of the Americas, COTA for short, welcomed F1. Built especially to attract F1 to Texas, its site in rolling hills just outside Austin gave the designers the chance to use gradient to make some of its corners all the more special.

The blast from the grid to the first corner is steeply uphill, into a broad hairpin at which drivers can take a variety of lines. Then the track immediately plunges downhill to turn 2. What comes next is a stretch of track inspired by Suzuka's S-Curves, albeit on the flat, with the track swerving its way to turn 9 before opening out for a simpler section along to the turn 11 hairpin.

The lap's longest straight follows, with cars reaching 193mph (310kph) before the drivers have to brake heavily for the 100-degree left at turn 12.

Then comes a run of tight corners until the track changes back to a more high-speed sweep around the base of the giant tower that offers amazing, if scary, views from its observation platform.

The lap ends with a 110-degree left on to the pit straight. A poor exit from here can both ruin a lap and wreck any chance of catching a slipstreaming tow from a rival in order to pull off a passing move into turn 1.

Location: The Circuit of the Americas lies in undulating countryside about 10 miles (16km) to the south-east of Austin, state capital of Texas.

Toughest corner: The esses that run from turn 3 to turn 6 are the greatest challenge for the drivers, as any deviation from the ideal line leaves them increasingly compromised.

Best passing spot: The first corner provides plenty of opportunity for passing thanks to the many lines that can be taken there, but turn 12 is the pick as it's a long straight into a heavy braking area.

COTA's greatest Grand Prix: Lewis Hamilton has good reason to remember the 2017 United States GP, as it was a race in which he had to catch and overtake Sebastian Vettel's race-leading Ferrari that had got past him at the start. He took his Mercedes past the German with a great move under braking into turn 12 and controlled things from there.

Greatest American driver: Phil Hill and Mario Andretti are the only Americans to be F1 champions, in 1961 and 1978 respectively, but the latter stands out as the greatest as he also won the Indianapolis 500 and four IndyCar titles. He also came close to winning the Le Mans 24 Hours in 1995, showing his adaptability.

CIRCUIT OF THE AMERICAS

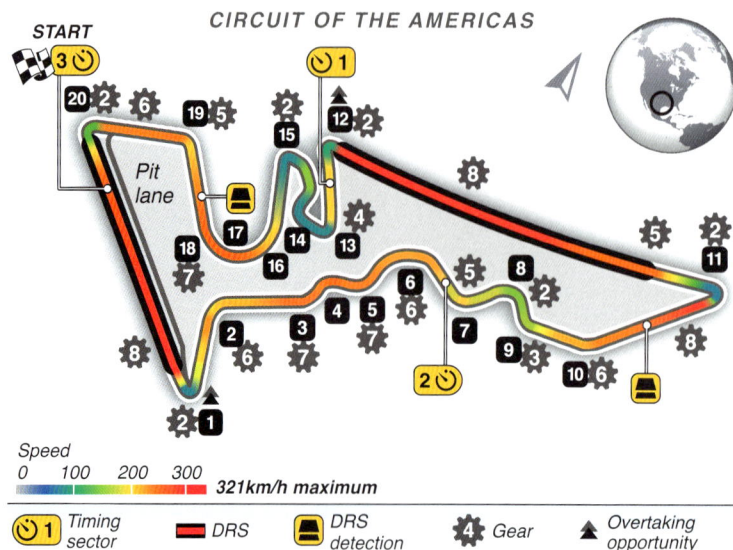

START

Pit lane

Speed
0   100   200   300
321km/h maximum

🕐1 *Timing sector* ▬ *DRS* *DRS detection* 4 *Gear* ▲ *Overtaking opportunity*

2024 POLE TIME: **NORRIS (MCLAREN), 1M32.330S, 133.567MPH/214.955KPH**
2024 WINNER'S AVERAGE SPEED: **120.827MPH/195.453KPH**
2024 FASTEST LAP: **OCON (ALPINE), 1M37.330S, 126.705MPH/203.912KPH**
LAP RECORD: **LECLERC (FERRARI), 1M36.169S, 128.235MPH/206.374KPH, 2019**

MEXICO CITY

Fast, wide and open, the Autodromo Hermanos Rodriguez is a great place for F1 to visit, as the track is a cracker and the wildly enthusiastic fans make the atmosphere electric.

The young, wealthy and extremely rapid Rodriguez brothers excited Mexican motor racing fans in the early 1960s and the local authorities moved swiftly to give the nation a circuit on which they could show their talents. Sadly, the younger, faster brother, Ricardo, was killed in practice for a trial, non-championship Mexican GP in 1962 and, tragically, brother Pedro would die nine years later.

In many ways, Monza was the circuit's template, not just in its choice of building it in a park, but also in its shape, making it a circuit of high-speed corners.

The lap starts with a long, broad straight, with drivers having to get into position for the first corner complex. This is three turns, right, left and right again, with enough space for assorted overtaking bids.

A second straight concludes with a sharp left followed immediately by a right, then a wide hairpin in front of the grandstands at Recorte Rebaque. Then comes a wonderful sequence of esses over a slight rise around the back of the park.

After taking a sharp right at turn 12, the track then offers something truly distinctive as it runs through a baseball stadium, snaking left to turn between the grandstands and out to rejoin the original circuit's key corner, the long, banked Peraltada. By entering it halfway around the Peraltada's course, it is not the fearsome challenge that it once was, but a good run through this long right-hander can set drivers up to make a slipstreaming run behind a rival down to the lap's fastest point; they can hit 210mph (336kph) on the approach to the first corner.

INSIDE TRACK

MEXICO CITY GRAND PRIX

Date:	**26 October**
Circuit name:	**Autodromo Hermanos Rodriguez**
Circuit length:	**2.675 miles/4.304km**
Number of laps:	**71**

PREVIOUS WINNERS

1992	**Nigel Mansell**	WILLIAMS
2015	**Nico Rosberg**	MERCEDES
2016	**Lewis Hamilton**	MERCEDES
2017	**Max Verstappen**	RED BULL
2018	**Max Verstappen**	RED BULL
2019	**Lewis Hamilton**	MERCEDES
2021	**Max Verstappen**	RED BULL
2022	**Max Verstappen**	RED BULL
2023	**Max Verstappen**	RED BULL
2024	**Carlos Sainz Jr**	FERRARI

Location: The Autodromo Hermanos Rodriguez is in the eastern suburbs of Mexico City, built in a municipal park.
Toughest corner: The esses on the return leg, running from turn 7 to 11, offer the lap's greatest challenge.
Best passing spot: With plenty of track width, the lap's first corner offers the best overtaking possibilities as drivers position themselves for the right/left/right three-corner esse after slipstreaming past the pits.
Mexico City's first Grand Prix: After a non-championship trial in 1962, Mexico's first World Championship round took place as the penultimate race of 1963. This was dominated by Lotus ace Jim Clark as he raced to the sixth victory of his title-winning campaign with Lotus.
Mexico City's greatest Grand Prix: Nothing has ever come close to the 1964 championship finale as Graham Hill, John Surtees and Jim Clark battled for the title, but recent history has been all about Max Verstappen and his victory in 2021 was the pick of his wins here. He did all the work in the first minute, as he braved it out around the outside of Valtteri Bottas' pole-starting Mercedes into the first corner and avoided the mayhem as the Finn was hit by Daniel Ricciardo's McLaren. The Dutch ace then went on to win as he pleased.

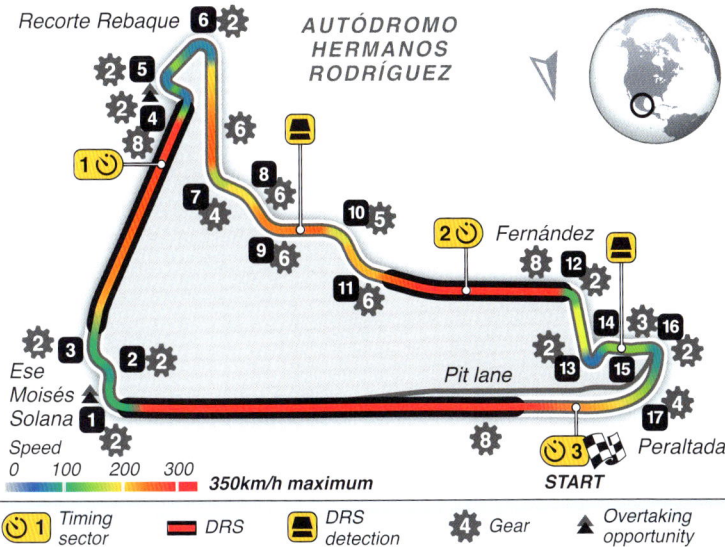

AUTÓDROMO HERMANOS RODRÍGUEZ

Recorte Rebaque

Ese Moisés Solana

Pit lane

Fernández

Peraltada

START

Speed
0   100   200   300   **350km/h maximum**

⏱1	Timing sector	▬ DRS	🖥 DRS detection	⚙4 Gear	▲ Overtaking opportunity

2024 POLE TIME: **SAINZ JR (FERRARI), 1M15.946S, 126.771MPH/204.018KPH**
2024 WINNER'S AVERAGE SPEED: **112.794MPH/181.524KPH**
2024 FASTEST LAP: **LECLERC (FERRARI), 1M18.336S, 122.889MPH/197.794KPH**
LAP RECORD: **BOTTAS (MERCEDES), 1M17.774S, 123.791KPH/199.223KPH, 2021**

INTERLAGOS

Rising and falling across its hillside site outside Sao Paulo, this circuit is one of the World Championship's gems, a place guaranteed to produce great racing in front of passionate fans.

Built in 1940, this is a circuit that retains the open flow that makes it one of the world's great tracks. Combine that with grandstands from which very vocal fans can see most of the lap, and it really is a special place to race, especially if there is a Brazilian driver in the mix.

The lap begins from the rising start/finish straight that is sunk between grandstands on the right and a lofty pit wall to the left, with drivers unable to see the exit of the first corner until they are into the braking zone. This is because this left-hander falls sharply away on its exit, with the cars plunging down the slope before turning almost immediately into a more open right.

Although still dropping down, the gradient is less extreme as the drivers arc to the left through the Curva do Sol and vie for position with the hope of pulling off a pass into Descida do Lago, a 90-degree left at the end of the straight. This is the lowest point of the lap, and the track then turns uphill.

The open right-hander just behind the narrow paddock at Ferradura is followed by a tighter right turn at Laranja which is the start of a twisting run of four corners as the track climbs and descends the hillside.

Then comes the final sweep into the homeward leg. This starts at third-gear Juncao and a clean exit from here is perhaps the most important element of the lap. It's flat-out from here all the way to the start of the following lap, with the fastest cars reaching 197mph (317kph) before having to brake for the first corner.

INSIDE TRACK

SAO PAULO GRAND PRIX

Date:	**9 November**
Circuit name:	**Autodromo Jose Carlos Pace**
Circuit length:	2.678 miles/4.309km
Number of laps:	71

PREVIOUS WINNERS

2014	**Nico Rosberg** MERCEDES
2015	**Nico Rosberg** MERCEDES
2016	**Lewis Hamilton** MERCEDES
2017	**Sebastian Vettel** FERRARI
2018	**Lewis Hamilton** MERCEDES
2019	**Max Verstappen** RED BULL
2021	**Lewis Hamilton** MERCEDES
2022	**George Russell** MERCEDES
2023	**Max Verstappen** RED BULL
2024	**Max Verstappen** RED BULL

Location: This circuit that was once in open countryside has long been enveloped by the urban spread of the southern suburbs of Sao Paulo.

Toughest corner: Juncao is the lap's trickiest corner as this 90-degree left-hander is the point at which drivers accelerate onto the curving rise that takes them all the way to the first corner.

Best passing spot: The first corner, Descida do Sol, is where most of the overtaking happens, and not just on the opening lap.

Interlagos' greatest Grand Prix: If the 2007 title decider here was packed with drama, it has been overshadowed by what happened 12 months later when Ferrari's Felipe Massa won and was champion for about 40 seconds; then Lewis Hamilton's McLaren flashed across the line in fifth and he took the title instead after gaining a position on the final lap. Massa continues to believe that he was the rightful champion and issued a legal challenge last year.

Rising Brazilian star: It was a race between Gabriel Bortoleto and Enzo Fittipaldi to become Brazil's next F1 driver, with FIA F2 champion Bortoleto taking on Emerson Fittipaldi's grandson Enzo in his third year in F1's feeder category. Bortoleto came out ahead to land a ride with Sauber.

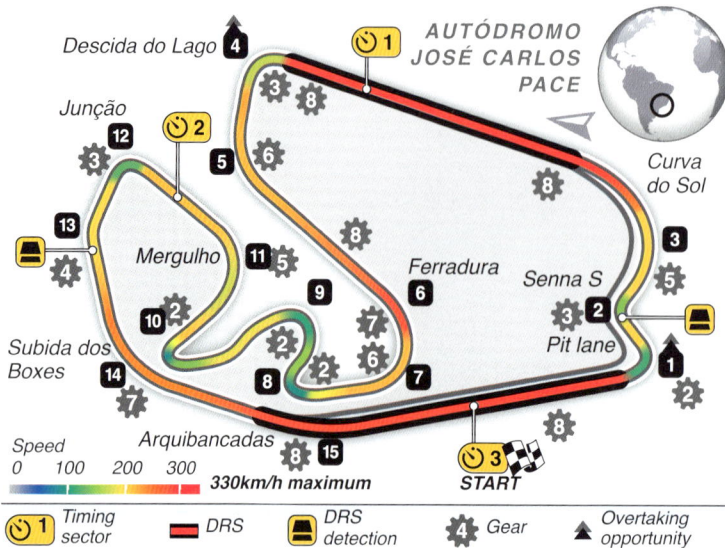

AUTÓDROMO JOSÉ CARLOS PACE

Descida do Lago
Junção
Mergulho
Subida dos Boxes
Arquibancadas
Ferradura
Senna S
Pit lane
Curva do Sol
START

Speed
0   100   200   300
330km/h maximum

Timing sector | DRS | DRS detection | Gear | Overtaking opportunity

2024 POLE TIME: **NORRIS (MCLAREN)**, 1M23.405S, 115.567MPH/185.988PH
2024 WINNER'S AVERAGE SPEED: 87.327MPH/140.540KPH
2024 FASTEST LAP: **VERSTAPPEN (RED BULL)**, 1M20.472S, 119.780MPH/192.767KPH
LAP RECORD: **BOTTAS (MERCEDES)**, 1M10.540S, 136.645MPH/219.909KPH, 2018

LAS VEGAS

Now bedded in after two races, this second-generation Las Vegas street circuit represents everything that has made this casino city famous – it's bold, brash and entertaining.

For decades since Las Vegas hosted a couple of Grands Prix at the start of the 1980s, there had been discussion about F1 making a return to this Nevada playground. Yet, there had also been much discussion about a Grand Prix in New York and other American cities. Then, in 2023, the race returned.

The circuit created to entice the World Championship could hardly be more different to its predecessor. That had been tucked away in the parking lot of the Caesars Palace casino, whereas this one is right on central stage, running along Las Vegas Boulevard, meaning that no one can ignore its temporary layout.

The lap starts with a left-hand hairpin, out of which the track kinks to the right before a flowing arc onto the back straight that takes the track down to one

of the many landmarks it passes: Caesars Forum. After slowing for a 90-degree right, the track then circumnavigates the MSG Sphere, with a chicane at turn 7/8.

Out of turn 9, the lap opens out and sweeps down to a tight left that has more relevance than you might think, as it is from here on that drivers are flat-out all the way along Las Vegas Boulevard, hitting 212mph (342kph) after passing Treasure Island, Caesars Palace and the Bellagio.

A left/right/left chicane follows before a simple end to the lap consisting of a straight and a left kink, with all of this looking dramatic as the spectacular buildings are lit up against the night sky.

There were problems on the first visit in 2023 when inspection covers were sucked out of their mounting points, causing damage to Carlos Sainz Jr's Ferrari.

INSIDE TRACK

LAS VEGAS GRAND PRIX

Date:	**22 November**
Circuit name:	Las Vegas Strip Circuit
Circuit length:	3.853 miles/6.201km
Number of laps:	50

PREVIOUS WINNERS

1981*	**Alan Jones**	WILLIAMS
1982*	**Michele Alboreto**	TYRRELL
2023	**Max Verstappen**	RED BULL
2024	**George Russell**	MERCEDES

* Held at the Caesars Palace circuit

Location: The first Grand Prix held in Las Vegas, in 1981 and 1982, was tucked away in the car park for the Caesars Palace casino, but the modern version is very much out in the open, running through the very heart of town.

Toughest corner: Positioning the car correctly for turn 9 is the lap's hardest challenge, as the drivers need to move across to their right as soon as they can after the turn 7/8 chicane.

Best passing spot: With its flat-out blast from turn 12 all the way along the Las Vegas Boulevard, turn 14 offers the clearest opportunity for drivers looking to gamble on making a passing move as the cars drop from over 212mph (338kph) to 55mph (88kph) for this tight left.

Las Vegas' first Grand Prix: This was in 1981, on a tight and twisty temporary circuit and Alan Jones got the jump on his pole-sitting Williams team-mate Carlos Reutemann and then won as he pleased as Reutemann faded and lost his title shot.

Deserving American star: Josef Newgarden has won races and titles in IndyCar but has never had a shot at F1. The 34-year-old raced in British Formula Ford and then the Europe-based GP3 series, suggesting that F1 would be his aim, but then elected to head home. He followed winning the Indy Lights title in 2011 with an IndyCar career that has yielded titles in 2017 and 2019 for Team Penske as well as victories in the Indianapolis 500 in 2023 and 2024.

85

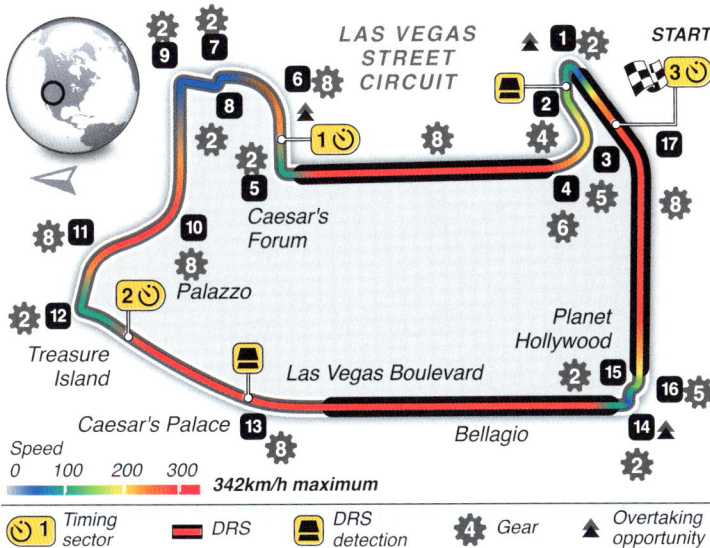

LAS VEGAS STREET CIRCUIT

START

Caesar's Forum

Palazzo

Treasure Island

Caesar's Palace

Las Vegas Boulevard

Bellagio

Planet Hollywood

Speed
0   100   200   300
342km/h maximum

| Timing sector | DRS | DRS detection | Gear | Overtaking opportunity |

2024 POLE TIME: RUSSELL (MERCEDES), 1M32.212S, 150.264MPH/241.827KPH
2024 WINNER'S AVERAGE SPEED: 140.755MPH/226.523KPH
2024 FASTEST LAP: NORRIS (MCLAREN), 1M34.876S, 146.203MPH/235.292KPH
LAP RECORD: NORRIS (MCLAREN), 1M34.876S, 146.203MPH/235.292KPH, 2024

LUSAIL

Moving this Grand Prix back by seven weeks so that it can be run in less extreme temperatures was a great help to drivers and tyres alike last year – so the timing is being repeated.

This year marks the fourth visit of the World Championship to Qatar as F1 continues to use the Arabian Peninsula as its fulcrum. This is the least visited of the four tracks used in the region, even though it opened for business as long ago as 2004, the same year as Bahrain's Sakhir.

The lap of Lusail International Circuit has an unusually good flow to it and would be a physical test for the drivers even if its race was run in cool conditions. So, with the usual searing heat, it is a real work-out.

The first corner is a long right-hander followed by an equivalent left. After a short straight, it's then time for the drivers to get considerably more busy as the 90-degree right-hander at turn 4 marks the start of a twisting seven-corner sequence in which the turn 6 hairpin is the tightest and the kink at turn 8 the most open.

Then the lap has a marked change and getting a good exit from turn 10 is crucial, as the lap enters a high-speed run of open right-handers, with turns 12 to 14 resembling three sides of a pentagon. The drivers have to resist the g-force of these seventh-gear corners which they found made them nauseous on F1's first visit, in 2021.

The lap is completed with two more corners, with the final turn a sharp right-hander on to the pit straight. As with so many modern circuits, the run past the pits is the fastest point on the lap, with cars hitting a top speed of 200mph (320kph) on the run down towards the first corner.

INSIDE TRACK

QATAR GRAND PRIX

Date:	**30 November**
Circuit name:	**Lusail International Circuit**
Circuit length:	**3.368 miles/5.419km**
Number of laps:	**57**

PREVIOUS WINNERS

2021	**Lewis Hamilton**	MERCEDES
2023	**Max Verstappen**	RED BULL
2024	**Max Verstappen**	RED BULL

Location: The circuit is north of capital Doha on the east coast of the Qatar peninsula.

Toughest corner: A clean exit from turn 10 is critical for a fast lap time as this left-hand hairpin leads on to a run of seventh-gear corners.

Best passing spot: The first corner is best for passing, with turn 4 another option.

Lusail's first Grand Prix: Run as the first of a three-race sequence of Grands Prix on the Arabian peninsula to conclude the 2021 World Championship, Lewis Hamilton knew that victory was required to close the points gap to Red Bull Racing's title leader Max Verstappen. Pole for the Mercedes team leader was the first step, and this was augmented by Verstappen lining up seventh after being hit with a five-place grid penalty. Although he reached second by lap 5, that was all he could achieve and so Hamilton cut his points deficit to eight.

Lusail's greatest Grand Prix: Soaring temperatures in October 2023 caused not only considerable driver discomfort but also had tyre supplier Pirelli mandating a maximum stint length. Through all this, Max Verstappen kept his cool to secure his third F1 title, with McLaren's Oscar Piastri and Lando Norris following him home.

Lusail's previous life: The circuit was opened in 2004, being used for motorcycle racing. The Grand Prix Masters single-seater series also used it, but it was only because the World Championship needed extra venues in 2021, when countries had travel restrictions in place, that it got its F1 break.

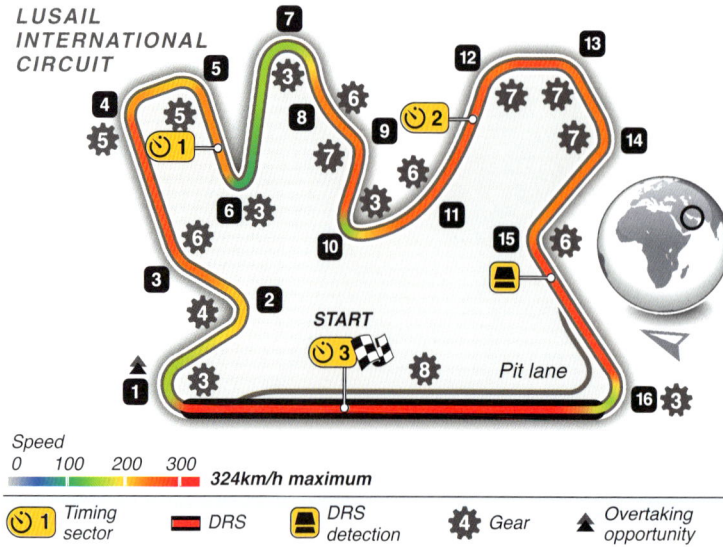

LUSAIL INTERNATIONAL CIRCUIT

Speed
0   100   200   300
324km/h maximum

- ⏱ 1 Timing sector
- ▬ DRS
- 🟡 DRS detection
- ⚙ Gear
- ▲ Overtaking opportunity

2024 POLE TIME: RUSSELL (MERCEDES), 1M20.575S, 150.442MPH/242.114KPH
2024 WINNER'S AVERAGE SPEED: 126.313MPH/203.281KPH
2024 FASTEST LAP: NORRIS (MCLAREN), 1M22.384S, 147.139MPH/236.798KPH
LAP RECORD: NORRIS (MCLAREN), 1M22.384S, 147.139MPH/236.798KPH, 2024

YAS MARINA

With the Abu Dhabi GP starting in daylight and ending after dark, the Yas Marina Circuit looks spectacular. Recent layout changes have at least offered more chances for overtaking.

The Yas Marina Circuit was world-beating when it opened for business in 2009, its facilities simply on another level to anywhere else. However, despite its money-no-object approach, the track offered little overtaking and this led to the track being modified and simplified in 2021.

The lap begins with the same 90-degree left and the same sweepers from turns 2 to 4, but the replacement of the original left/right chicane before the first hairpin has been a good thing, as it offers a chasing driver more chance of trying an overtaking manoeuvre into it.

Then comes the lap's longest straight, with cars reaching 200mph (320kph) before having to brake for second-gear turn 6. The entry to this corner tends to be the most likely passing place.

After two tight corners, the lap opens out again onto a long blast down to the other main point of modification, with the original chicane having being replaced by one long corner. This brings the track to the edge of the marina around which the lap has a change of format and is completed with a series of twists and a blast under a link between two parts of the Yas Viceroy Hotel. A clean exit from the final corner can offer at least the hope of lining up a passing manoeuvre into the first corner.

Abu Dhabi's wealth has secured its race the treasured slot of being the last race of the year, hopefully as the title decider, but question marks remain about whether its layout is suitable for generating the excitement and overtaking opportunities deserving of that.

INSIDE TRACK

ABU DHABI GRAND PRIX

Date:	**7 December**
Circuit name:	**Yas Marina Circuit**
Circuit length:	**3.282 miles/5.281km**
Number of laps:	**58**

PREVIOUS WINNERS

2015	**Nico Rosberg** MERCEDES
2016	**Lewis Hamilton** MERCEDES
2017	**Valtteri Bottas** MERCEDES
2018	**Lewis Hamilton** MERCEDES
2019	**Lewis Hamilton** MERCEDES
2020	**Max Verstappen** RED BULL
2021	**Max Verstappen** RED BULL
2022	**Max Verstappen** RED BULL
2023	**Max Verstappen** RED BULL
2024	**Lando Norris** McLAREN

Location: The Yas Island to the east of the capital includes a sports resort, of which the circuit is the centrepiece.

Toughest corner: Getting the run through turn 2 right is more important now that there is a longer run to the first hairpin.

Best passing spot: Turn 5 has become more of an overtaking hotspot than the left-hander at the end of the straight that follows it. This is thanks to the less complicated approach since the removal of the two-part chicane that used to slow cars before getting there.

Yas Marina's greatest Grand Prix: It's not often that four drivers arrive at an F1 finale in with a shot at the title, but this was the case in 2010. Points leader Fernando Alonso was frustrated in traffic and could finish only seventh, while second place wasn't enough for McLaren's Lewis Hamilton. Red Bull Racing's Mark Webber languished in eighth, while Sebastian Vettel won both race and title.

Rising Emirati star: With Middle Eastern series for both Formula Regional and Formula 4, a trickle of young drivers from the United Arab Emirates is starting to flow. The best of these is 17-year-old Keanu Al Azhari who ranked third in F4 UAE then shone in Spanish F4 by finishing as runner-up.

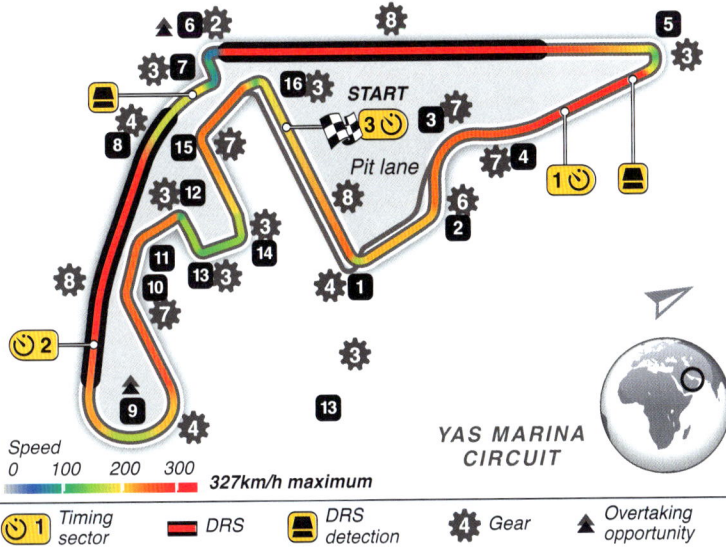

YAS MARINA CIRCUIT

Speed
0   100   200   300
327km/h maximum

⏱ 1 Timing sector	▬ DRS	🔋 DRS detection	⚙ 4 Gear	▲ Overtaking opportunity

2024 POLE TIME: **NORRIS (McLAREN), 1M22.595S, 143.026MPH/230.178KPH**
2024 WINNER'S AVERAGE SPEED: **131.883MPH/212.246KPH**
2024 FASTEST LAP: **MAGNUSSEN (HAAS), 1M25.637S, 137.945MPH/222.002KPH**
LAP RECORD: **MAGNUSSEN (HAAS), 1M25.637S, 137.945MPH/222.002KPH, 2024**

// REVIEW OF THE 2024 SEASON

Last year started off with Max Verstappen and Red Bull Racing making it look as though they would power off into the distance for a third year in succession. However, things changed as three other teams got in on the act. Ferrari, McLaren and Mercedes would rue their poor starts, and wonder what might have been.

For Red Bull Racing to have won seven of the 2024 season's first ten races and not to have ended the year as the champion constructor is extraordinary. Max Verstappen did all he could and produced some exceptional performances, but the team lacked any meaningful support from its second driver, Sergio Perez, whose form disintegrated.

But what prevented another runaway success for the team from Milton Keynes was a trio of rival teams also finding a winning touch, albeit not consistently, although between them they won ten races in a row between the Austrian and Mexico City GPs before Verstappen beat them all in the wet in Brazil.

The team that came on the most strongly was McLaren, with both Lando Norris and second-year F1 racer Oscar Piastri. But Norris' form dipped in Brazil and his outside shot at the drivers' title was extinguished at the Las Vegas GP. With two wins in the bag, Piastri showed that he might be Norris' most serious threat in 2025.

Ferrari began the year with one of its drivers already feeling less than happy. This was Carlos Sainz Jr, who caught wind of Lewis Hamilton's arrival to fill his seat this year. However, he drove with dignity and no little speed as team-mate Charles Leclerc responded by finally winning his home Grand Prix.

Mercedes was the least convincing of the top four teams, largely because it took until midway through the season to really get going with a run of three wins from four races, but then their form fluctuated, with Hamilton claiming that his car's handling was so bad in Brazil that he almost quit. George Russell seemed happier, which is good as he will be team leader this year.

Aston Martin ranked fifth for a second year in a row, but the team's 2024 showing was a far cry from its 2023 performance when Fernando Alonso gathered podium finishes seemingly for fun. His best result last year was a fifth place.

Alpine was a team going nowhere fast, usually marooned outside the points, but there were signs of a late-season upswing in form before the extraordinary wet race at Interlagos; the team's decision, like Verstappen's, not to pit for new tyres was rewarded when the race was red-flagged, allowing them to gain a free change of rubber before the restart. Their prize was a 33-point haul as Esteban Ocon and Pierre Gasly came home second and third and a huge boost from ninth in the points table to sixth.

Haas F1 was a team that appeared to be set on making its new-found place in F1's midfield, with Nico Hulkenberg usually qualifying well and grabbing consecutive sixth places to boost the team.

RB, formerly AlphaTauri, was often in with a chance of points, with Yuki Tsunoda rather than Daniel Ricciardo leading the way. Then, instead of proving that he was ready to take Perez's place at Red Bull Racing, the Australian was dropped and Liam Lawson brought in.

Williams ended up ranked ninth overall, two places down on 2023. This was despite strong form shown by Alex Albon, although Logan Sargeant disappointed in the team's second car. He was replaced by Argentinian rookie Franco Colapinto, who promptly scored some points. The team endured an awful close to its season with a run of car-wrecking shunts.

Sauber looked like a team treading water as it waits for Audi to arrive in 2026. Neither Valtteri Bottas nor Zhou Guanyu could do much with the Swiss team's car.

There was suggestion last autumn that the lowered cost cap had led to an improvement of the competition, allowing more teams to close the gap to the teams at the front of the field. If so, that is a welcome development.

BAHRAIN GP

Liberty Media wanted the season to start brightly, and it did, but not for the right reasons, with Red Bull Racing chief Christian Horner fending off accusations of harassment from a team member. But Max Verstappen stayed focused and kicked off with a dominant win.

After pre-season testing had made it look all set to be another strong year for Red Bull Racing, the team arrived in Bahrain under a cloud. Although team boss Christian Horner had just been cleared by an internal Red Bull investigation of harassing a female employee, his arrival at Sakhir was met with the release of seemingly incriminating messages that put the matter into the public arena.

Out on the track, though, the Red Bull drivers were the ones with a smile on their faces, their pace perhaps even further clear of their rivals than it had been in 2023. With pole position going to Verstappen by 0.228 seconds from Ferrari's Charles Leclerc, and George Russell another 0.1 seconds down in third place, just a whisker ahead of Carlos Sainz Jr's Ferrari, it looked as though Horner might take some pleasure from the season's opening round – especially if Sergio Perez could get the second Red Bull to advance from fifth on the grid.

Indeed, this is what transpired, as Perez was up to second place after the first round of pit stops and Verstappen led every single lap as he built a lead over his team-mate. In fact, the race was so straightforward for the Dutch ace that he asked what the lap record was so that he had something on which to focus.

The Ferraris filled the next two positions, with Sainz Jr making a point as he moved ahead of Leclerc, with the Spaniard having just discovered that Lewis Hamilton would be replacing him at Ferrari in 2025. A disenchanted Russell fell back to fifth.

While the spotlight remained on Red Bull's internal saga, the team's rivals headed off to Saudi Arabia with any slight pre-season optimism crushed. Adrian Newey's RB20, was setting new standards that meant that they appeared to have not closed the gap but fallen away.

SAKHIR ROUND 1

DATE: **2 MARCH 2024**

Laps: **57** • Distance: **191.530 miles/308.238km** • Weather: **Warm & dry**

Pos	Driver	Team	Result	Stops	Qualifying Time	Grid
1	**Max Verstappen**	Red Bull	1h31m44.742s	2	1m29.179s	1
2	**Sergio Perez**	Red Bull	1h32m07.199s	2	1m29.537s	5
3	**Carlos Sainz Jr**	Ferrari	1h32m09.852s	2	1m29.507s	4
4	**Charles Leclerc**	Ferrari	1h32m24.411s	2	1m29.407s	2
5	**George Russell**	Mercedes	1h32m31.530s	2	1m29.485s	3
6	**Lando Norris**	McLaren	1h32m33.200s	2	1m29.614s	7
7	**Lewis Hamilton**	Mercedes	1h32m35.066s	2	1m29.710s	9
8	**Oscar Piastri**	McLaren	1h32m40.824s	2	1m29.683s	8
9	**Fernando Alonso**	Aston Martin	1h32m59.629s	2	1m29.542s	6
10	**Lance Stroll**	Aston Martin	1h33m17.958s	2	1m30.200s	12
11	**Zhou Guanyu**	Sauber	56 laps	2	1m30.757s	17
12	**Kevin Magnussen**	Haas	56 laps	2	1m30.529s	15
13	**Daniel Ricciardo**	RB	56 laps	2	1m30.278s	14
14	**Yuki Tsunoda**	RB	56 laps	2	1m30.129s	11
15	**Alex Albon**	Williams	56 laps	2	1m30.221s	13
16	**Nico Hulkenberg**	Haas	56 laps	3	1m30.502s	10
17	**Esteban Ocon**	Alpine	56 laps	2	1m30.793s	19
18	**Pierre Gasly**	Alpine	56 laps	3	1m30.948s	20
19	**Valtteri Bottas**	Sauber	56 laps	2	1m30.756s	16
20	**Logan Sargeant**	Williams	55 laps	3	1m30.770s	18

FASTEST LAP: VERSTAPPEN, 1M32.608S, 130.726MPH/210.383KPH ON LAP 39 • RACE LEADERS: VERSTAPPEN 1-57

Max Verstappen leads the 20-car field into the first corner on the opening lap of the 2024 season.

SAUDI ARABIAN GP

There were again no challengers to Red Bull Racing's attack and Max Verstappen led home a second straight one-two. The talk was instead focused on Ollie Bearman, who stepped in at short notice to replace Carlos Sainz Jr and shone by finishing seventh.

Although all went smoothly for Red Bull Racing on the track, the team was still in choppy waters in the paddock. Long-standing team consultant Helmut Marko arrived in Saudi Arabia with disciplinary proceedings ahead of him and Verstappen said that he would leave the team if the Austrian was forced out. The matter continued to dominate all on-track action.

Fortunately for the sport, but not fortunately for Carlos Sainz Jr, news broke on Friday morning that the Spaniard had been sidelined by suspected appendicitis and this led to instant promotion to his race seat for F2 star Ollie Bearman. The 18-year-old Briton became F1's third youngest debutant, older only than Max Verstappen and Lance Stroll had been, and slotted in with remarkable maturity, having only the third practice session in which to acclimatize himself ahead of qualifying. That this was happening on a circuit that requires more commitment than most made matters all the more difficult, yet he only missed out on reaching the final qualifying session by 0.036 seconds, pipped by Lewis Hamilton.

Verstappen made it two pole positions from two, this time with Charles Leclerc second and team-mate Sergio Perez third. But the Mexican didn't take long to get into second place, earning a Red Bull one-two.

As this was a one-stop race, there was little scope for place-gaining strategy, but Lance Stroll offered a chance for some when his Aston Martin clipped a wall and brought out the safety car. Almost everybody pitted, but Lando Norris and Lewis Hamilton elected to save their stop until late in the race. This meant that they were on fresher rubber and they started hauling in Bearman, who was seventh. They put him under huge pressure, but he earned great praise by resisting their challenge.

Verstappen made it two from two when he beat team-mate Perez and Ferrari's Leclerc in Jeddah.

JEDDAH ROUND 2

DATE: 9 MARCH 2024

Laps: 50 • Distance: 191.662 miles/308.450km • Weather: Hot & dry

Pos	Driver	Team	Result	Stops	Qualifying Time	Grid
1	Max Verstappen	Red Bull	1h20m43.273s	1	1m27.472s	1
2	Sergio Perez !	Red Bull	1h20m56.916s	1	1m27.807s	3
3	Charles Leclerc	Ferrari	1h21m01.912s	1	1m27.791s	2
4	Oscar Piastri	McLaren	1h21m15.280s	1	1m28.089s	5
5	Fernando Alonso	Aston Martin	1h21m19.032s	1	1m27.846s	4
6	George Russell	Mercedes	1h21m23.209s	1	1m28.316s	7
7	Ollie Bearman	Ferrari	1h21m25.952s	1	1m28.642s	11
8	Lando Norris	McLaren	1h21m28.981s	1	1m28.132s	6
9	Lewis Hamilton	Mercedes	1h21m30.664s	1	1m28.460s	8
10	Nico Hulkenberg	Haas	1h22m00.269s	1	no time	15
11	Alex Albon	Williams	1h22m11.627s	1	1m28.980s	12
12	Kevin Magnussen *, !!	Haas	1h22m29.010s	1	1m29.020s	13
13	Esteban Ocon	Alpine	49 laps	1	1m29.475s	17
14	Logan Sargeant	Williams	49 laps	1	1m29.526s	19
15	Yuki Tsunoda !	RB	49 laps	1	1m28.547s	9
16	Daniel Ricciardo	RB	49 laps	1	1m29.025s	14
17	Valtteri Bottas	Sauber	49 laps	2	1m29.179s	16
18	Zhou Guanyu	Sauber	49 laps	1	no time	20
R	Lance Stroll	Aston Martin	5 laps/accident	0	1m28.572s	10
R	Pierre Gasly	Alpine	1 lap/gearbox	0	1m29.479s	18
W	Carlos Sainz Jr	Ferrari	appendicitis	-	-	-

FASTEST LAP: LECLERC, 1M31.632S, 150.720MPH/242.561KPH ON LAP 50 • RACE LEADERS: VERSTAPPEN 1-7 & 13-50, NORRIS 8-12
! 5S PENALTY FOR UNSAFE RELEASE • * 10S PENALTY FOR CAUSING A COLLISION • !! 10S PENALTY FOR GAINING AN ADVANTAGE BY LEAVING TRACK INCORRECTLY

A fortnight after having his appendix removed, Carlos Sainz Jr not only overtook Max Verstappen for the lead but went on to command a Ferrari one-two after the points leader retired with a brake problem after only three laps. McLaren finished third and fourth.

Everyone was delighted to see a winner other than Max Verstappen and doubly so that it was Carlos Sainz Jr who climbed onto the top step of the podium. He had had to miss the Saudi Arabian GP after his appendix flared up and was obviously going to feel less than comfortable in the car on his return, but the Spaniard got on with the job.

Starting second on the grid behind Verstappen, Sainz settled into second place then swept past on lap 2. Something was clearly wrong with the Red Bull and the world champion radioed his pit, then smoke started spewing from the rear brakes and he would soon retire, his locked brakes now on fire.

Sainz proving himself once again to be the faster of the Ferrari drivers will have been bittersweet following the pre-season announcement that he was going to be replaced for 2025 by Lewis Hamilton. Judging by his start to the 2024 campaign, Hamilton would have been licking his lips in anticipation, as he was uncompetitive in his Mercedes, qualifying only 11th, and followed Verstappen into retirement.

McLaren had reason to smile as its drivers scooped 27 points, with Lando Norris third and Oscar Piastri fourth.

Sergio Perez finished another 20 seconds back after his car's aerodynamics were hampered by a tear-off visor lodged in its floor. Behind him, Fernando Alonso and George Russell were fighting over sixth place going into the last lap, but neither would claim the position as the Aston Martin driver appeared to brake early for turn 9 and Russell's Mercedes, clipping the wall in avoidance, ended up on its side. Alonso was hit after the race with a 20-second penalty that dropped him to eighth in the rankings and promoted team-mate Lance Stroll to sixth and RB's Yuki Tsunoda to seventh.

Carlo Sainz Jr bounced back from being too unwell to race in Jeddah to triumph in Melbourne.

MELBOURNE ROUND 3

DATE: **24 MARCH 2024**

Laps: **58** • Distance: **190.216 miles/306.124km** • Weather: **Hot & sunny**

Pos	Driver	Team	Result	Stops	Qualifying Time	Grid
1	**Carlos Sainz Jr**	Ferrari	1h20m26.843s	2	1m16.185s	2
2	**Charles Leclerc**	Ferrari	1h20m29.209s	2	1m16.435s	4
3	**Lando Norris**	McLaren	1h20m32.747s	2	1m16.315s	3
4	**Oscar Piastri**	McLaren	1h21m02.613s	2	1m16.572s	5
5	**Sergio Perez !**	Red Bull	1h21m23.152s	2	1m16.274s	6
6	**Lance Stroll**	Aston Martin	1h22m00.065s	2	1m17.072s	9
7	**Yuki Tsunoda**	RB	1h22m02.444s	2	1m16.788s	8
8	**Fernando Alonso ***	Aston Martin	1h22m07.835s	2	1m17.552s	10
9	**Nico Hulkenberg**	Haas	1h22m11.396s	2	1m17.976s	16
10	**Kevin Magnussen**	Haas	57 laps	2	1m17.427s	14
11	**Alex Albon**	Williams	57 laps	2	1m17.167s	12
12	**Daniel Ricciardo**	RB	57 laps	2	1m18.085s	18
13	**Pierre Gasly**	Alpine	57 laps	2	1m17.982S	17
14	**Valtteri Bottas**	Sauber	57 laps	2	1m17.340s	13
15	**Zhou Guanyu !!**	Sauber	57 laps	2	1m18.188s	19
16	**Esteban Ocon**	Alpine	57 laps	3	1m17.697s	15
R	**George Russell**	Mercedes	56 laps/accident	2	1m16.724s	7
R	**Lewis Hamilton**	Mercedes	15 laps/power unit	1	1m16.960s	11
R	**Max Verstappen**	Red Bull	3 laps/brakes	0	1m15.915s	1
W	**Logan Sargeant**	Williams	Car given to Albon	-	-	-

FASTEST LAP: LECLERC, 1M19.813S, 147.927MPH/238.066KPH ON LAP 56 • RACE LEADERS: VERSTAPPEN 1, SAINZ 2-58 • ! 3-PLACE GRID PENALTY FOR IMPEDING HULKENBERG • !! HAD TO START FROM PIT LANE FOR CAR BEING MODIFIED IN PARC FERME • * 20S PENALTY FOR CAUSING AN ACCIDENT

JAPANESE GP

Normal service was resumed as Max Verstappen dominated, leading Mercedes chief Toto Wolff to declare the title already won. With Sergio Perez second, the only remaining prize on offer was third place, with Carlos Sainz Jr beating his Ferrari team-mate Charles Leclerc again.

With a Red Bull lock-out of the front row, 18 of the 20 drivers didn't really fancy their chances. Correctly, as it proved, and their numbers were reduced by two on the opening lap as Daniel Ricciardo's RB came together with Alex Albon's Williams on their way out of turn 2. This brought out the red flags to stop the race while the tyre wall was repaired.

At the second time of asking, Verstappen led away again and, although Lando Norris followed along in third place, his McLaren was hungrier on its tyres. Norris became the first of the front runners to make the first of their two planned pit stops, followed a lap later by team-mate Oscar Piastri.

Fernando Alonso's Aston Martin was next to pit and then the Red Bulls, with the race under control. By staying out longest, Charles Leclerc rose from eighth on the grid to lead for four laps, and his frugality put him close to the Red Bulls – but not close enough. The Monegasque driver dropped to third and then, with seven laps to go, was demoted from the final place on the podium as team-mate Carlos Sainz Jr got past him.

Norris wasn't far behind in fifth, but in this race of tyre strategy, McLaren didn't have a car that could manage its rubber as well as Ferrari did. Despite finishing only sixth, Alonso felt that he had got everything from his Aston Martin, with the Mercedes drivers perhaps even more disappointed in their cars' performance around this twisting and testing circuit.

Perhaps the loudest cheer of the day came from the grandstands when local hero Yuki Tsunoda secured the final point for RB. Nico Hulkenberg just missed out on scoring for Haas, and he was far happier than the beleaguered Alpine drivers who couldn't even dream of scoring.

SUZUKA ROUND 4

DATE: **7 APRIL 2024**

Laps: **53** · Distance: **191.053 miles/307.471km** · Weather: **Warm but overcast**

Pos	Driver	Team	Result	Stops	Qualifying Time	Grid
1	**Max Verstappen**	Red Bull	1h54m23.566s	3	1m28.197s	1
2	**Sergio Perez**	Red Bull	1h54m36.101s	3	1m28.263s	2
3	**Carlos Sainz Jr**	Ferrari	1h54m44.432s	3	1m28.682s	4
4	**Charles Leclerc**	Ferrari	1h54m50.088s	2	1m28.786s	8
5	**Lando Norris**	McLaren	1h54m53.266s	3	1m28.489s	3
6	**Fernando Alonso**	Aston Martin	1h55m07.838s	3	1m28.686s	5
7	**George Russell**	Mercedes	1h55m09.517s	3	1m29.008s	9
8	**Oscar Piastri**	McLaren	1h55m11.091s	3	1m28.760s	6
9	**Lewis Hamilton**	Mercedes	1h55m12.192s	3	1m28.766s	7
10	**Yuki Tsunoda**	RB	52 laps	3	1m29.413s	10
11	**Nico Hulkenberg**	Haas	52 laps	3	1m29.494s	12
12	**Lance Stroll**	Aston Martin	52 laps	4	1m30.024s	16
13	**Kevin Magnussen**	Haas	52 laps	2	1m30.131s	18
14	**Valtteri Bottas**	Sauber	52 laps	3	1m29.593s	13
15	**Esteban Ocon**	Alpine	52 laps	3	1m29.816s	15
16	**Pierre Gasly**	Alpine	52 laps	3	1m30.119s	17
17	**Logan Sargeant**	Williams	52 laps	4	1m30.139s	19
R	**Zhou Guanyu**	Sauber	12 laps/gearbox	3	1m30.143	20
R	**Daniel Ricciardo**	RB	0 laps/collision	0	1m29.472s	11
R	**Alex Albon**	Williams	0 laps/collision	0	1m29.714s	14

FASTEST LAP: **VERSTAPPEN, 1M33.706S, 138.623MPH/223.093KPH ON LAP 50** · RACE LEADERS: **VERSTAPPEN 1-16, 21-34, 36-53, LECLERC 17-20, SAINZ JR 35**

The Red Bull RB20s of Verstappen and Perez fill the front row at the start of the Japanese GP.

CHINESE GP

Max Verstappen made it four wins from five starts, but the story of F1's return to China for the first time since pre-COVID days was the improved form of McLaren, with Lando Norris following the Dutchman home after making the most of the timing of a virtual safety car period.

After winning the sprint race on the Saturday, Verstappen soon had the first Grand Prix at the Shanghai International Circuit since 2019 under control as he pulled clear in the lead. Sergio Perez was passed at the start by Aston Martin's Fernando Alonso and it took several laps for the Mexican to make it back to second.

After the first round of pit stops, the deployment of a virtual safety car offered a boost for those drivers who had been light on their first set of tyres and had yet to pit. The safety car occurred because Valtteri Bottas' Sauber suffered engine failure and couldn't be moved from the track at the tight left at turn 11 as it was jammed in gear. Pitting during the safety car period produced a gain of nigh on ten seconds for both Lando Norris and Charles Leclerc, and this moved them up to second and third places respectively.

Verstappen was all set to lead away when the safety car withdrew, but this was complicated by Alonso locking up and triggering a chain reaction, with Alonso's team-mate Lance Stroll failing to notice what was happening and slamming into the tail of RB's Daniel Ricciardo. The Australian soon pulled off into retirement, doubly disappointed as he had been running in ninth place when it happened, hoping to score points to spike talks of him being replaced by Liam Lawson.

Verstappen then eased clear from Norris, while Perez took eight laps to catch and pass Leclerc for third. However, he couldn't catch the Englishman, who was astonished to secure a podium position as McLaren hadn't reckoned that it would be competitive here. Team-mate Oscar Piastri also scored, finishing eighth. George Russell was cheered by coming sixth just behind the Ferraris in the last race before a Mercedes upgrade.

Lando Norris was happy to be able to bring his McLaren home second, behind Verstappen.

SHANGHAI ROUND 5

DATE: 21 APRIL 2024

Laps: 56 • Distance: **189.559 miles/305.066km** • Weather: **Warm but cloudy**

Pos	Driver	Team	Result	Stops	Grid	Sprint
1	**Max Verstappen**	Red Bull	1h40m52.554s	2	1	1
2	**Lando Norris**	McLaren	1h41m06.327s	1	4	6
3	**Sergio Perez**	Red Bull	1h41m11.714s	2	2	3
4	**Charles Leclerc**	Ferrari	1h41m16.177s	1	6	4
5	**Carlos Sainz Jr**	Ferrari	1h41m26.537s	1	7	5
6	**George Russell**	Mercedes	1h41m31.278s	2	8	8
7	**Fernando Alonso**	Aston Martin	1h41m35.968s	3	3	20
8	**Oscar Piastri**	McLaren	1h41m48.752s	2	5	7
9	**Lewis Hamilton**	Mercedes	1h41m50.540s	2	18	2
10	**Nico Hulkenberg**	Haas	1h41m53.030s	2	9	19
11	**Esteban Ocon**	Alpine	1h41m55.366s	2	13	13
12	**Alex Albon**	Williams	1h41m58.060s	2	14	17
13	**Pierre Gasly**	Alpine	1h42m01.777s	3	15	15
14	**Zhou Guanyu**	Sauber	1h42m04.243s	3	16	9
15	**Lance Stroll**	Aston Martin	1h42m15.340s	4	11	14
16	**Kevin Magnussen** !	Haas	1h42m20.087s	2	17	10
17	**Logan Sargeant** *, !!	Williams	1h42m27.664s	2	20	18
R	**Daniel Ricciardo**	RB	33 laps/Crash damage	2	12	11
R	**Yuki Tsunoda**	RB	26 laps/Accident	2	19	16
R	**Valtteri Bottas**	Sauber	19 laps/Engine	1	10	12

FASTEST LAP: ALONSO, 1M37.810S, 124.665MPH/200.629KPH ON LAP 45 • RACE LEADERS: VERSTAPPEN 1-13 & 19-56, NORRIS 14-18
* REQUIRED TO START FROM PIT LANE AS CAR MODIFIED UNDER PARC FERME CONDITIONS • ! 10S PENALTY FOR CAUSING A COLLISION WITH TSUNODA • !! 10S PENALTY FOR SAFETY CAR INFRINGEMENT

MIAMI GP

After 15 podium visits spread across his first five-and-a-bit seasons of F1, Lando Norris broke his F1 duck at his 110th attempt by taking a hugely popular victory, which put McLaren back on top in a race where he beat Max Verstappen fair and square.

A first-time winner will always gain the plaudits, but the scenes after the race were extraordinary, with every driver finding Lando to join in his celebrations, with Ferrari team principal Frederic Vasseur donning a McLaren cap as he sprayed champagne.

There is no doubting that Lando's ready smile and keen sense of humour is one reason for this outbreak of joy. The other reason was undoubtedly that the Red Bull Racing juggernaut had been brought to a halt. Sure, Carlos Sainz Jr won in Australia, but that was after Verstappen broke down. This time, it was different.

The portents for anything other than another Verstappen victory were not good, as the Dutch ace won the sprint race, a part of the weekend that veteran Fernando Alonso said he considered increasingly less worthwhile. Verstappen then went on to set pole for good measure, with the Ferraris second and third fastest.

Verstappen duly led away, followed by Charles Leclerc, Norris' fast-starting team-mate Oscar Piastri and Sainz. Sergio Perez ran fifth in the second Red Bull ahead of Norris. By not pushing his rubber too hard as he acknowledged there would be few chances to pass, Lando was able to stretch his opening stint longer than his rivals. Then, on lap 27, he was presented with a gift: the safety car was deployed after Logan Sargeant and Kevin Magnussen collided at turn 3. The advantage of pitting while his rivals were lapping at abated pace meant that he came back out at the head of the pack.

Ordinarily, Verstappen would have expected to catch and pass Norris in the remaining half of the race, but the latest upgrades introduced by McLaren were clearly effective, as he could make no impact, slowed by floor damage from an off-track excursion at the chicane. Indeed, Norris pulled away, never to be caught.

MIAMI ROUND 6
DATE: 5 MAY 2024

Laps: 57 • **Distance:** 191.585 miles/308.326km • **Weather:** **Warm & sunny**

Pos	Driver	Team	Result	Stops	Grid	Sprint
1	**Lando Norris**	McLaren	1h30m49.876s	1	5	R
2	**Max Verstappen**	Red Bull	1h30m57.488s	1	1	1
3	**Charles Leclerc**	Ferrari	1h30m59.796s	1	2	2
4	**Sergio Perez**	Red Bull	1h31m04.526s	2	4	3
5	**Carlos Sainz Jr !**	Ferrari	1h31m06.283s	1	3	5
6	**Lewis Hamilton**	Mercedes	1h31m06.461s	1	8	16
7	**Yuki Tsunoda**	RB	1h31m16.061s	1	10	8
8	**George Russell**	Mercedes	1h31m24.665s	1	7	12
9	**Fernando Alonso**	Aston Martin	1h31m26.983s	1	15	17
10	**Esteban Ocon**	Alpine	1h31m29.622s	1	13	15
11	**Nico Hulkenberg**	Haas	1h31m30.665s	2	9	7
12	**Pierre Gasly**	Alpine	1h31m34.834s	1	12	9
13	**Oscar Piastri**	McLaren	1h31m39.632s	2	6	6
14	**Zhou Guanyu**	Sauber	1h31m39.855s	1	19	11
15	**Daniel Ricciardo ***	RB	1h31m40.832s	1	20	4
16	**Valtteri Bottas**	Sauber	1h31m42.232s	2	16	14
17	**Lance Stroll !!**	Aston Martin	1h31m45.049s	2	11	R
18	**Alex Albon**	Williams	1h32m05.967s	2	14	13
19	**Kevin Magnussen !!!**	Haas	1h32m14.559s	3	18	18
R	**Logan Sargeant**	Williams	27 laps/accident		17	10

FASTEST LAP: PIASTRI, 1M30.634S, 133.573MPH/214.965KPH ON LAP 43 • RACE LEADERS: VERSTAPPEN 1-22, PIASTRI 23-26, NORRIS 27-57 • 3-PLACE GRID PENALTY FOR OVERTAKING UNDER SAFETY CAR CONDITIONS AT CHINESE GP • ! 5S PENALTY FOR COLLIDING WITH PIASTRI • !! 10S PENALTY FOR LEAVING THE TRACK & GAINING AN ADVANTAGE • !!! 10S PENALTY FOR COLLIDING WITH SARGEANT & 20S PENALTY FOR ENTERING PITS DURING A SAFETY CAR PERIOD & NOT CHANGING TYRES

One race later, Norris claimed the first win of his F1 career on a day when McLaren hit form.

// EMILIA ROMAGNA GP

Max Verstappen returned to winning form, but he was chased all the way to the finish by Lando Norris, proving that McLaren's victory in Miami was no isolated success and that any further progress by the team from Woking could make life a little more tricky for him.

Round seven meant pole number seven of the season for Max Verstappen, but the Dutch ace knew that the tide was turning and that McLaren was truly finding its feet, with its drivers qualifying second and third. Unfortunately for Oscar Piastri, just 0.074 seconds down on the three-time world champion, he had impeded Kevin Magnussen and the impressive Australian was put back three places, behind teammate Lando Norris plus the Ferraris of Charles Leclerc and Carlos Sainz Jr.

On the other side of the Red Bull Racing garage, Sergio Perez was doing little to act as support, qualifying only 11th.

Boosted by his breakthrough win in Miami, Norris knew that his best chance of beating Verstappen again was to get ahead at the start, as this picturesque old-school track offers few passing opportunities. He tried, but Verstappen had it all covered and gradually eased clear in the lead, building the gap to five seconds before he dived into the pits for his planned stop.

Norris had already come in, but was then frustrated to emerge behind Perez who at least did his bit for the team by delaying the English racer, and that looked to be that, as Norris was still ahead of the Ferraris when they resumed, but still behind Verstappen.

Then things got interesting, as Norris began to be reeled in my Leclerc, but he had been nursing his tyre life and then attacked as the race went into its final stages, chipping away at Verstappen's lead. Down it came until viewers imagined that Norris would be close enough to pounce if there had been just a couple of laps more.

However, Verstappen held on, winning by 0.725 seconds, but now fully aware that the McLaren challenge had become bona fide. Fortunately, Verstappen's points tally of 161 put him 60 clear of Norris.

IMOLA ROUND 7

DATE: 19 MAY 2024

Laps: **63** • Distance: **192.034 miles/309.049km** • Weather: **Warm & sunny**

Pos	Driver	Team	Result	Stops	Qualifying Time	Grid
1	**Max Verstappen**	Red Bull	1h25m25.252s	1	1m14.746s	1
2	**Lando Norris**	McLaren	1h25m25.977s	1	1m14.837s	2
3	**Charles Leclerc**	Ferrari	1h25m33.168s	1	1m14.970s	3
4	**Oscar Piastri** *	McLaren	1h25m39.384s	1	1m14.820s	5
5	**Carlos Sainz Jr**	Ferrari	1h25m47.577s	1	1m15.233s	4
6	**Lewis Hamilton**	Mercedes	1h26m00.356s	1	1m15.504s	8
7	**George Russell**	Mercedes	1h26m12.406s	2	1m15.234s	6
8	**Sergio Perez**	Red Bull	1h26m20.028s	1	1m15.706s	11
9	**Lance Stroll**	Aston Martin	1h26m44.808s	1	1m15.992s	13
10	**Yuki Tsunoda**	RB	62 laps	1	1m15.465s	7
11	**Nico Hulkenberg**	Haas	62 laps	1	1m15.980s	10
12	**Kevin Magnussen**	Haas	62 laps	1	1m16.854s	18
13	**Daniel Ricciardo**	RB	62 laps	1	1m15.706s	9
14	**Esteban Ocon**	Alpine	62 laps	1	1m15.906s	12
15	**Zhou Guanyu**	Sauber	62 laps	1	1m16.834s	17
16	**Pierre Gasly**	Alpine	62 laps	2	1m16.381s	15
17	**Logan Sargeant**	Williams	62 laps	1	No time	19
18	**Valtteri Bottas**	Sauber	62 laps	1	1m16.626s	16
19	**Fernando Alonso** !	Aston Martin	62 laps	3	1m16.917s	20
R	**Alex Albon**	Williams	51 laps/withdrew	4	1m16.200s	14

FASTEST LAP: RUSSELL, 1M18.589S, 139.782MPH/224.871KPH ON LAP 54 • RACE LEADERS: VERSTAPPEN 1-24 & 28-63, SAINZ JR 25-27 * 3-PLACE GRID PENALTY FOR IMPEDING MAGNUSSEN4 • ! REQUIRED TO START FROM PIT LANE AS CAR MODIFIED UNDER PARC FERME CONDITIONS

Max Verstappen was out on his own at Imola, his Red Bull galloping clear at this scenic track.

MONACO GP

After claiming pole position, vital at this race, Charles Leclerc could begin to dream that he might win his home race at his seventh attempt. There was a red flag when Sergio Perez was pitched off on the opening lap, but Leclerc kept his cool to bring it home.

This was a race that started with a bang and ended with a fanfare as Charles Leclerc became the first Monegasque driver to win at home.

Leclerc got away well from pole and led into Sainte Devote. Oscar Piastri and Carlos Sainz Jr brushed wheels behind him, resulting in the Ferrari pulling off at Casino Square with a puncture. There was also a midfield sort-out, when Esteban Ocon hit Alpine team-mate Pierre Gasly at Portier.

Most notably, right at the back, there was contact between Sergio Perez and Kevin Magnussen on the climb to Massenet, with the Mexican's car being wrecked and bringing out the red flags. Nico Hulkenberg was also caught in the incident to make it a doubly bad day for Haas. Gallingly for the German, he had qualified ninth but, like his team-mate, had been put to the rear of the grid because their rear wings had an oversized DRS opening.

Leclerc pulled clear at the restart and the race became a stalemate. Indeed, the fact that the top ten cars were in the same order at race's end for the first time showed how difficult overtaking is on this street circuit, especially as they had made their one tyre-change before the restart.

Verstappen said he was bored as he sat in the queue in sixth, with many suggesting that it was hardly racing, with the cars around four seconds off their ultimate pace to save their tyres and almost no chance to overtake. Oscar Piastri, from second on the grid, followed Leclerc home with Sainz Jr, who had been fortunate that he was able to change tyres before the restart, taking the final podium place.

However, the sheer joy at Leclerc's victory on his home turf and the sight of Prince Albert spraying champagne on the podium made up for the processional race.

Charles Leclerc celebrated when he took pole on home ground and even more so after he won.

MONTE CARLO ROUND 8

DATE: **26 MAY 2024**

Laps: **78** • Distance: **161.734 miles/260.286km** • Weather: **Warm & sunny**

Pos	Driver	Team	Result	Stops	Qualifying Time	Grid
1	**Charles Leclerc**	Ferrari	2h23m15.554s	1	1m10.270s	1
2	**Oscar Piastri**	McLaren	2h23m22.706s	1	1m10.424s	2
3	**Carlos Sainz Jr**	Ferrari	2h23m23.139s	1	1m10.518s	3
4	**Lando Norris**	McLaren	2h23m24.204s	1	1m10.542s	4
5	**George Russell**	Mercedes	2h23m28.863s	1	1m10.543s	5
6	**Max Verstappen**	Red Bull	2h23m29.407s	2	1m10.567s	6
7	**Lewis Hamilton**	Mercedes	2h23m30.462s	2	1m10.621s	7
8	**Yuki Tsunoda**	RB	77 laps	1	1m10.858s	8
9	**Alex Albon**	Williams	77 laps	1	1m10.948s	9
10	**Pierre Gasly**	Alpine	77 laps	1	1m11.311s	10
11	**Fernando Alonso**	Aston Martin	76 laps	1	1m12.019s	14
12	**Daniel Ricciardo**	RB	76 laps	1	1m11.482s	12
13	**Valtteri Bottas**	Sauber	76 laps	2	1m12.512s	17
14	**Lance Stroll**	Aston Martin	76 laps	3	1m11.563s	13
15	**Logan Sargeant**	Williams	76 laps	2	1m12.020s	15
16	**Zhou Guanyu**	Sauber	76 laps	2	1m13.028s	18
R	**Esteban Ocon**	Alpine	0 laps/accident damage	1	1m11.285s	11
R	**Nico Hulkenberg** !	Haas	0 laps/accident	0	no time	19
R	**Kevin Magnussen** !	Haas	0 laps/accident	0	no time	20
R	**Sergio Perez**	Red Bull	0 laps/accident	0	1m12.060s	16

FASTEST LAP: **HAMILTON, 1M14.165S, 100.649MPH/161.979KPH ON LAP 63** • RACE LEADERS: **LECLERC 1-78** • **! PUT TO BACK OF GRID FOR A REAR WING INFRINGEMENT**

Charles Leclerc leads Oscar Piastri and Carlos Sainz Jr past the yachts at the 2024 Monaco GP.

Wet/dry conditions seldom fail to enliven proceedings, and this was the case in Montreal as it set up a five-way late-race charge to the finish on a treacherous track. Max Verstappen emerged in front to edge out Lando Norris and pole-starter George Russell.

The one-third mark of the season proved to be a sweet spot for Mercedes, as its rich form continued and McLaren was right in the mix too. George Russell set the fastest time in qualifying for the first time since 2022 and then Max Verstappen equalled it, but pole went to the Mercedes driver as he set his time first.

Neither Ferrari driver made it through to the third qualifying session, while Sergio Perez didn't even get out of the first session, with Red Bull advisor Helmut Marko saying that it was a psychological matter.

Russell led away on a wet track, but it began to dry, with Lando Norris passing Verstappen and then getting by Russell for the lead in a move that had Russell sliding wide and losing a further place to the Dutchman.

Norris' hopes of a second win were dashed when Logan Sargeant went off and the safety car was sent out just after Norris had passed the pit entry, leaving him to endure a slow lap before pitting and rejoining in third. When the safety car withdrew, Verstappen edged clear, but then was reeled in, before a slip from both Norris and Russell, who stayed out longest before pitting for slicks, made life easier for him.

Then Carlos Sainz brought the red flags out on lap 53, when he slid off at turn 6 and collected Alex Albon's Williams.

The restart came with 11 laps to go, and this was when the action really hotted up as it allowed the pack to close in and Mercedes to fit fresh tyres. With his grip advantage, Russell caught the McLarens but ran wide when trying to pass Piastri at the chicane and had to mount his attack all over again. However, the damage was done, and he could make it back only to third.

George Russell led early on, but Max Verstappen took the honours after a five-way battle to the finish.

MONTREAL ROUND 9

DATE: **9 JUNE 2024**

Laps: **70** • Distance: **189.686 miles/305.270km** • Weather: **Warm & wet**

Pos	Driver	Team	Result	Stops	Qualifying Time	Grid
1	**Max Verstappen**	Red Bull	1h45m47.927s	2	1m12.000s	2
2	**Lando Norris**	McLaren	1h45m51.806s	2	1m12.021s	3
3	**George Russell**	Mercedes	1h45m52.244s	3	1m12.000s	1
4	**Lewis Hamilton**	Mercedes	1h45m52.842s	3	1m12.280s	7
5	**Oscar Piastri**	McLaren	1h45m58.126s	2	1m12.103s	4
6	**Fernando Alonso**	Aston Martin	1h46m05.437s	2	1m12.228s	6
7	**Lance Stroll**	Aston Martin	1h46m11.552s	2	1m12.701s	9
8	**Daniel Ricciardo**	RB	1h46m16.599s	2	1m12.178s	5
9	**Pierre Gasly**	Alpine	1h46m17.948s	2	1m12.940s	15
10	**Esteban Ocon** !	Alpine	1h46m18.240s	1	1m13.435s	18
11	**Nico Hulkenberg**	Haas	1h46m18.751s	3	1m13.978s	17
12	**Kevin Magnussen**	Haas	1h46m19.180s	4	1m12.916s	14
13	**Valtteri Bottas** !!	Sauber	1h46m28.414s	1	1m13.366s	19
14	**Yuki Tsunoda**	RB	1h46m40.621s	1	1m12.414s	8
15	**Zhou Guanyu** !!	Sauber	69 laps	3	1m14.292s	20
R	**Carlos Sainz Jr**	Ferrari	52 laps/accident damage	2	1m12.728s	12
R	**Alex Albon**	Williams	52 laps/accident	2	1m12.796s	10
R	**Sergio Perez**	Red Bull	51 laps/accident damage	2	1m13.326s	16
R	**Charles Leclerc**	Ferrari	40 laps/engine	3	1m12.691s	11
R	**Logan Sargeant**	Williams	23 laps/accident	0	1m12.736s	13

FASTEST LAP: HAMILTON, 1M14.856S, 130.320MPH/209.730KPH ON LAP 70 • RACE LEADERS: RUSSELL 1-20, NORRIS 21-25 & 45-47, VERSTAPPEN 26-44 & 48-70 • ! 5-PLACE GRID PENALTY FOR COLLIDING WITH GASLY IN MONACO GP • !! REQUIRED TO START FROM PIT LANE AS CAR MODIFIED IN PARC FERME

SPANISH GP

Lando Norris wasted his pole position and George Russell grabbed the lead, but Max Verstappen rose to the task again and, although perhaps no longer having the fastest car, still managed to muscle his way into the lead and kept Norris at bay. No one else was in the hunt.

McLaren's form continued to blossom and Lando Norris reckoned that he had given his all to produce the lap that gave him pole. With Max Verstappen starting alongside him, and aware how hard it is to overtake at this circuit, Lando knew that he could not let Verstappen ease ahead. Perhaps he was so busy watching for the Dutchman and edging him across towards the grass on the inside of the track that he didn't notice a bold move coming from George Russell, whose Mercedes swept around the outside to grab the lead.

Worse still, Verstappen also got ahead by the first corner, with Lewis Hamilton's attack spoiled as he had to lift off a little in avoidance.

Although Mercedes was increasingly finding performance in the middle stage of the season, Russell was hunted down easily by Verstappen and the Red Bull driver flashed by into the lead into turn 1 as they started lap 3.

Still upset about his start, Norris needed to get past Russell to go after Verstappen, but it took until lap 35 after the first of two pit stops to do so, and the time he lost behind his compatriot cost him. Russell then had a tyre problem and this let Hamilton claim third.

The racing was closer than normal at this circuit where processional races are the norm, but the sight of the cars cruising around ten seconds off their qualifying pace was less than exciting.

The Ferrari drivers didn't enjoy each other's company as they squabbled over fifth, with Carlos Sainz Jr notably vexed.

Sergio Perez was again woeful in the second Red Bull, making one wonder why the team had just extended his contract by two years. Having qualified only eighth, he was given a three-place grid penalty, yet still made it only back to eighth.

BARCELONA ROUND 10

DATE: 23 JUNE 2024

Laps: **66** · Distance: **190.907 miles/307.236km** · Weather: **Hot & bright**

Pos	Driver	Team	Result	Stops	Qualifying Time	Grid
1	**Max Verstappen**	Red Bull	1h28m20.227s	2	1m11.403s	2
2	**Lando Norris**	McLaren	1h28m22.446s	2	1m11.383s	1
3	**Lewis Hamilton**	Mercedes	1h28m38.017s	2	1m11.701s	3
4	**George Russell**	Mercedes	1h28m42.547s	2	1m11.703s	4
5	**Charles Leclerc**	Ferrari	1h28m42.936s	2	1m11.731s	5
6	**Carlos Sainz Jr**	Ferrari	1h28m51.255s	2	1m11.736s	6
7	**Oscar Piastri**	McLaren	1h28m53.987s	2	no time	9
8	**Sergio Perez** !	Red Bull	1h29m19.751s	3	1m12.061s	11
9	**Pierre Gasly**	Alpine	1h29m22.252s	2	1m11.857s	7
10	**Esteban Ocon**	Alpine	1h29m32.116s	2	1m12.125s	8
11	**Nico Hulkenberg** *	Haas	1h29m39.442s	2	1m123.10s	13
12	**Fernando Alonso**	Aston Martin	65 laps	2	1m12.128s	10
13	**Zhou Guanyu**	Sauber	65 laps	2	1m12.738s	15
14	**Lance Stroll**	Aston Martin	65 laps	2	1m12.372s	14
15	**Daniel Ricciardo**	RB	65 laps	2	1m13.075s	18
16	**Valtteri Bottas**	Sauber	65 laps	2	1m12.227s	12
17	**Kevin Magnussen**	Haas	65 laps	2	1m12.937s	16
18	**Alex Albon** !!	Williams	65 laps	2	1m13.153s	20
19	**Yuki Tsunoda** *	RB	65 laps	3	1m12.985s	17
20	**Logan Sargeant** !!!	Williams	64 laps	2	1m13.509s	19

FASTEST LAP: NORRIS, 1M17.115S, 135.089MPH/217.405KPH ON LAP 51 · RACE LEADERS: RUSSELL 1-2, VERSTAPPEN 3-17, 24-44 & 48-66, NORRIS 18-23 & 45-47 · * 5S PENALTY FOR SPEEDING IN THE PIT LANE · ! 3-PLACE GRID PENALTY FOR DRIVING A CAR IN AN UNSAFE CONDITION AT PREVIOUS RACE · !! REQUIRED TO START FROM PIT LANE AS CAR MODIFIED IN PARC FERME · !!! 3-PLACE GRID PENALTY FOR IMPEDING STROLL IN QUALIFYING

Lando Norris squandered his pole position and Max Verstappen nipped through to beat him.

AUSTRIAN GP

A late-race clash between a battling Max Verstappen and a win-chasing Lando Norris opened the door for George Russell to claim Mercedes' first victory since the 2022 Brazilian GP. Norris was livid with the driver who had been his closest friend in F1.

With the pendulum of form still swinging away from Red Bull Racing and towards McLaren, Max Verstappen knew that he was going to have a fight on his hands to resist Lando Norris through the 71-lap race distance. He had pulled out the stops to claim pole position, but McLaren's increasing competitiveness across a Grand Prix distance had him concerned.

Verstappen led away and worked hard to build an advantage, but he had a slow second pit stop and was then reeled in and realized that the English racer had the performance advantage needed to get past him. They tussled for a dozen laps, with Verstappen's defensive moves becoming ever more desperate as he struggled for grip with a scrubbed set of tyres rather than fresh ones. Then, on lap

64, they clashed at turn 3, with Verstappen moving across on Norris. In a flash, George Russell swept by and would race on to victory, while Verstappen limped back to the pits to have a flat tyre replaced and Norris, whose car also had a puncture, retired to the pits with car damage, complaining that the world champion's behaviour had been both reckless and a little desperate. Whether Verstappen and Norris could return to being friends became a matter for conversation.

Oscar Piastri drove a great race to at least give McLaren something to smile about, as he rose from seventh to second, closing to within two seconds of Russell by flagfall, with Carlos Sainz Jr completing the podium. His team-mate, Charles Leclerc pitted four times and ended up out of the points. This helped Nico Hulkenberg rise to sixth place, just ahead of Sergio Perez's damaged Red Bull, and Haas F1's great day was boosted further by Kevin Magnussen finishing eighth to increase their points advantage over Alpine, Williams and Sauber.

George Russell was running third until Verstappen and Norris clashed and he dived by to win.

RED BULL RING ROUND 11

DATE: **30 JUNE 2024**

Laps: **71** • Distance: **190.420 miles/306.452km** • Weather: **Warm & cloudy**

Pos	Driver	Team	Result	Stops	Grid	Sprint
1	**George Russell**	Mercedes	1h24m22.798s	2	3	4
2	**Oscar Piastri**	McLaren	1h24m24.24.704s	2	7	2
3	**Carlos Sainz Jr**	Ferrari	1h24m27.331s	2	4	5
4	**Lewis Hamilton**	Mercedes	1h24m45.940s	2	5	6
5	**Max Verstappen !!!**	Red Bull	1h25m00.051s	3	1	1
6	**Nico Hulkenberg**	Hass	1h25m16.886s	2	9	19
7	**Sergio Perez**	Red Bull	1h25m17.470s	2	8	8
8	**Kevin Magnussen**	Haas	1h25m23.153s	2	12	9
9	**Daniel Ricciardo**	RB	1h25m23.967s	2	11	14
10	**Pierre Gasly**	Alpine	1h25m24.564s	2	13	12
11	**Charles Leclerc**	Ferrari	1h25m29.854s	4	6	7
12	**Esteban Ocon**	Alpine	1h25m31.123s	2	10	11
13	**Lance Stroll**	Aston Martin	70 laps	2	17	10
14	**Yuki Tsunoda**	RB	70 laps	2	14	13
15	**Alex Albon !**	Williams	70 laps	2	16	17
16	**Valtteri Bottas**	Sauber	70 laps	2	18	18
17	**Zhou Guanyu ***	Sauber	70 laps	2	20	20
18	**Fernando Alonso**	Aston Martin	70 laps	3	15	15
19	**Logan Sargeant**	Williams	69 laps	3	19	16
R	**Lando Norris !!**	McLaren	64 laps/collision damage	3	2	3

FASTEST LAP: **ALONSO, 1M07.694S, 142.687MPH/229.633KPH ON LAP 70** • RACE LEADERS: **VERSTAPPEN 1-23 & 25-63, PIASTRI 24, RUSSELL 64-71** • * MADE TO START FROM PIT LANE AS CAR MODIFIED IN PARC FERME • ! 5S PENALTY FOR CROSSING PIT ENTRY LINE !! 5S PENALTY FOR EXCEEDING TRACK LIMITS • !!! 10S PENALTY FOR COLLIDING WITH NORRIS

BRITISH GP

Lewis Hamilton's sheer emotion when he won the British GP for the ninth time was clear evidence of what it meant to end his victory drought as Mercedes' strong form continued. McLaren had less reason to be pleased after getting its race strategy calls wrong.

For a driver with 103 Grand Prix wins to his name to consider that he might never win again, as Lewis Hamilton admitted after the race, this was a Grand Prix that made him sob with joy. And so it should, as 57 Grands Prix had passed since he had last won, in the 2021 Saudi Arabian GP.

It began with good form in qualifying, as he shared the front row with Mercedes team-mate George Russell, with Lando Norris making it three British drivers in the top three places and Max Verstappen only fourth.

At the start, Russell led away and Mercedes had the race under control. The first of two rain showers arrived on lap 17 and Hamilton chose his moment to pass Russell into Stowe for the lead. This was also the point at which the McLarens started to shine, with Oscar Piastri demoting Verstappen.

However, the track was soon slippery and both Mercedes slid off at the start of lap 19, allowing Norris to pass Russell then Hamilton too at the start of lap 20, soon followed by Piastri.

While McLaren and Mercedes braved it out on slicks, Verstappen changed to intermediate tyres. A lap later, Norris, Hamilton and Russell did the same, but Piastri was told to stay out for one more lap and it cost him ten seconds.

Russell retired and Verstappen and Hamilton pitted on lap 38, but McLaren dithered and cost Norris the lead. Worse was to follow, as Norris had been put on to soft tyres, whereas Verstappen's hards worked better and he grabbed second with four laps to go.

For Sergio Perez, a career-changing decision seemed to be just around the corner as the Mexican qualified only 19th after spinning and trailed home in 17th, with his underachievement relative to Verstappen now gargantuan.

SILVERSTONE ROUND 12

DATE: 7 JULY 2024

Laps: **52** • Distance: **190.262 miles/306.198km** • Weather: **Warm with rain**

Pos	Driver	Team	Result	Stops	Qualifying Time	Grid
1	Lewis Hamilton	Mercedes	1h22m27.059s	2	1m25.990s	2
2	Max Verstappen	Red Bull	1h22m28.524s	2	1m26.203s	4
3	Lando Norris	McLaren	1h22m34.606s	2	1m26.030s	3
4	Oscar Piastri	McLaren	1h22m39.488s	2	1m26.237s	5
5	Carlos Sainz Jr	Ferrari	1h23m14.377s	3	1m26.509s	7
6	Nico Hulkenberg	Haas	1h23m22.781s	2	1m26.338s	6
7	Lance Stroll	Aston Martin	1h23m23.628s	2	1m26.585s	8
8	Fernando Alonso	Aston Martin	1h23m30.636s	2	1m26.917s	10
9	Alex Albon	Williams	1h23m35.446s	2	1m26.640s	9
10	Yuki Tsunoda	RB	1h23m46.362s	2	1m27.269s	13
11	Logan Sargeant	Williams	1h23m56.019s	2	1m27.175s	12
12	Kevin Magnussen	Haas	1h23m57.212s	2	1m32.905s	17
13	Daniel Ricciardo	RB	51 laps	2	1m27.949s	15
14	Charles Leclerc	Ferrari	51 laps	3	1m27.097s	11
15	Valtteri Bottas	Sauber	51 laps	2	1m32.431s	16
16	Esteban Ocon	Alpine	50 laps	4	1m34.557s	18
17	Sergio Perez !	Red Bull	50 laps	4	1m39.804s!	19
18	Zhou Guanyu	Sauber	50 laps	4	1m27.867s	14
R	George Russell	Mercedes	33 laps/water system	1	1m25.819s	1
NS	Pierre Gasly !!	Alpine	0 laps/gearbox	0	1m39.804s	20

FASTEST LAP: **SAINZ, 1M28.293S, 149.250MPH/240.195KPH ON LAP 52** • RACE LEADERS: **RUSSELL 1-17, HAMILTON 18-19 & 40-52, NORRIS 20-27 & 29-39, PIASTRI 28** • **!** REQUIRED TO START FROM PIT LANE AS CAR MODIFIED IN PARC FERME • **!!** REQUIRED TO START FROM REAR OF GRID AS ADDITIONAL POWER UNIT ELEMENTS FITTED

The fans rise to applaud Lewis Hamilton as he heads for a record ninth British GP victory.

HUNGARIAN GP

It took a lengthy call from the pit wall to Lando Norris, but he eventually agreed to honour an agreement, rue his poor start and let team-mate Oscar Piastri through to take his maiden F1 victory. Behind them, Lewis Hamilton survived an attack from Max Verstappen to take third.

McLaren locked out the front row and, at this track on which overtaking is difficult, must have fancied their chances. Before the race, Lando Norris rued his several missed winning opportunities and said he was focused on not blowing any more.

Then came the start and he blundered, with team-mate Oscar Piastri getting away better to take the lead. Worse still for Norris, Max Verstappen got past too. However, it was adjudged that Verstappen had gained an advantage from running off the track at turn 1 and was asked to hand back the position.

Piastri was in control, though, and the 23-year-old Australian was still in front once the leading half-dozen drivers had made their first pit stop. Verstappen voiced his dissatisfaction at the timing of his stop, as Lewis Hamilton had moved ahead by being the first of the group to pit on a day when track temperatures were very high and tyre degradation a major factor.

McLaren's mid-season developments made their cars the pick of the bunch and they elected to bring Norris in first for their second planned pit stops, in order to help him stay ahead of Hamilton. He was thus in front after Piastri pitted two laps later.

Then the radio messages began to fly between Norris and his race engineer, asking him to let Piastri back ahead as he had been in control before the second round of stops. The language heated up but, eventually, with three laps to go, Norris moved aside.

The challenge from behind had by this stage dissipated as Hamilton had come under pressure from Verstappen, with the reigning world champion making a dive up his inside into turn 1, locking up and vaulting over the Mercedes driver's front right wheel. Both continued, but Verstappen lost a position to Charles Leclerc as he recovered.

HUNGARORING ROUND 13

DATE: **21 JULY 2024**

Laps: **70** · Distance: **190.531 miles/306.630km** · Weather: **Hot & sunny**

Pos	Driver	Team	Result	Stops	Qualifying Time	Grid
1	**Oscar Piastri**	McLaren	1h38m01.989s	2	1m15.249s	2
2	**Lando Norris**	McLaren	1h38m04.130s	2	1m15.227s	1
3	**Lewis Hamilton**	Mercedes	1h38m16.869s	2	1m15.854s	5
4	**Charles Leclerc**	Ferrari	1h38m21.675s	2	1m15.905s	6
5	**Max Verstappen**	Red Bull	1h38m23.338s	2	1m15.273s	3
6	**Carlos Sainz Jr**	Ferrari	1h38m25.062s	2	1m15.696s	4
7	**Sergio Perez**	Red Bull	1h38m14.781s	2	1m17.886s	16
8	**George Russell**	Mercedes	1h38m44.357s	2	1m17.968s	17
9	**Yuki Tsunoda**	RB	1h39m19.248s	1	1m16.477s	10
10	**Lance Stroll**	Aston Martin	1h39m19.965s	2	1m16.244s	8
11	**Fernando Alonso**	Aston Martin	1h39m24.449s	2	1m16.043s	7
12	**Daniel Ricciardo**	RB	69 laps	2	1m16.447s	9
13	**Nico Hulkenberg**	Haas	69 laps	2	1m16.317s	11
14	**Alex Albon**	Williams	69 laps	2	1m16.429s	13
15	**Kevin Magnussen**	Haas	69 laps	2	1m16.548s	15
16	**Valtteri Bottas**	Sauber	69 laps	2	1m16.384s	12
17	**Logan Sargeant**	Williams	69 laps	3	1m16.543s	14
18	**Esteban Ocon**	Alpine	69 laps	3	1m18.049s	19
19	**Zhou Guanyu**	Sauber	69 laps	2	1m18.037s	18
R	**Pierre Gasly ***	Alpine	33 laps/hydraulics	2	1m18.166s	20

FASTEST LAP: RUSSELL, 1M20.305S, 122.035MPH/196.396KPH ON LAP 55 · RACE LEADERS: PIASTRI 1-18, 24-27 & 68-70, VERSTAPPEN 19-21 & 48-49, LECLERC 22-23, NORRIS 50-67 · * REQUIRED TO START FROM PIT LANE FOR USInG ADDITIONAL POWER UNIT ELEMENTS & CAR BEING WORKED ON IN PARC FERME

McLaren celebrate after Lando Norris agreed to hand the lead back to Oscar Piastri for his first win.

BELGIAN GP

This was the best race of 2024 so far, with the eight top cars going at it all race and victory going to George Russell, who made a one-stop strategy work. However, his car was found to be underweight and the 25 points went to team-mate Lewis Hamilton instead.

With Max Verstappen having to start 11th due to a ten-place grid penalty, it was a chance for his rivals to try and take a bite out of his championship lead.

Charles Leclerc, promoted to pole, put his Ferrari into the lead, with Lewis Hamilton getting past Sergio Perez and Lando Norris running wide at the first corner and falling behind team-mate Oscar Piastri, George Russell and Carlos Sainz. Verstappen gained a few places as he began his charge.

On lap 3, Hamilton motored past Leclerc. Seven laps later, Russell was the first of the front runners to pit, followed a lap later by Hamilton, with this strategy getting Hamilton into the lead once Sainz finally came in. Amazingly, Russell decided that tyre degradation wasn't bad and so started considering a one-stop strategy.

Piastri botched his second pit stop by overshooting his marks and, but for that, might have got ahead of Hamilton and been able to challenge Russell. The Australian was again impressive, going around the outside of Leclerc at Les Combes. Then it was the turn of Norris and Verstappen to try to pass the Ferrari driver, but they couldn't.

When Sainz passed Perez in the closing laps, there was much discussion that Red Bull would drop him for the second half of the season.

In the closing laps, Hamilton and Piastri moved on to Russell's tail, but he hung on and was ecstatic as he took the chequered flag. Two hours later, he was in despair, as his F1 W15 was found to be 3.3lb (1.5kg) underweight.

Unusually, because of Spa's longer than usual lap distance, there is no cool down lap, and this might have been what caught out Mercedes, as drivers usually use the lap to drive over discarded rubber to add weight to their cars before the post-race weigh-in.

George Russell thought he had won, but victory went to Mercedes team-mate Hamilton instead.

105

SPA-FRANCORCHAMPS ROUND 14 DATE: 28 JULY 2024
Laps: 44 • Distance: 191.414 miles/308.052km • Weather: Hot & bright

Pos	Driver	Team	Result	Stops	Qualifying Time	Grid
1	Lewis Hamilton	Mercedes	1h19m57.566s	2	1m53.835s	3
2	Oscar Piastri	McLaren	1h19m58.213s	2	1m54.027s	5
3	Charles Leclerc	Ferrari	1h20m05.589s	2	1m53.754s	1
4	Max Verstappen *	Red Bull	1h20m06.266s	2	1m53.159s	11
5	Lando Norris	McLaren	1h20m06.890s	2	1m53.981s	4
6	Carlos Sainz Jr	Ferrari	1h20m16.835s	2	1m54.477s	7
7	Sergio Perez	Red Bull	1h20m40.235s	3	1m53.765s	2
8	Fernando Alonso	Aston Martin	1h20m47.003s	1	1m54.765s	8
9	Esteban Ocon	Alpine	1h20m49.592s	2	1m54.810s	9
10	Daniel Ricciardo	RB	1h20m51.966s	2	1m54.682s	13
11	Lance Stroll	Aston Martin	1h21m00.051s	1	1m55.716s	15
12	Alex Albon	Williams	1h21m00.691s	2	1m54.473s	10
13	Pierre Gasly	Alpine	1h21m01.405s	2	1m54.635s	12
14	Kevin Magnussen	Haas	1h21m03.671s	1	1m56.500s	17
15	Valtteri Bottas	Sauber	1h21m07.678s	2	1m54.764s	14
16	Yuki Tsunoda !!	RB	1h21m13.777s	1	1m56.593s	20
17	Logan Sargeant	Williams	1h21m23.097s	2	1m57.230s	18
18	Nico Hulkenberg	Haas	1h21m25.873s	2	1m56.308s	16
R	Zhou Guanyu !	Sauber	5 laps/electrical	1	1m57.775s	19
DQ	George Russell	Mercedes	1h19m57.040s/underweight1		1m54.184s	6

FASTEST LAP: PEREZ, 1M44.701S, 149.640MPH/240.822KPH ON LAP 44 • RACE LEADERS: LECLERC 1-2 & 11-12, HAMILTON 3-10 & 20-26, SAINZ 13-19, PIASTRI 27-30, RUSSELL 31-44 • * 10-PLACE GRID PENALTY FOR USING AN ADDITIONAL POWER UNIT ELEMENT ! 3-PLACE GRID PENALTY FOR IMPEDING VERSTAPPEN IN QUALIFYING • !! REQUIRED TO START FROM BACK OF GRID FOR USING ADDITIONAL POWER UNIT ELEMENTS

DUTCH GP

Max Verstappen has made a habit of winning his home Grand Prix. This time, though, not only was he beaten but he was thrashed, as Lando Norris recovered from being passed to rocket off into the distance to send the army of orange fans home disappointed.

The McLaren MCL38 was clearly more competitive than before, after its first upgrade since the Miami GP. Norris put his on pole by more than a third of a second over Verstappen, with Oscar Piastri third on the grid just ahead of George Russell's Mercedes.

Yet Norris made it hard for himself again when he got wheelspin at the start and was passed before the first corner by Verstappen. Such was Norris' performance advantage though, that he didn't have to try to use clever tactics to get back into the lead – not needing to wait until the one planned pit stop to move ahead. His passing move came on lap 18 when he dived down the inside of the Red Bull into the first corner, Tarzan, with Verstappen, who was already struggling on tyres that had become 'numb', not offering much resistance. Norris was in control from then on. Indeed, he was able to stretch clear not just by a few seconds but by enough to finish with an almost 23 seconds' advantage.

Piastri hampered his chances by falling behind Russell at the start and so couldn't make the most of his upgraded car's performance. It was then decided that he should run a long first stint to put him in a position to pick off rivals later in the race, but this didn't work.

Charles Leclerc was surprised to finish third ahead of Piastri after Ferrari race strategy brought him out ahead of the Australian, with set-up tweaks for the race finally giving him some performance. Red Bull advisor Helmut Marko described the McLarens' pace as 'alarming' and there was a feeling that the performance advantage had swung away from Red Bull to the extent that even Verstappen's progress towards a fourth drivers' title might be in doubt.

Lando Norris lost out to Verstappen at the start but got back in front to score a dominant victory.

ZANDVOORT ROUND 15

DATE: **25 AUGUST 2024**

Laps: **72** · Distance: **190.504 miles/306.587km** · Weather: **Warm & bright**

Pos	Driver	Team	Result	Stops	Qualifying Time	Grid
1	**Lando Norris**	McLaren	1h30m45.519s	1	1m09.673s	1
2	**Max Verstappen**	Red Bull	1h31m08.415s	1	1m10.029s	2
3	**Charles Leclerc**	Ferrari	1h31m10.958s	1	1m10.582s	6
4	**Oscar Piastri**	McLaren	1h31m12.856s	1	1m10.172s	3
5	**Carlos Sainz Jr**	Ferrari	1h31m17.656s	1	1m10.914s	10
6	**Sergio Perez**	Red Bull	1h31m25.061s	1	1m10.416s	5
7	**George Russell**	Mercedes	1h31m30.136s	2	1m10.244s	4
8	**Lewis Hamilton** !	Mercedes	1h31m35.118s	2	1m10.948s	14
9	**Pierre Gasly**	Alpine	71 laps	1	1m10.977s	9
10	**Fernando Alonso**	Aston Martin	71 laps	1	1m10.633s	7
11	**Nico Hulkenberg**	Haas	71 laps	1	1m11.215s	12
12	**Daniel Ricciardo**	RB	71 laps	1	1m11.943s	13
13	**Lance Stroll** *	Aston Martin	71 laps	1	1m10.857s	8
14	**Alex Albon** !!	Williams	71 laps	2	no time	19
15	**Esteban Ocon**	Alpine	71 laps	1	1m11.995s	15
16	**Logan Sargeant**	Williams	71 laps	1	no time	18
17	**Yuki Tsunoda**	RB	71 laps	2	1m10.955s	11
18	**Kevin Magnussen** !!!	Haas	71 laps	1	1m11.295s	20
19	**Valtteri Bottas**	Sauber	70 laps	2	1m21.168s	16
20	**Zhou Guanyu**	Sauber	70 laps	2	1m13.261s	17

FASTEST LAP: NORRIS, 1M13.817S, 129.084MPH/207.708KPH ON LAP 72 · RACE LEADERS: VERSTAPPEN 1-17, PIASTRI 29-32, NORRIS 18-28 & 33-72 · ! 3-PLACE GRID PENALTY FOR IMPEDING PEREZ IN QUALIFYING · !! DISQUALIFIED FROM QUALIFYING FOR FLOOR BODY BEING TOO LARGE · !!! CAR HAD TO START FROM PIT LANE AS CAR MODIFIED IN PARC FERME & ADDITIONAL POWER UNIT ELEMENTS USED * 5S PENALTY FOR SPEEDING IN PIT LANE

ITALIAN GP

This was a result that sent the *tifosi* wild with delight. The McLarens were fastest here but Ferrari out-thought them and Charles Leclerc did the rest to make a one-stop run work, holding off Piastri and Norris for a famous win.

While McLaren's ascendancy continued and they locked out the front row of the grid, so Red Bull Racing's decline became ever more apparent. Max Verstappen now joined Sergio Perez in claiming that the once all-conquering RB20 had become undriveable as he was able to qualify only seventh, fully 0.876 seconds off pole.

Oscar Piastri challenged pole-starting Lando Norris on the run down to the first chicane, but then moved left to block an ambitious George Russell, who bent his front wing in the process. But Norris got loose on the exit of the chicane, and this allowed Piastri to get a better run up to the second chicane where he simply forced his way around the outside into the lead. Worse still for Norris, he was offline out of there too and Charles Leclerc motored past into second. This added to the English driver's woeful record of having started on pole for the sixth time and yet not led at the end of the opening lap in any of them. It also meant that this golden opportunity to eat into Verstappen's points lead had been made a whole lot harder.

The key element that prevented Piastri from pulling clear and going on to win was tyre wear. The Ferraris appeared to be lighter on their tyres and Leclerc was confident enough to go for a one-stop strategy, which was enough for him to assume the lead when Piastri came in for his second set of new tyres. Then, although the McLarens were closing in on him rapidly at the end of the race, the Monegasque driver hung on to trigger massed exultation in the grandstands.

Franco Colapinto drove an impressive race to come home 12th on his debut on a day when team-mate Alex Albon grabbed valuable points for Williams.

MONZA ROUND 16

DATE: **1 SEPTEMBER 2024**

Laps: **53** · Distance: **190.587 miles/306.720km** · Weather: **Warm**

Pos	Driver	Team	Result	Stops	Qualifying Time	Grid
1	Charles Leclerc	Ferrari	1h14m40.727s	1	1m19.461s	4
2	Oscar Piastri	McLaren	1h14m43.391s	2	1m19.436s	2
3	Lando Norris	McLaren	1h14m46.880s	2	1m19.327s	1
4	Carlos Sainz Jr	Ferrari	1h14m56.348s	1	1m19.467s	5
5	Lewis Hamilton	Mercedes	1h15m03.547s	2	1m19.513s	6
6	Max Verstappen	Red Bull	1h15m18.659s	2	1m20.022s	7
7	George Russell	Mercedes	1h15m20.442s	2	1m19.440s	3
8	Sergio Perez	Red Bull	1h15m34.875	2	1m20.062s	8
9	Alex Albon	Williams	1h15m48.183s	1	1m20.299s	9
10	Kevin Magnussen *	Haas	1h15m49.029s	1	1m20.698s	13
11	Fernando Alonso	Aston Martin	1h15m49.222s	2	1m20.421s	11
12	Franco Colapinto	Williams	1h16m02.035s	1	1m21.061s	18
13	Daniel Ricciardo **	RB	1h16m14.179s	1	1m20.479s	12
14	Esteban Ocon	Alpine	52 laps	1	1m20.766s	15
15	Pierre Gasly	Alpine	52 laps	2	1m20.738s	14
16	Valtteri Bottas	Sauber	52 laps	1	1m21.101s	19
17	Nico Hulkenberg	Haas	52 laps	2	1m20.339s	10
18	Zhou Guanyu	Sauber	52 laps	1	1m21.445s	20
19	Lance Stroll	Aston Martin	52 laps	3	1m21.013s	17
R	Yuki Tsunoda	RB	7 laps/crash damage	1	1m20.945s	16

FASTEST LAP: NORRIS, 1M21.432S, 159.133MPH/256.100KPH ON LAP 53 · RACE LEADERS: PIASTRI 1-16 & 23-38, SAINZ 17-18, VERSTAPPEN 19-21, PEREZ 22, LECLERC 39-53 · * 10S PENALTY FOR CAUSING A COLLISION · ** 5S PENALTY FOR FORCING ANOTHER DRIVER OFF TRACK + 10S PENALTY FOR FAILING TO SERVE TIME PENALTY CORRECTLY

Charles Leclerc saved his tyres and held off a late attack from Oscar Piastri to send the *tifosi* wild.

Oscar Piastri revelled in the glory of his second win, as it came not only without team orders but after he displayed his skill in resisting all that Charles Leclerc could throw at him. Lando Norris bounced back from a qualifying disaster to still outscore Max Verstappen.

This was an event peppered with incident all weekend. Firstly, title challenger Lando Norris failed to get his final lap in at the end of the first qualifying session as there were waved yellow flags to warn of Esteban Ocon's slow-moving Alpine, leaving him only 17th fastest. Essential work on Lewis Hamilton's Mercedes meant that he had to start from the pit lane. Max Verstappen's increasing concerns over Red Bull Racing's declining level of competitiveness meant that he could qualify only sixth – even two places behind a driver he almost invariably outpaces, his team-mate Sergio Perez.

Charles Leclerc arrived fresh from victory in Monza and grabbed pole position. He then led away, but Piastri was able to hit the front after making his one planned pit stop, helped by Norris delaying Perez enough to be sure that Piastri would have a chance of being in front once all the front runners had pitted. He still had to pass Leclerc and did so on lap 20.

Late in the race, Leclerc's tyre performance fell way and Piastri was left in the clear while the Monegasque driver fell back towards the battle over third place between Perez and Carlos Sainz. The Spaniard grabbed third but when the Mexican tried to get the place back with two laps to go, they clashed and were both out of the race.

This promoted George Russell to third. Next to the chequered flag was Norris, who had passed Verstappen with three laps remaining, pleased that he had at least scored more points than the Dutchman, but regretting that he had had to start so far down the grid.

A notable performance came from Williams, taking seventh and eighth places, while Ollie Bearman shone on a one-off outing for Haas, coming home ahead of team-mate Nico Hulkenberg in tenth.

Oscar Piastri's second win was achieved without team interference and tasted all the sweeter.

BAKU ROUND 17

DATE: **15 SEPTEMBER 2024**

Laps: **51** • Distance: **190.170 miles/306.049km** • Weather: **Hot & sunny**

Pos	Driver	Team	Result	Stops	Qualifying Time	Grid
1	**Oscar Piastri**	McLaren	1h32m58.007s	1	1m41.686s	2
2	**Charles Leclerc**	Ferrari	1h33m08.917s	1	1m41.365s	1
3	**George Russell**	Mercedes	1h33m29.335s	1	1m41.874s	5
4	**Lando Norris**	McLaren	1h33m34.150s	1	1m43.609s	15
5	**Max Verstappen**	Red Bull	1h34m15.105s	2	1m42.023s	6
6	**Fernando Alonso**	Aston Martin	1h34m23.475s	1	1m42.369s	7
7	**Alex Albon**	Williams	1h34m25.403s	1	1m42.859s	9
8	**Franco Colapinto**	Williams	1h34m27.548s	1	1m42.530s	8
9	**Lewis Hamilton !!**	Mercedes	1h34m30.408s	1	1m42.289s	19
10	**Ollie Bearman**	Haas	1h34m31.134s	1	1m42.968s	10
11	**Nico Hulkenberg**	Haas	1h34m31.472s	1	1m43.191s	12
12	**Pierre Gasly ***	Alpine	1h34m55.196s	1	no time	18
13	**Daniel Ricciardo**	RB	1h35m24.914s	1	1m43.547s	14
14	**Zhou Guanyu !**	Sauber	1h35m26.848s	1	1m44.246s	17
15	**Esteban Ocon !!**	Alpine	50 laps	1	1m44.504s	20
16	**Valtteri Bottas**	Sauber	50 laps	1	1m43.618s	16
R	**Sergio Perez**	Red Bull	49 laps/accident	0	1m41.813s	4
R	**Carlos Sainz Jr**	Ferrari	49 laps/accident	0	1m41.805s	3
R	**Lance Stroll**	Aston Martin	45 laps/brakes	2	1m43.404s	13
R	**Yuki Tsunoda**	RB	14 laps/crash damage	1	1m43.035s	11

FASTEST LAP: NORRIS, 1M45.255S, 127.578MPH/205.318KPH ON LAP 42 • RACE LEADERS: LECLERC 1-16 & 18-19, SAINZ 17, PIASTRI 20-51
! REQUIRED TO START FROM BACK OF GRID AS EXTRA POWER UNIT ELEMENTS USED • !! REQUIRED TO START FROM PIT LANE AS CAR MODIFIED IN PARC FERME • * DISQUALIFIED FROM QUALIFYING FOR EXCEEDING FUEL MASS FLOW LIMIT

SINGAPORE GP

This was a great race for Lando Norris, not just because he won but because he won by fully 21 seconds. However, his joy was kept in check by the identity of the driver in second, Max Verstappen, but the win brought the title race gap down to 52 points.

Pole position is always extra important when the World Championship visits street circuits, so there was extra pressure on Lando Norris not to blow this one, as he had four others up to this point of the season.

Fortunately for McLaren fans, he did not, keeping Max Verstappen behind him on the short blast to the left/right/left sequence of the first three corners. In fact, his form was so superior that he simply edged ever further clear from there and was never to be caught. His only issues were the two occasions when he locked up and clipped the barriers, but his concerns about front wing damage didn't appear to slow him.

What stood out on the opening lap was the flying start made by Franco Colapinto in the second Williams, with the Argentinian rising from 12th position on the grid to ninth, while team-mate Alex Albon dropped four places to 15th.

Third in the constructors' championship, Ferrari had an awful time in qualifying, with neither driver setting a time in the third qualifying session as Carlos Sainz crashed and then Charles Leclerc had his only lap scrubbed for exceeding track limits, leaving them to start ninth and tenth on the grid.

Oscar Piastri's pit stop was delayed until later in the race than his rivals and he then made the most of fresher rubber to catch, attack and pass both Mercedes to secure the final podium position. Leclerc also made a move late on and got past Hamilton to finish fifth.

Daniel Ricciardo, suspecting that this might be his final Grand Prix, was called in by Red Bull's junior team to fit new rubber and go for fastest lap. This he achieved and so denied Norris the bonus point, a point that many thought might prove critical at season's end.

MARINA BAY ROUND 18 — DATE: 22 SEPTEMBER 2024

Laps: **62** · Distance: **190.228 miles/306.143km** · Weather: **Very hot & humid**

Pos	Driver	Team	Result	Stops	Qualifying Time	Grid
1	**Lando Norris**	McLaren	1h40m52.571s	1	1m29.525s	1
2	**Max Verstappen**	Red Bull	1h41m13.516s	1	1m29.728s	2
3	**Oscar Piastri**	McLaren	1h41m34.394s	1	1m29.953s	5
4	**George Russell**	Mercedes	1h41m53.611s	1	1m29.867s	4
5	**Charles Leclerc**	Ferrari	1h41m55.001s	1	no time	9
6	**Lewis Hamilton**	Mercedes	1h42m17.819s	1	1m29.841s	3
7	**Carlos Sainz Jr**	Ferrari	1h42m28.610s	1	no time	10
8	**Fernando Alonso**	Aston Martin	61 laps	1	1m30.214s	7
9	**Nico Hulkenberg**	Haas	61 laps	1	1m30.115s	6
10	**Sergio Perez**	Red Bull	61 laps	1	1m30.579s	13
11	**Franco Colapinto**	Williams	61 laps	1	1m30.481s	12
12	**Yuki Tsunoda**	RB	61 laps	1	1m30.354s	8
13	**Esteban Ocon**	Alpine	61 laps	1	1m30.769s	15
14	**Lance Stroll**	Aston Martin	61 laps	1	1m31.094s	17
15	**Zhou Guanyu**	Sauber	61 laps	1	1m32.054s	20
16	**Valtteri Bottas**	Sauber	61 laps	1	1m31.572s	19
17	**Pierre Gasly**	Alpine	61 laps	1	1m31.312s	18
18	**Daniel Ricciardo**	RB	61 laps	3	1m31.085s	16
R	**Kevin Magnussen**	Haas	57 laps/withdrew	2	1m30.653s	14
R	**Alex Albon**	Williams	15 laps/overheating	1	1m30.474s	11

FASTEST LAP: **RICCIARDO, 1M34.486S, 116.953MPH/188.218KPH ON LAP 60** · RACE LEADERS: **NORRIS 1-62**

Lando Norris leads from Verstappen and Hamilton and would go on to score valuable points.

Ferrari looked strong all meeting and came away with a one-two finish, led home by Charles Leclerc. Hit with a five-second penalty for leaving the track late in the race while passing Max Verstappen, who ran wide too, Lando Norris was furious to lose ground in their title scrap.

The season's endgame was clear: Lando Norris had to outscore Max Verstappen by nine points at each of the final six Grands Prix. Any event at which this didn't happen would make the mountain he had to scale to overhaul the Dutchman all the steeper. And, here in Texas, he stumbled.

Firstly, Lando shed a couple of points to his rival by finishing third in the sprint race won by Max. More damaging, though, was the fact that Lando also ended the Grand Prix behind Max, despite starting from pole.

The first corner set the tone, as Max dived up the inside of Lando, both went wide, and Charles Leclerc's Ferrari nipped through the gap. Lando suggested that the stewards should make Max give the place back, but they didn't.

Alex Albon's race was wrecked when he was hit by Valtteri Bottas at the first corner. Then, a lap later, Lewis Hamilton did something he almost never does and crashed out of the race.

After Carlos Sainz Jr pitted before Max and emerged in second place, the title protagonists' scrap intensified when Lando closed in on Verstappen and went for a passing move into turn 12 on lap 52. He was on the outside line and Max was having none of it, with both going wide and Lando making his passing move when both were off the track. Opinions were divided, but the stewards hit Lando with a five-second penalty. Perhaps it would have been wiser to have given the place back and tried again over the remaining four laps, but McLaren elected to press on and Lando fell 0.9 seconds short of negating it.

Fortunately for Lando, finishing behind Max meant a three-point deficit rather than the seven-point difference he would have suffered had they finished in first and second ahead of the Ferraris.

CIRCUIT OF THE AMERICAS ROUND 19 DATE: 20 OCTOBER 2024

Laps: 56 • Distance: **191.634 miles/308.405km** • Weather: **Warm & bright**

Pos	Driver	Team	Result	Stops	Grid	Sprint
1	Charles Leclerc	Ferrari	1h35m09.639s	1	4	4
2	Carlos Sainz Jr	Ferrari	1h35m18.201s	1	3	2
3	Max Verstappen	Red Bull	1h35m29.051s	1	2	1
4	Lando Norris *	McLaren	1h35m29.993s	1	1	3
5	Oscar Piastri	McLaren	1h35m31.560s	1	5	10
6	George Russell !	Mercedes	1h36m05.934s	1	20	5
7	Sergio Perez	Red Bull	1h36m08.711s	1	9	9
8	Nico Hulkenberg	Haas	1h36m12.596s	1	11	8
9	Liam Lawson !!	RB	1h36m20.202s	1	19	16
10	Franco Colapinto	Williams	1h36m21.618s	1	15	12
11	Kevin Magnussen	Haas	1h36m29.421s	2	8	7
12	Pierre Gasly *	Alpine	1h36m40.197s	1	6	14
13	Fernando Alonso	Aston Martin	55 laps	1	7	18
14	Yuki Tsunoda **	RB	55 laps	1	10	11
15	Lance Stroll	Aston Martin	55 laps	1	13	13
16	Alex Albon	Williams	55 laps	2	14	17
17	Valtteri Bottas	Sauber	55 laps	1	16	20
18	Esteban Ocon	Alpine	55 laps	2	12	15
19	Zhou Guanyu !!!	Sauber	55 laps	2	18	19
R	Lewis Hamilton	Mercedes	1 lap/accident	0	17	6

FASTEST LAP: OCON, 1M37.330S, 126.705MPH/203.912KPH ON LAP 53 • RACE LEADERS: LECLERC 1-26 & 32-56, NORRIS 27-31 • * 5S PENALTY FOR LEAVING THE TRACK & GAINING AN ADVANTAGE • ** 5S PENALTY FOR FORCING ALBON OFF THE TRACK • ! REQUIRED TO START FROM PIT LANE AS CAR MODIFIED IN PARC FERME • !! REQUIRED TO START FROM BACK OF GRID AS ADDITIONAL POWER UNIT ELEMENTS USED !!! 5-PLACE GRID PENALTY AS ADDITIONAL POWER UNIT ELEMENT USED

This one-two finish for Charles Leclerc and Carlos Sainz Jr was a huge boost to Ferrari's season.

MEXICO CITY GP

In Mexico City Max Verstappen was penalized not once but twice for being overly assertive, dropping him to an eventual sixth. Meanwhile title rival Lando Norris remained between the white lines to climb to second place behind Carlos Sainz Jr, who was supreme for Ferrari.

Max Verstappen wasn't hanging around at the start and he pressured pole-starter Carlos Sainz Jr to brake too late for the first corner complex, with the Spaniard leaving the track and rejoining in front but dutifully handing the place back.

For Alex Albon, it was the second time in three races that he was forced to retire, this time because his Williams was hit on the run to the first corner by Yuki Tsunoda's RB, triggering a safety car period.

However, it was soon clear that Verstappen didn't have the pace of the Ferraris or of Lando Norris' McLaren, with Sainz moving into the lead at turn 1 a lap after the safety car withdrew. Then Norris began to pressure his title rival and Verstappen forced the McLaren driver off the track twice, notably at the start of the esses. Two ten-second penalties served at his pit stop dropped him way down the order.

Norris' quest was then to score as many points as he could, catching and passing Charles Leclerc's Ferrari to move into second place with nine laps to go.

With both drivers on the podium, Ferrari moved ahead of Red Bull Racing into second in the constructors' championship, something facilitated by Sergio Perez's awful form. He had hoped to bounce back in front of his home crowd, but did the reverse, qualifying poorly yet again, being penalised for lining up ahead of his grid box and trailing home last of the 17 finishers.

Mercedes finished fourth and fifth, with George Russell dropping behind Lewis Hamilton as he had a damaged front wing, but was still far enough ahead to finish ahead of Verstappen.

Haas was a happy camp, as Kevin Magnussen had his best run in a long while to finish seventh and Nico Hulkenberg ninth, with Oscar Piastri advancing to eighth after starting 17th.

Once Carlos Sainz Jr assumed the lead for Ferrari, he stayed there for his second win of 2024.

MEXICO CITY ROUND 20

DATE: **27 OCTOBER 2024**

Laps: **71** • Distance: **189.738 miles/305.354km** • Weather: **Warm & sunny**

Pos	Driver	Team	Result	Stops	Qualifying Time	Grid
1	Carlos Sainz Jr	Ferrari	1hm40m55.800s	1	1m15.946s	1
2	Lando Norris	McLaren	1h41m00.505s	1	1m16.260s	3
3	Charles Leclerc	Ferrari	1h41m30.187s	2	1m16.265s	4
4	Lewis Hamilton	Mercedes	1h41m40.580s	1	1m16.651s	6
5	George Russell	Mercedes	1h41m44.336s	1	1m16.356s	5
6	Max Verstappen	Red Bull	1h41m55.358s	1	1m16.171s	2
7	Kevin Magnussen	Haas	1h41m59.442s	1	1m16.886s	7
8	Oscar Piastri	McLaren	1h42m00.728s	1	1m17.597s	17
9	Nico Hulkenberg	Haas	70 laps	1	1m17.365s	10
10	Pierre Gasly	Alpine	70 laps	1	1m16.892s	8
11	Lance Stroll	Aston Martin	70 laps	1	1m17.294s	14
12	Franco Colapinto !	Williams	70 laps	1	1m17.558s	16
13	Esteban Ocon *	Alpine	70 laps	1	1m17.617s	20
14	Valtteri Bottas	Sauber	70 laps	1	1m17.817s	15
15	Zhou Guanyu	Sauber	70 laps	1	1m18.072s	19
16	Liam Lawson	RB	70 laps	2	1m17.162s	12
17	Sergio Perez	Red Bull	70 laps	3	1m17.611s	18
R	Fernando Alonso	Aston Martin	15 laps/brakes	1	1m17.168s	13
R	Alex Albon	Williams	0 laps/accident	0	1m17.065s	9
R	Yuki Tsunoda	RB	0 laps/accident	0	1m17.129s	11

FASTEST LAP: LECLERC, 1M18.336S, 122.903MPH/197.794KPH ON LAP 71 • RACE LEADERS: VERSTAPPEN 1-8, SAINZ JR 9-71
* REQUIRED TO START FROM PIT LANE AS CAR MODIFIED IN PARC FERME & ADDITIONAL POWER UNIT ELEMENTS USED • ! 10S PENALTY FOR CAUSING A COLLISION

Max Verstappen mastered soaking
conditions to dominate the Sao Paulo GP.

This was an astonishing turnaround. Lando Norris started from pole and Max Verstappen from 17th, yet it was the Dutch ace who won and the McLaren driver who ended up sixth in a race that pivoted around the rule that allows teams to change tyres after a red flag.

For Norris, this race was all about cutting Verstappen's points lead. Winning the sprint gained him a few. He was also starting from pole, while Verstappen – who had qualified 12th after a red flag stopped his run – was moved back five places as his car had been fitted with a new power unit. This meant that the stage, albeit a wet stage, was set.

Aston Martin's form continued to be average at best and got worse before the start when Lance Stroll spun going into the first corner on the formation lap and then beached his car, causing an aborted start.

When the lights went green, George Russell sprinted past Norris to take the lead, while Verstappen advanced six places on lap 1 and kept advancing.

The rain became heavier and Nico Hulkenberg spun his Haas and triggered a virtual safety car period, with Russell, against his will, and Norris called in for a pit stop. Vitally, Verstappen and both the Alpine drivers stayed out, moving into the top three positions, their teams reckoning that ever heavier rain would bring out the red flag. And it did come out a few laps later when Franco Colapinto crashed. This meant that Verstappen, Esteban Ocon and Pierre Gasly would be able to have new tyres fitted and yet keep their position at the front of the field.

A second safety car period followed after Carlos Sainz crashed at Laranja and Verstappen took the lead from Ocon on the restart, then drove away to finish nearly 20 seconds clear in appalling conditions in a fabulous display of wet weather driving.

The Alpine drivers deserved almost as much praise as Verstappen and the 33 points they collected lifted their beleaguered team from ninth to sixth in the constructors' table, thus earning it a great deal more end-of-season prize money.

Alpine's season was saved by second and third places for its overjoyed drivers at Interlagos.

INTERLAGOS ROUND 21

DATE: 3 NOVEMBER 2024

Laps: **69** • Distance: **184.709 miles/297.261km** • Weather: **Warm & very wet**

Pos	Driver	Team	Result	Stops	Grid	Sprint
1	Max Verstappen *	Red Bull	2h06m54.430s	1	17	4
2	Esteban Ocon	Alpine	2h07m13.907s	1	4	13
3	Pierre Gasly	Alpine	2h07m16.962s	1	13	7
4	George Russell	Mercedes	2h07m17.695s	2	2	6
5	Charles Leclerc	Ferrari	2h07m24.607s	2	6	3
6	Lando Norris	McLaren	2h07m25.802s	2	1	1
7	Yuki Tsunoda	RB	2h07m36.486s	2	3	15
8	Oscar Piastri !	McLaren	2h07m39.373s	2	8	2
9	Liam Lawson	RB	2h07m44.882s	2	5	9
10	Lewis Hamilton	Mercedes	2h07m45.183s	2	14	11
11	Sergio Perez	Red Bull	2h07m45.961s	2	12	8
12	Ollie Bearman	Haas	2h07m51.515s	2	15	14
13	Valtteri Bottas	Sauber	2h07m58.018s	1	11	16
14	Fernando Alonso	Aston Martin	2h08m12.479s	2	9	18
15	Zhou Guanyu	Sauber	2h08m14.079s	4	19	17
R	Carlos Sainz Jr !!	Ferrari	38 laps/accident	2	20	5
R	Franco Colapinto	Williams	30 laps/accident	2	16	12
DQ	Nico Hulkenberg	Haas	30 laps/outside assistance	3	18	R
NS	Alex Albon	Williams	Accident	-	7	10
NS	Lance Stroll	Aston Martin	Spun off	-	10	19

FASTEST LAP: VERSTAPPEN, 1M20.472S, 119.780MPH/192.767KPH ON LAP 67 • RACE LEADERS: RUSSELL 1-28, OCON 29-42, VERSTAPPEN 43-69 • * 5-PLACE GRID PENALTY FOR USING ADDITIONAL POWER UNIT ELEMENTS • ! 10S PENALTY FOR CAUSING A COLLISION WITH LAWSON • !! REQUIRED TO START FROM PIT LANE FOR USING ADDITIONAL POWER UNIT ELEMENTS & RESTRICTED NUMBER COMPONENT

LAS VEGAS GP

Cooler temperatures and a low-grip track clearly suited Mercedes as George Russell won from pole and Lewis Hamilton was the driver of the race as he rose from tenth to second. However, the one celebrating the most was Max Verstappen, as he landed his fourth F1 title.

In this year of fluctuating form among the top four teams, the balance shifted again as Mercedes returned to the front. George Russell did everything asked of him to qualify on pole and control the race from there, resisting an early challenge from Ferrari's Charles Leclerc and, in the closing stages, from his own team-mate who was left to rue his poor qualifying position as he passed car after car. Then, just when he was taking chunks out of Russell's lead, a minor error cost him time and meant that second was as high as he could climb.

Pierre Gasly had high hopes when he qualified his improving Alpine third but it wasn't to finish the race, pulling out early on.

Ferrari was the other team with cars in the hunt, but it made a mistake and left Sainz out for a lap too long before his second pit stop, losing him a place to Lewis Hamilton. Team-mate Leclerc had to settle for fourth.

Finishing in fifth place would usually make Max Verstappen furious, but he knew that all he had to do to be champion again was to finish ahead of McLaren's Lando Norris, which he did, so he forgot about the fact his Red Bull had struggled for form at this Nevada street circuit. Sergio Perez had to fight even to climb to tenth to take the final point.

McLaren was also at sea in Las Vegas and just couldn't get Norris ahead of his title rival. However, realizing that this wasn't going to happen, Norris pitted close to the end to have new tyres put on so that he could go for the extra point for fastest lap. However, it was a mere gesture as it came too late to stop Verstappen becoming champion again.

LAS VEGAS ROUND 22

DATE: 23 NOVEMBER 2024

Laps: **50** · Distance: **192.599 miles/309.958km** · Weather: **Mild & dry**

Pos	Driver	Team	Result	Stops	Qualifying Time	Grid
1	George Russell	Mercedes	1h22m05.969s	2	1m32.312s	1
2	Lewis Hamilton	Mercedes	1h22m13.282s	2	1m48.106s	10
3	Carlos Sainz Jr	Ferrari	1h22m17.875s	2	1m32.410s	2
4	Charles Leclerc	Ferrari	1h22m20.252s	2	1m32.783s	4
5	Max Verstappen	Red Bull	1h22m22.551s	2	1m32.797s	5
6	Lando Norris	McLaren	1h22m49.354s	2	1m33.008s	6
7	Oscar Piastri	McLaren	1h22m57.334s	2	1m33.033s	8
8	Nico Hulkenberg	Haas	1h23m05.777s	2	1m33.062s	9
9	Yuki Tsunoda	RB	1h23m08.777s	2	1m33.029s	7
10	Sergio Perez	Red Bull	1h23m09.083s	2	1m34.155s	15
11	Fernando Alonso	Aston Martin	1h23m15.164s	2	1m34.258s	16
12	Kevin Magnussen	Haas	1h23m15.772s	1	1m33.297s	12
13	Zhou Guanyu	Sauber	1h23m20.054s	2	1m33.566s	13
14	Franco Colapinto *	Williams	1h23m21.141s	2	1m33.749s	20
15	Lance Stroll	Aston Martin	1h23m30.071s	2	1m34.484s	18
16	Liam Lawson	RB	1h23m36.974s	2	1m34.257s	14
17	Esteban Ocon	Alpine	49 laps	3	1m33.221s	11
18	Valtteri Bottas !	Sauber	49 laps	2	1m34.430s	19
R	Alex Albon	Williams	26 laps/power unit	0	1m34.425s	17
R	Pierre Gasly	Alpine	16 laps/power unit	0	1m32.664s	3

FASTEST LAP: NORRIS, 1M34.876S, 146.203MPH/235.292KPH ON LAP 50 · RACE LEADERS: RUSSELL 1-12 & 14-50, HAMILTON 13
* REQUIRED TO START FROM PIT LANE AS CAR MODIFIED IN PARC FERME · ! 5-PLACE GRID PENALTY FOR USING ADDITIONAL POWER UNIT ELEMENTS

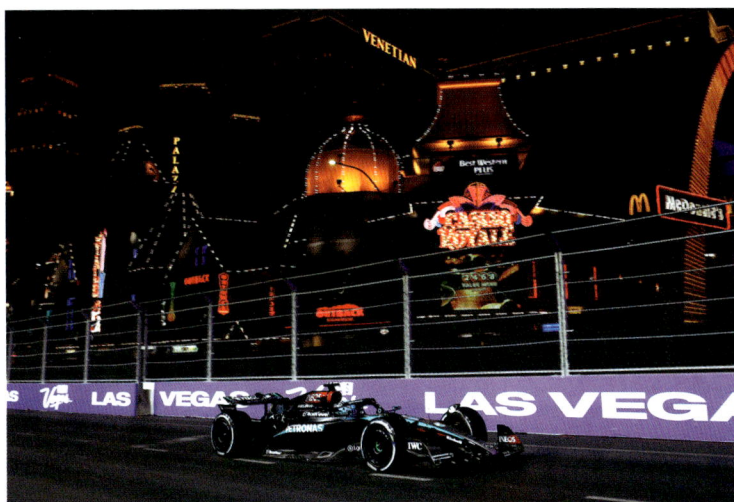

Mercedes came good in Las Vegas' cooler conditions and George Russell led home a team one-two.

QATAR GP

Max Verstappen was angered by George Russell getting him demoted from pole, but he channelled that frustration to take the lead at the start. He remained there through three safety-car periods and was given breathing space when Lando Norris was hit with a ten-second penalty.

Fired up with indignation, Verstappen made a brilliant start to out-drag Russell to turn 1, but Norris made an even better one and almost passed both before tucking into second place.

At the tail of the field, Nico Hulkenberg lost the rear of his Haas and clipped Franco Colapinto, who then took out Esteban Ocon. Hulkenberg was able to continue, although having to pit to replace a punctured tyre.

There was no change to the lead order until Russell was called in to be the first front runner to pit, doing so on lap 23, but his day was wrecked by a slow stop that dropped him to the tail of the top ten.

Just before his rivals were expected to pit, Alex Albon's Williams shed a mirror on the main straight and Verstappen noted that, under yellow flags, Norris had closed in. Then, two laps later, the mirror was hit by Valtteri Bottas' Sauber, with both Carlos Sainz Jr and Lewis Hamilton picking up punctures from the debris; the Mercedes driver also served a five-second penalty, rejoining in last place but one.

This brought out the safety car and, although Norris made a bid for the lead when it withdrew, Verstappen resisted him. Then the safety car was called out again after Hulkenberg spun off and Verstappen made a better escape this time. Then he was given a major helping hand as Norris was hit with a ten-second penalty for failing to slow under yellow flags, ending his challenge and scuppering McLaren's hopes of securing the constructors' title with a round to spare.

Charles Leclerc was promoted to second and Oscar Piastri to third, where they remained to the finish, with Russell a disappointed fourth.

Hamilton's race was then made pointless as he was given a drivethrough penalty for speeding in the pit lane, dropping him to 12th.

Max Verstappen's ninth win of 2024 was made easier when Lando Norris was given a penalty.

LUSAIL ROUND 23

DATE: **1 DECEMBER 2024**

Laps: **57** • Distance: **191.762 miles/308.611km** • Weather: **Cool & windy**

Pos	Driver	Team	Result	Stops	Grid	Sprint
1	**Max Verstappen** *	Red Bull	1h31m05.323s	3	2	8
2	**Charles Leclerc**	Ferrari	1h31m11.354s	3	5	5
3	**Oscar Piastri**	McLaren	1h31m12.142s	3	4	1
4	**George Russell** !	Mercedes	1h31m19.427s	4	1	3
5	**Pierre Gasly**	Alpine	1h31m22.105s	3	11	9
6	**Carlos Sainz Jr**	Ferrari	1h31m22.799s	3	7	4
7	**Fernando Alonso**	Aston Martin	1h31m25.190s	3	8	11
8	**Zhou Guanyu**	Sauber	1h31m30.683s	3	12	19
9	**Kevin Magnussen**	Haas	1h31m37.500s	3	10	10
10	**Lando Norris**	McLaren	1h31m41.085s	4	3	2
11	**Valtteri Bottas**	Sauber	1h31m55.566s	3	13	12
12	**Lewis Hamilton**	Mercedes	1h32m01.445s	4	6	6
13	**Yuki Tsunoda**	RB	1h32m06.423s	4	14	17
14	**Liam Lawson**	RB	1h32m07.979s	4	17	16
15	**Alex Albon**	Williams	56 laps	4	16	15
R	**Nico Hulkenberg**	Haas	39 laps/spun off	4	18	7
R	**Sergio Perez**	Red Bull	38 laps/spun off	0	9	20
R	**Lance Stroll**	Aston Martin	10 laps/crash damage	0	15	13
R	**Franco Colapinto**	Williams	0 laps/accident	0	19	18
R	**Esteban Ocon**	Alpine	0 laps/accident	0	20	14

FASTEST LAP: **NORRIS, 1M22.384S, 147.139MPH/236.798KPH ON LAP 56** • RACE LEADERS: **VERSTAPPEN 1-57** • * 1-PLACE GRID PENALTY FOR DRIVING UNNECESSARILY SLOWLY • ! 5S PENALTY FOR FALLING MORE THAN 10 CAR LENGTHS BEHIND THE SAFETY CAR

ABU DHABI GP

An all-McLaren front row suggested that the British team ought to be able to cruise to the constructors' title, but Max Verstappen took Oscar Piastri at the first corner. Yet Lando Norris resisted all pressure from Carlos Sainz Jr and did just enough to clinch the deal.

Norris led away, but McLaren's plans were wrecked almost immediately as Verstappen dived up the inside of Piastri into turn 1, sending both cars spinning. Sainz Jr nipped into second as they rotated and Pierre Gasly grabbed third, George Russell fourth and Nico Hulkenberg fifth. Verstappen got going and rejoined outside the top ten, with Piastri dropping to the tail of the field.

The most spectacular aspect of the opening lap, though, came from Charles Leclerc, who had to start from the back of the grid and yet was up to eighth by halfway around lap 1.

Sergio Perez's last run for Red Bull Racing didn't last a lap, as his car was hit by Valtteri Bottas' Sauber.

After a brief VSC period, Norris controlled the restart ahead of Sainz, and Gasly did just enough to resist Russell. The Alpine driver stayed ahead until his first pit stop, frustrating the Mercedes driver as the first two escaped, with Norris building a lead of four seconds.

Then Piastri clipped Franco Colapinto as he fought back, puncturing one of the Williams' tyres and, in time, landing the Australian with a ten-second penalty.

His was the second to be issued, as Verstappen had already been hit with a ten-second penalty for his first corner error.

In the run towards the pit stops, when some of the teams went away from the expected one-stop strategy, Leclerc kept on making up places, rising to fourth when the Haas duo came in early.

Lewis Hamilton was the only driver to start on hard compound tyres to shoot for points. It was slow to start with, but paid dividends late on, with Hamilton passing Russell on the last lap.

The Ferraris fell away and Norris was able to cruise clear and gave McLaren its first constructors' title since 1998.

YAS MARINA ROUND 24

DATE: **8 DECEMBER 2024**

Laps: **58** · Distance: **190.253 miles/306.183km** · Weather: **Warm & dry**

Pos	Driver	Team	Result	Stops	Qualifying Time	Grid
1	**Lando Norris**	McLaren	1h26m33.291s	1	1m22.595s	1
2	**Carlos Sainz Jr**	Ferrari	1h26m39.123s	1	1m22.824s	3
3	**Charles Leclerc ***	Ferrari	1h27m05.219s	1	1m23.833s	19
4	**Lewis Hamilton**	Mercedes	1h27m09.774s	1	1m23.887s	16
5	**George Russell**	Mercedes	1h27m10.829s	1	1m23.132s	6
6	**Max Verstappen**	Red Bull	1h27m23.138s	1	1m22.945s	4
7	**Pierre Gasly**	Alpine	1h27m45.851s	1	1m22.984s	5
8	**Nico Hulkenberg !**	McLaren	1h27m48.845s	1	1m22.886s	7
9	**Fernando Alonso**	Aston Martin	1h27m55.664s	2	1m23.196s	8
10	**Oscar Piastri**	McLaren	1h27m57.112s	2	1m22.804s	2
11	**Alex Albon !!**	Williams	57 laps	1	1m23.821s	18
12	**Yuki Tsunoda**	RB	57 laps	1	1m23.419s	11
13	**Zhou Guanyu**	Sauber	57 laps	2	1m23.880s	15
14	**Lance Stroll ^**	Aston Martin	57 laps	2	1m23.784s	13
15	**Jack Doohan**	Alpine	57 laps	1	1m24.105s	17
16	**Kevin Magnussen**	Haas	57 laps	4	1m23.877s	14
17	**Liam Lawson**	RB	55 laps/brakes	2	1m23.472s	12
R	**Valtteri Bottas**	Sauber	32 laps/crash damage	0	1m23.204s	9
R	**Franco Colapinto !!**	Williams	28 laps/power unit	0	1m23.912s	20
R	**Sergio Perez**	Red Bull	0 laps/spun off	0	1m23.264s	10

FASTEST LAP: **MAGNUSSEN, 1M25.637S, 137.945MPH/222.002KPH ON LAP 57** · RACE LEADERS: NORRIS 1-58 · * 10-PLACE GRID PENALTY FOR USING ADDITIONAL POWER UNIT ELEMENT · ! 3-PLACE GRID PENALTY FOR OVERTAKING IN THE PIT EXIT TUNNEL · !! 5-PLACE GRID PENALTY FOR USING ADDITIONAL GEARBOX COMPONENTS · ^ 5S PENALTY FOR EXCEEDING TRACK LIMITS

McLaren principal Zak Brown and race winner Lando Norris celebrate ending their campaign in style.

POS	DRIVER	NAT		CAR-ENGINE	R1	R2	R3	R4	R5	R6	R7
1	MAX VERSTAPPEN	NED		RED BULL-HONDA RB20	1PF	1P	RP	1PF	1P	2P	1P
2	LANDO NORRIS	GBR		McLAREN-MERCEDES MCL38	6	8	3	5	2	1	2
3	CHARLES LECLERC	MON		FERRARI SF24	4	3F	2F	4	4	3	3
4	OSCAR PIASTRI	AUS		McLAREN-MERCEDES MCL38	8	4	4	8	8	13F	4
5	CARLOS SAINZ JR	SPA		FERRARI SF24	3	-	1	3	5	5	5
6	GEORGE RUSSELL	GBR		MERCEDES F1 W15	5	6	R	7	6	8	7F
7	LEWIS HAMILTON	GBR		MERCEDES F1 W15	7	9	R	9	9	6	6
8	SERGIO PEREZ	MEX		RED BULL-HONDA RB20	2	2	5	2	3	4	8
9	FERNANDO ALONSO	SPA		ASTON MARTIN-MERCEDES AMR24	9	5	8	6	7F	9	19
10	PIERRE GASLY	FRA		ALPINE-RENAULT A524	18	R	13	16	13	12	16
11	NICO HULKENBERG	GER		HAAS-FERRARI VF-24	16	10	9	11	10	11	11
12	YUKI TSUNODA	JPN		RB-HONDA VCARB01	14	15	7	10	R	7	10
13	LANCE STROLL	CDN		ASTON MARTIN-MERCEDES AMR24	10	R	6	12	15	17	9
14	ESTEBAN OCON	FRA		ALPINE-RENAULT A524	17	13	16	15	11	10	14
15	KEVIN MAGNUSSEN	DEN		HAAS-FERRARI VF-24	12	12	10	13	16	19	12
16	ALEX ALBON	GBR/THA		WILLIAMS-MERCEDES FW46	15	11	11	R	12	18	R
17	DANIEL RICCIARDO	AUS		RB-HONDA VCARB01	13	16	12	R	R	15	13
18	OLIVER BEARMAN	GBR		FERRARI SF24	-	7	-	-	-	-	-
				HAAS-FERRARI VF-24	-	-	-	-	-	-	-
19	FRANCO COLAPINTO	ARG		WILLIAMS-MERCEDES FW46	-	-	-	-	-	-	-
20	ZHOU GUANYU	PRC		SAUBER-FERRARI C44	11	18	15	R	14	14	15
21	LIAM LAWSON	NZL		RB-HONDA VCARB01	-	-	-	-	-	-	-
22	VALTTERI BOTTAS	FIN		SAUBER-FERRARI C44	19	17	14	14	R	16	18
23	LOGAN SARGEANT	USA		WILLIAMS-MERCEDES FW46	20	14	W	17	17	R	17
24	JACK DOOHAN	AUS		ALPINE-RENAULT A524	-	-	-	-	-	-	-

SCORING

1st	25 points
2nd	18 points
3rd	15 points
4th	12 points
5th	10 points
6th	8 points
7th	6 points
8th	4 points
9th	2 points
10th	1 point
Fastest lap	1 point*

SPRINT RACE POINTS

1st	8 points
2nd	7 points
3rd	6 points
4th	5 points
5th	4 points
6th	3 points
7th	2 points
8th	1 point

* if in top 10 finishers

POS	TEAM-ENGINE	R1	R2	R3	R4	R5	R6	R7
1	McLAREN-MERCEDES	6/8	4/8	3/4	5/8	2/8	1/13	2/4
2	FERRARI	3/4	3/7	1/2	3/4	4/5	3/5	3/5
3	RED BULL-HONDA	1/2	1/2	5/R	1/2	1/3	2/4	1/8
4	MERCEDES	5/7	6/9	R/R	7/9	6/9	6/8	6/7
5	ASTON MARTIN-MERCEDES	9/10	5/R	6/8	6/12	7/15	9/17	9/19
6	ALPINE-RENAULT	17/18	13/R	13/16	15/16	11/13	10/12	14/16
7	HAAS-FERRARI	12/16	12/10	9/10	11/13	10/16	11/19	11/12
8	RB-HONDA	13/14	15/16	7/12	10/R	R/R	7/15	10/13
9	WILLIAMS-MERCEDES	15/20	11/14	11/W	17/R	12/17	18/R	17/R
10	SAUBER-FERRARI	11/19	17/18	14/15	14/R	14/R	14/16	15/18

SYMBOLS AND GRAND PRIX KEY

ROUND 1	BAHRAIN GP	ROUND 7	EMILIA ROMAGNA GP	ROUND 13	HUNGARIAN GP
ROUND 2	SAUDI ARABIAN GP	ROUND 8	MONACO GP	ROUND 14	BELGIAN GP
ROUND 3	AUSTRALIAN GP	ROUND 9	CANADIAN GP	ROUND 15	DUTCH GP
ROUND 4	JAPANESE GP	ROUND 10	SPANISH GP	ROUND 16	ITALIAN GP
ROUND 5	CHINESE GP	ROUND 11	AUSTRIAN GP	ROUND 17	AZERBAIJAN GP
ROUND 6	MIAMI GP	ROUND 12	BRITISH GP	ROUND 18	SINGAPORE GP

ROUND 19	UNITED STATES GP
ROUND 20	MEXICO CITY GP
ROUND 21	SAO PAULO GP
ROUND 22	LAS VEGAS GP
ROUND 23	QATAR GP
ROUND 24	ABU DHABI GP

D DISQUALIFIED   **F** FASTEST LAP   **NC** NOT CLASSIFIED   **NS** NON-STARTER   **P** POLE POSITION   **R** RETIRED   **W** WITHDRAWN

R8	R9	R10	R11	R12	R13	R14	R15	R16	R17	R18	R19	R20	R21	R22	R23	R24	TOTAL
6	1	1	5P	2	5	4	2	6	5	2	3	6	1F	5	1	6	437
4	2	2PF	R	3	2P	5	1PF	3PF	4F	1P	4P	2	6P	6F	10F	1P	374
1P	R	5	11	14	4	3P	3	1	2P	5	1	3F	5	4	2	3	356
2	5	7	2	4	1	2	4	2	1	3	5	8	8	7	3	10	292
3	R	6	3	5F	6	6	5	4	R	7	2	1P	R	3	5	2	290
5	3P	4	1	RP	8F	D	7	7	3	4	6	5	4	1P	4	5	245
7F	4F	3	4	1	3	1	8	5	9	6	R	4	10	2	12	4	223
R	R	8	7	17	7	7F	6	8	R	10	7	17	11	10	R	R	152
11	6	12	18F	8	11	8	10	11	6	8	13	R	14	11	7	9	70
10	9	9	10	R	R	13	9	15	12	17	12	10	3	R	5	7	42
R	11	11	6	6	13	18	11	17	11	9	8	9	DQ	8	R	8	41
8	14	19	14	10	9	16	17	R	R	12	14	R	7	9	13	12	30
14	7	14	13	7	10	11	13	19	R	14	15	11	NS	15	R	14	24
R	10	10	12	16	18	9	15	14	15	13	18	13	2	17	R	-	23
R	12	17	8	12	15	14	18	10	-	R	11	7	W	12	9	16F	16
9	R	18	15	9	14	12	14	9	7	R	16	R	NS	R	15	11	12
12	8	15	9	13	12	10	12	13	13	18F	-	-	-	-	-	-	12
-	-	-	-	-	-	-	-	-	-	-	-	-	-	-	-	-	7
-	-	-	-	-	-	-	-	10	-	-	-	-	12	-	-	-	
-	-	-	-	-	-	-	-	12	8	11	10	12	R	14	R	R	5
16	15	13	17	18	19	R	20	18	14	15	19	15	15	13	8	13	4
-	-	-	-	-	-	-	-	-	-	-	9	16	9	16	14	17	4
13	13	16	16	15	16	15	19	16	16	16	17	14	13	18	11	R	0
15	R	20	19	11	17	17	16	-	-	-	-	-	-	-	-	-	0
-	-	-	-	-	-	-	-	-	-	-	-	-	-	-	-	15	0

R8	R9	R10	R11	R12	R13	R14	R15	R16	R17	R18	R19	R20	R21	R22	R23	R24	TOTAL
2/4	2/5	2/7	2/R	3/4	1/2	2/5	1/4	2/3	1/4	1/3	4/5	2/8	6/8	6/7	3/10	1/10	666
1/3	R/R	5/6	3/11	5/14	4/6	3/6	3/5	1/4	2/R	5/7	1/2	1/3	5/R	3/4	2/6	2/3	652
6/R	1/R	1/8	5/7	2/17	5/7	4/7	2/6	6/8	5/R	2/10	3/7	6/17	1/11	5/10	1/R	6/R	589
5/7	3/4	3/4	1/4	1/R	3/8	1/D	7/8	5/7	3/9	4/6	6/R	4/5	4/10	1/2	4/12	4/5	468
11/14	6/7	12/14	13/18	7/8	10/11	8/11	10/13	11/19	6/R	8/14	13/15	11/R	14/NS	11/15	7/R	9/14	94
10/R	9/10	9/10	10/12	16/R	18/R	9/13	9/15	14/15	12/15	13/17	12/18	10/13	2/3	17/R	5/R	7/15	65
R/R	11/12	11/17	6/8	6/12	13/15	14/18	11/18	10/17	10/11	9/R	8/11	7/9	12/DQ	8/12	9/R	8/16	58
8/12	9/14	15/19	9/14	10/13	9/12	10/16	12/17	13/R	13/R	12/18	9/14	16/R	7/9	9/16	13/14	12/R	46
9/15	R/R	18/20	15/19	9/11	14/17	12/17	14/16	9/12	7/8	11/R	10/16	12/R	R/NS	14/R	15/R	11/R	17
13/16	13/15	13/16	16/17	15/18	16/19	15/R	19/20	16/18	14/16	15/16	17/19	14/15	13/15	13/18	8/11	13/R	4

FORMULA ONE RECORDS

STARTS

DRIVERS

401	Fernando Alonso	(SPA)	185	Kevin Magnussen	(DEN)		Clay Regazzoni	(SWI)
356	Lewis Hamilton	(GBR)	183	Nick Heidfeld	(GER)	128	Mario Andretti	(USA)
349	Kimi Raikkonen	(FIN)	180	Ralf Schumacher	(GER)		Lando Norris	(GBR)
325	Rubens Barrichello	(BRA)	179	Romain Grosjean	(FRA)		George Russell	(GBR)
306	Jenson Button	(GBR)	176	Graham Hill	(GBR)		Adrian Sutil	(GER)
	Michael Schumacher	(GER)		Jacques Laffite	(FRA)	126	Jack Brabham	(AUS)
299	Sebastian Vettel	(GER)	171	Niki Lauda	(AUT)	123	Ronnie Peterson	(SWE)
281	Sergio Perez	(MEX)	166	Lance Stroll	(CDN)	118	Pierluigi Martini	(ITA)
269	Felipe Massa	(BRA)	163	Thierry Boutsen	(BEL)	116	Jacky Ickx	(BEL)
257	Daniel Ricciardo	(AUS)		Jacques Villeneuve	(CDN)		Alan Jones	(AUS)
256	Riccardo Patrese	(ITA)	161	Mika Hakkinen	(FIN)	115	Damon Hill	(GBR)
252	Jarno Trulli	(ITA)		Ayrton Senna	(BRA)	114	Keke Rosberg	(FIN)
246	Valtteri Bottas	(FIN)	160	Johnny Herbert	(GBR)		Patrick Tambay	(FRA)
	David Coulthard	(GBR)	158	Martin Brundle	(GBR)	112	Denny Hulme	(NZL)
229	Giancarlo Fisichella	(ITA)	157	Olivier Panis	(FRA)		Jody Scheckter	(RSA)
227	Nico Hulkenberg	(GER)	156	Heinz-Harald Frentzen	(GER)	111	Heikki Kovalainen	(FIN)
215	Mark Webber	(AUS)		Esteban Ocon	(FRA)		John Surtees	(GBR)
210	Gerhard Berger	(AUT)	153	Pierre Gasly	(FRA)	110	Daniil Kvyat	(RUS)
209	Max Verstappen	(NED)	152	John Watson	(GBR)	109	Philippe Alliot	(FRA)
208	Andrea de Cesaris	(ITA)	149	Rene Arnoux	(FRA)		Mika Salo	(FIN)
206	Nico Rosberg	(GER)	147	Charles Leclerc	(MON)	108	Elio de Angelis	(ITA)
	Carlos Sainz Jr	(SPA)	146	Carlos Reutemann	(ARG)	106	Jos Verstappen	(NED)
204	Nelson Piquet	(BRA)		Derek Warwick	(GBR)	104	Alex Albon	(GBR/THA)
201	Jean Alesi	(FRA)	145	Eddie Irvine	(GBR)		Jo Bonnier	(SWE)
199	Alain Prost	(FRA)	144	Emerson Fittipaldi	(BRA)		Pedro de la Rosa	(SPA)
194	Michele Alboreto	(ITA)	134	Jean-Pierre Jarier	(FRA)		Jochen Mass	(GER)
187	Nigel Mansell	(GBR)	132	Eddie Cheever	(USA)			

CONSTRUCTORS

1,098	Ferrari	590	Sauber (formerly Sauber including BMW Sauber then Alfa Romeo II)	382	Arrows
970	McLaren			227	March
839	Williams			197	BRM
761	Alpine (formerly Toleman then Benetton then Renault II, Lotus II & Renault III)	527	Red Bull (formerly Stewart then Jaguar Racing)	190	Haas
				132	Osella
715	RB (formerly Minardi then Toro Rosso then AlphaTauri)	492	Mercedes GP (formerly BAR then Honda Racing then Brawn GP)	129	Renault
		491	Lotus		
625	Aston Martin II (formerly Jordan then Midland then Spyker then Force India then Racing Point)	430	Tyrrell		
		409	Prost (nee Ligier)		
		394	Brabham		

120

MOST WINS

DRIVERS

105	Lewis Hamilton	(GBR)	16	Stirling Moss	(GBR)		Jody Scheckter	(RSA)
91	Michael Schumacher	(GER)	15	Jenson Button	(GBR)	9	Mark Webber	(AUS)
63	Max Verstappen	(NED)	14	Jack Brabham	(AUS)	8	Denny Hulme	(NZL)
53	Sebastian Vettel	(GER)		Emerson Fittipaldi	(BRA)		Jacky Ickx	(BEL)
51	Alain Prost	(FRA)		Graham Hill	(GBR)		Charles Leclerc	(MON)
41	Ayrton Senna	(BRA)	13	Alberto Ascari	(ITA)		Daniel Ricciardo	(AUS)
32	Fernando Alonso	(SPA)		David Coulthard	(GBR)	7	Rene Arnoux	(FRA)
31	Nigel Mansell	(GBR)	12	Mario Andretti	(USA)		Juan Pablo Montoya	(COL)
27	Jackie Stewart	(GBR)		Alan Jones	(AUS)	6	Tony Brooks	(GBR)
25	Jim Clark	(GBR)		Carlos Reutemann	(ARG)		Jacques Laffite	(FRA)
	Niki Lauda	(AUT)	11	Rubens Barrichello	(BRA)		Riccardo Patrese	(ITA)
24	Juan Manuel Fangio	(ARG)		Felipe Massa	(BRA)		Sergio Perez	(MEX)
23	Nelson Piquet	(BRA)		Jacques Villeneuve	(CDN)		Jochen Rindt	(AUT)
	Nico Rosberg	(GER)	10	Gerhard Berger	(AUT)		Ralf Schumacher	(GER)
22	Damon Hill	(GBR)		Valtteri Bottas	(FIN)		John Surtees	(GBR)
21	Kimi Raikkonen	(FIN)		James Hunt	(GBR)		Gilles Villeneuve	(CDN)
20	Mika Hakkinen	(FIN)		Ronnie Peterson	(SWE)			

CONSTRUCTORS

248	Ferrari	17	BRM		Wolf
189	McLaren	16	Cooper	2	RB (including Minardi, Toro Rosso & AlphaTauri)
129	Mercedes GP (including Honda Racing & Brawn GP)	15	Renault		Honda
123	Red Bull Racing (including Stewart)	10	Alfa Romeo	1	BMW Sauber
		9	Ligier		Eagle
114	Williams		Maserati		Hesketh
79	Lotus		Matra		Penske
50	Alpine (including Benetton, Renault II, Lotus II & Renault III)		Mercedes		Porsche
			Vanwall		Shadow
35	Brabham	5	Aston Martin II (including Jordan & Racing Point)		
23	Tyrrell	3	March		

Lewis Hamilton remains the driver with the most grand prix wins, 105, with the first coming with McLaren in the 2007 Canadian GP.

MOST WINS IN ONE SEASON

DRIVERS

Wins	Driver	Year	Wins	Driver	Year	Wins	Driver	Year
19	Max Verstappen	2023		Michael Schumacher	2001		Alberto Ascari	1952
15	Max Verstappen	2022		Max Verstappen	2024		Jenson Button	2009
13	Michael Schumacher	2004	8	Mika Hakkinen	1998		Jim Clark	1965
	Sebastian Vettel	2013		Lewis Hamilton	2021		Juan Manuel Fangio	1954
11	Lewis Hamilton	2014		Damon Hill	1996		Damon Hill	1994
	Lewis Hamilton	2018		Michael Schumacher	1994		James Hunt	1976
	Lewis Hamilton	2019		Ayrton Senna	1988		Nigel Mansell	1987
	Lewis Hamilton	2020	7	Fernando Alonso	2005		Kimi Raikkonen	2007
	Michael Schumacher	2002		Fernando Alonso	2006		Felipe Massa	2008
	Sebastian Vettel	2011		Jim Clark	1963		Nico Rosberg	2015
10	Lewis Hamilton	2015		Alain Prost	1984		Michael Schumacher	1998
	Lewis Hamilton	2016		Alain Prost	1988		Michael Schumacher	2003
	Max Verstappen	2021		Alain Prost	1993		Michael Schumacher	2006
9	Lewis Hamilton	2017		Kimi Raikkonen	2005		Ayrton Senna	1989
	Nigel Mansell	1992		Michael Schumacher	2006		Ayrton Senna	1990
	Nico Rosberg	2016		Ayrton Senna	1991		Jackie Stewart	1969
	Michael Schumacher	1995		Jacques Villeneuve	1997		Jackie Stewart	1971
	Michael Schumacher	2000	6	Mario Andretti	1978			

CONSTRUCTORS

Wins	Constructor	Year	Wins	Constructor	Year	Wins	Constructor	Year
21	Red Bull	2023	10	Ferrari	2000		Lotus	1978
19	Mercedes GP	2016		McLaren	2005		McLaren	1991
17	Red Bull	2022		McLaren	1989		McLaren	2007
16	Mercedes GP	2014		Williams	1992		Renault	2005
	Mercedes GP	2015		Williams	1993		Renault	2006
15	Ferrari	2002	9	Ferrari	2001		Williams	1997
	Ferrari	2004		Ferrari	2006	7	Ferrari	1952
	McLaren	1988		Ferrari	2007		Ferrari	1953
	Mercedes GP	2019		McLaren	1998		Lotus	1963
13	Mercedes GP	2020		Mercedes GP	2021		Lotus	1973
	Red Bull	2013		Red Bull	2010		McLaren	1999
12	McLaren	1984		Red Bull	2024		McLaren	2000
	Mercedes GP	2017		Williams	1986		McLaren	2012
	Red Bull	2011		Williams	1987		Red Bull	2012
	Williams	1996	8	Benetton	1994		Tyrrell	1971
11	Benetton	1995		Brawn GP	2009		Williams	1991
	Mercedes GP	2018		Ferrari	2003		Williams	1994
	Red Bull	2021		Ferrari	2008			

Sergio Perez took two of Red Bull Racing's record 21 wins in 2023.

Ayrton Senna didn't know it at the time, but this victory celebration after the 1993 Australian GP with McLaren was to be his last before his death.

MOST POLE POSITIONS

DRIVERS

104	Lewis Hamilton	(GBR)	24	Niki Lauda	(AUT)		Rubens Barrichello	(BRA)
68	Michael Schumacher	(GER)		Nelson Piquet	(BRA)		James Hunt	(GBR)
65	Ayrton Senna	(BRA)	22	Fernando Alonso	(SPA)		Ronnie Peterson	(SWE)
57	Sebastian Vettel	(GER)	20	Valtteri Bottas	(FIN)	13	Jack Brabham	(AUS)
40	Max Verstappen	(NED)		Damon Hill	(GBR)		Graham Hill	(GBR)
33	Jim Clark	(GBR)	18	Mario Andretti	(USA)		Jacky Ickx	(BEL)
	Alain Prost	(FRA)		Rene Arnoux	(FRA)		Juan Pablo Montoya	(COL)
32	Nigel Mansell	(GBR)		Kimi Raikkonen	(FIN)		Jacques Villeneuve	(CDN)
30	Nico Rosberg	(GER)	17	Jackie Stewart	(GBR)		Mark Webber	(AUS)
29	Juan Manuel Fangio	(ARG)	16	Felipe Massa	(BRA)	12	Gerhard Berger	(AUT)
26	Mika Hakkinen	(FIN)		Stirling Moss	(GBR)		David Coulthard	(GBR)
	Charles Leclerc	(MON)	14	Alberto Ascari	(ITA)	10	Jochen Rindt	(AUT)

CONSTRUCTORS

253	Ferrari	14	Tyrrell	3	Shadow
164	McLaren	12	Alfa Romeo		Toyota
141	Mercedes GP (including	11	BRM	2	Lancia
	Brawn GP, Honda Racing, BAR)		Cooper	1	Arrows
128	Williams	10	Maserati		BMW Sauber
107	Lotus	9	Ligier		Haas
104	Red Bull	8	Mercedes		Lola
39	Brabham	7	Vanwall		Porsche
36	Alpine (including Toleman,	5	March		RB (including Minardi, Toro
	Benetton, Renault II, Lotus II	4	Aston Martin (including Jordan,		Rosso & AlphaTauri)
	& Renault III)		Force India & Racing Point)		Wolf
31	Renault		Matra		

Pole starter Michael Schumacher rockets away from his Ferrari team-mate Rubens Barrichello at the start of the 2004 Australian GP in Melbourne.

MOST FASTEST LAPS

DRIVERS

77	Michael Schumacher	(GER)	21	Gerhard Berger	(AUT)	13	Jacky Ickx	(BEL)
67	Lewis Hamilton	(GBR)	20	Nico Rosberg	(GER)		Alberto Ascari	(ITA)
46	Kimi Raikkonen	(FIN)	19	Valtteri Bottas	(FIN)		Alan Jones	(AUS)
41	Alain Prost	(FRA)		Damon Hill	(GBR)		Riccardo Patrese	(ITA)
38	Sebastian Vettel	(GER)		Stirling Moss	(GBR)	12	Rene Arnoux	(FRA)
33	Max Verstappen	(NED)		Ayrton Senna	(BRA)		Jack Brabham	(AUS)
30	Nigel Mansell	(GBR)		Mark Webber	(AUS)		Juan Pablo Montoya	(COL)
28	Jim Clark	(GBR)	18	David Coulthard	(GBR)		Lando Norris	(GBR)
26	Fernando Alonso	(SPA)	17	Rubens Barrichello	(BRA)		Sergio Perez	(MEX)
25	Mika Hakkinen	(FIN)		Daniel Ricciardo	(AUS)	11	John Surtees	(GBR)
24	Niki Lauda	(AUT)	15	Felipe Massa	(BRA)	10	Mario Andretti	(USA)
23	Juan Manuel Fangio	(ARG)		Clay Regazzoni	(SWI)		Graham Hill	(GBR)
	Nelson Piquet	(BRA)		Jackie Stewart	(GBR)		Charles Leclerc	(MON)

CONSTRUCTORS

263	Ferrari	41	Brabham		Force India)		
171	McLaren	20	Tyrrell		Prost (including Ligier)		
133	Williams	18	Renault	9	Mercedes		
104	Mercedes GP (including Brawn GP, BAR & Honda Racing)	15	BRM	7	Sauber (including BMW Sauber & Alfa Romeo II)		
			Maserati		March		
99	Red Bull	14	Alfa Romeo	7	Vanwall		
71	Lotus		Cooper				
57	Alpine (including Toleman, Benetton, Renault, Lotus II & Renault III)	12	Matra				
		10	Aston Martin (including Jordan &				

MOST POINTS (this figure is gross tally, i.e. including scores that were later dropped)

DRIVERS

4,862.5	Lewis Hamilton	(GBR)	798.5	Alain Prost	(FRA)		Jackie Stewart	(GBR)
3,098	Sebastian Vettel	(GER)	714	George Russell	(GBR)	329	Ralf Schumacher	(GER)
3,023.5	Max Verstappen	(NED)	658	Rubens Barrichello	(BRA)	310	Carlos Reutemann	(ARG)
2,337	Fernando Alonso	(SPA)	614	Ayrton Senna	(BRA)	307	Juan Pablo Montoya	(COL)
1,873	Kimi Raikkonen	(FIN)	571	Nico Hulkenberg	(GER)	292	Lance Stroll	(CDN)
1,797	Valtteri Bottas	(FIN)	535	David Coulthard	(GBR)	289	Graham Hill	(GBR)
1,638	Sergio Perez	(MEX)	485.5	Nelson Piquet	(BRA)	281	Emerson Fittipaldi	(BRA)
1,594.5	Nico Rosberg	(GER)	482	Nigel Mansell	(GBR)		Riccardo Patrese	(ITA)
1,566	Michael Schumacher	(GER)	445	Esteban Ocon	(FRA)	277.64	Juan Manuel Fangio	(ARG)
1,430	Charles Leclerc	(MON)	436	Pierre Gasly	(FRA)	275	Giancarlo Fisichella	(ITA)
1,329	Daniel Ricciardo	(AUS)	420.5	Niki Lauda	(AUT)	274	Jim Clark	(GBR)
1,272.5	Carlos Sainz Jr	(SPA)	420	Mika Hakkinen	(FIN)		Robert Kubica	(POL)
1,235	Jenson Button	(GBR)	391	Romain Grosjean	(FRA)	261	Jack Brabham	(AUS)
1,167	Felipe Massa	(BRA)	389	Oscar Piastri	(AUS)	259	Nick Heidfeld	(GER)
1,047.5	Mark Webber	(AUS)	385	Gerhard Berger	(AUT)	255	Jody Scheckter	(RSA)
1,007	Lando Norris	(GBR)	360	Damon Hill	(GBR)			

CONSTRUCTORS

10,324	Ferrari	2,120	Aston Martin (including Jordan, Midland, Spyker, Force India & Racing Point)	433	BRM	
8,195.5	Mercedes GP (including BAR, Honda Racing & Brawn GP)			423	Prost (including Ligier)	
				342	Cooper	
7,933	Red Bull (including Stewart, Jaguar Racing)	1,368	Lotus	312	Renault	
		1,018	Sauber (including BMW Sauber & Alfa Romeo II)	307	Haas	
6,957.5	McLaren			278.5	Toyota	
3,637	Williams	893	RB (including Minardi, Toro Rosso & AlphaTauri)	173.5	March	
3,561.5	Alpine (including Toleman, Benetton, Renault II, Lotus II & Renault III)	864	Brabham	167	Arrows	
		621	Tyrrell	163	Matra	

CHAMPIONSHIP TITLES

DRIVERS

7	Lewis Hamilton	(GBR)		Jenson Button	(GBR)
	Michael Schumacher	(GER)		Giuseppe Farina	(ITA)
5	Juan Manuel Fangio	(ARG)		Mike Hawthorn	(GBR)
4	Alain Prost	(FRA)		Damon Hill	(GBR)
	Sebastian Vettel	(GER)		Phil Hill	(USA)
	Max Verstappen	(NED)		Denny Hulme	(NZL)
3	Jack Brabham	(AUS)		James Hunt	(GBR)
	Niki Lauda	(AUT)		Alan Jones	(AUS)
	Nelson Piquet	(BRA)		Nigel Mansell	(GBR)
	Ayrton Senna	(BRA)		Kimi Raikkonen	(FIN)
	Jackie Stewart	(GBR)		Jochen Rindt	(AUT)
2	Fernando Alonso	(SPA)		Keke Rosberg	(FIN)
	Alberto Ascari	(ITA)		Nico Rosberg	(FIN)
	Jim Clark	(GBR)		Jody Scheckter	(RSA)
	Emerson Fittipaldi	(BRA)		John Surtees	(GBR)
	Mika Hakkinen	(FIN)		Jacques Villeneuve	(CDN)
	Graham Hill	(GBR)			
1	Mario Andretti	(USA)			

CONSTRUCTORS

16	Ferrari		Renault
9	McLaren	1	Benetton
	Williams		Brawn
8	Mercedes GP		BRM
7	Lotus		Matra
6	Red Bull		Tyrrell
2	Brabham		Vanwall
	Cooper		

NB. The Lotus stats listed are based on the team that ran from 1958-1994, whereas those listed as Lotus II are for the team that ran from 2012-2015. Those marked as Alpine are for the team based at Enstone that started as Toleman in 1981, became Benetton in 1986, then Renault II in 2002, Lotus II in 2012 and Renault III in 2016. The Renault listings are for the team that ran from 1977 to 1985, the stats for Red Bull Racing include those of the Stewart Grand Prix and Jaguar Racing teams from which it evolved, and those for Mercedes GP for the team that started as BAR in 1999, ran as Honda GP from 2006 and then as Brawn GP in 2009. Aston Martin II's stats include those of Jordan, Midland, Spyker, Force India and Racing Point, while RB's include those of its forerunner Minardi, Scuderia Toro Rosso and AlphaTauri. Alfa Romeo II's figures are for the team created in 2019 from Sauber, with no connection to the two iterations of the works team that ran from 1950-1951 and 1979-1985.

DRIVER	TEAM	Round 1 – 16 March AUSTRALIAN GP	Round 2 – 23 March CHINESE GP	Round 3 - 6 April JAPANESE GP	Round 4 – 13 April BAHRAIN GP	Round 5 – 20 April SAUDI ARABIAN GP	Round 6 – 4 May MIAMI GP	Round 7 – 18 May EMILIA ROMAGNA GP	Round 8 – 25 May MONACO GP	Round 9 – 1 June SPANISH GP	Round 10 – 15 June CANADIAN GP
LANDO NORRIS	McLaren										
OSCAR PIASTRI	McLaren										
CHARLES LECLERC	Ferrari										
LEWIS HAMILTON	Ferrari										
MAX VERSTAPPEN	Red Bull										
LIAM LAWSON	Red Bull										
GEORGE RUSSELL	Mercedes										
ANDREA KIMI ANTONELLI	Mercedes										
FERNANDO ALONSO	Aston Martin										
LANCE STROLL	Aston Martin										
PIERRE GASLY	Alpine										
JACK DOOHAN	Alpine										
ESTEBAN OCON	Haas										
OLIVER BEARMAN	Haas										
YUKI TSUNODA	RB										
ISACK HADJAR	RB										
ALEX ALBON	Williams										
CARLOS SAINZ JR	Williams										
NICO HULKENBURG	Sauber										
GABRIEL BORTOLETO	Sauber										

SCORING SYSTEM:
25, 18, 15, 12, 10, 8, 6, 4, 2, 1 POINTS FOR THE FIRST 10 FINISHERS IN EACH GRAND PRIX
8, 7, 6, 5, 4, 3, 2, 1 POINTS FOR THE FIRST 8 DRIVERS IN EACH SPRINT RACE

Round 11 – 29 June AUSTRIAN GP	Round 12 – 6 July BRITISH GP	Round 13 – 27 July BELGIAN GP	Round 14 – 3 August HUNGARIAN GP	Round 15 – 31 August DUTCH GP	Round 16 – 7 September ITALIAN GP	Round 17 –21 September AZERBAIJAN GP	Round 18 – 5 October SINGAPORE GP	Round 19 – 19 October UNITED STATES GP	Round 20 – 26 October MEXICAN GP	Round 21 – 9 November SÃO PAULO GP	Round 22 – 22 November LAS VEGAS GP	Round 23 – 30 November QATAR GP	Round 24 – 7 December ABU DHABI GP	POINTS TOTAL

128

The publishers would like to thank the following sources for their kind permission to reproduce the photographs and artwork in this book.

GRAPHIC NEWS: 11T, 12R, 13R, 17T, 18R, 19R, 21T, 22R, 23R, 25T, 26R, 27R, 29T, 30R, 31R, 35T, 36R, 37R, 39T, 40R, 41R, 43T, 44R, 45R, 47T, 48R, 49R, 51T, 52R, 53R, 62, 63, 64, 65, 66, 67, 68, 69, 70, 71, 72, 73, 76, 77, 78, 79, 80, 81, 82, 83, 84, 85, 86, 87,

GETTY IMAGES: 21B, 44TL, 47B, 55TR, 55C, 103, 123; Sam Bagnall/LAT Images 13TL, 34, 57B; Sam Bloxham/LAT Images 20, 27TL, 45TL, 50, 59TR, 96, 97, 101, 102, 105, 106, 128; Charles Coates 55TL; Glenn Dunbar/LAT Images 10, 38, 46, 55BR, 88-89; Jakob Ebrey/LAT Images 59C; Steve Etherington/LAT Images 8-9, 55BL, 90, 121; Simon Galloway/LAT Images 6-7, 18TL, 19TL, 22TL, 23TL, 30TL, 36TL, 41TL, 48TL, 52TL, 53TL; Andy Hone/LAT Images 16, 24, 39B, 42, 43B, 59B, 74-75, 98-99, 100, 116; Yasushi Ishihara/LAT Images 93; Daniel Kalisz/Sutton Images 25B; Zak Mauger/LAT Images 12TL, 14-15, 31TL, 32-33, 49TL, 92, 94, 104, 107, 108, 111, 112-113, 114, 115; James Moy/Sutton Images 124; Rainer Schlegelmilch 35B; Alastair Staley/LAT Images 37TL; Sutton Images 11B, 17B, 29B, 51B, 57C, 59TL; Mark Sutton/Sutton Images 26TL, 40TL, 60-61, 91, 109, 122; Michael Tee/LAT Images 57TL; Steven Tee/LAT Images 5, 28, 95, 110, 117

SHUTTERSTOCK: Daily Mail 57TR

Every effort has been made to acknowledge correctly and contact the source and/or copyright holder of each picture. Any unintentional errors or omissions will be corrected in future editions of this book.

McLaren sophomore racer Oscar Piastri scored the first of his two F1 wins in Hungary last year.